LOOKING AFTER LITERACY

CAROLINE WALKER-GLEAVES AND DAVID WAUGH

LOOKING AFTER LITERACY

A WHOLE CHILD APPROACH TO EFFECTIVE LITERACY INTERVENTIONS

SAGE | LearningMatters

Learning Matters
An imprint of SAGE Publications Ltd
1 Oliver's Yard
55 City Road
London EC1Y 1SP

SAGE Publications Inc.
2455 Teller Road
Thousand Oaks, California 91320

SAGE Publications India Pvt Ltd
B 1/I 1 Mohan Cooperative Industrial Area
Mathura Road
New Delhi 110 044

SAGE Publications Asia-Pacific Pte Ltd
3 Church Street
#10-04 Samsung Hub
Singapore 049483

Editor: Amy Thornton
Production controller: Chris Marke
Project management: Deer Park
Marketing manager: Lorna Patkai
Cover design: Wendy Scott
Typeset by: C&M Digitals (P) Ltd, Chennai, India
Printed in the UK

Library of Congress Control Number: 2017950167

British Library Cataloguing in Publication Data

A catalogue record for this book is available from the
British Library

ISBN 978-1-4739-7163-9 (pbk)
ISBN 978-1-4739-7162-2

At SAGE we take sustainability seriously. Most of our products are printed in the UK using FSC papers and boards.
When we print overseas we ensure sustainable papers are used as measured by the PREPS grading system.
We undertake an annual audit to monitor our sustainability.

Contents

Contents

List of figures and tables

Figures

Tables

About the editors and contributors

Caroline Walker-Gleaves is Professor of Education at Newcastle University and was formerly a Deputy Pro Vice Chancellor in the Faculty of Social Sciences and Health at Durham University. She has worked as a secondary teacher in schools and secure settings in the UK and overseas, and as an adviser in special educational needs, the educational attainment of looked-after and adopted children, and parental involvement in their children's education. Caroline researches in the area of educational experiences of looked-after children.

David Waugh is Associate Professor and Subject Leader for Primary English at Durham University. He has published extensively in primary English. David is a former deputy head teacher, was Head of the Education department at the University of Hull, and was Regional Adviser for ITT for the National Strategies from 2008 to 2010. He has written and co-written or edited more than forty books on primary education. As well as his educational writing, David also writes children's stories and regularly teaches in schools.

Kate Allott is a Lecturer in primary English at York St John University. Her teaching experience includes Early Years, Key Stage 1 and Further Education. She worked as a literacy consultant in a local authority from the inception of the National Literacy Strategy, returning to teacher education at York St John University. More recently, she spent two years as a regional adviser with the Primary National Strategy, working on the Communication, Language and Literacy Development initiative.

Kirsty Anderson is an Assistant Professor at Durham University where she teaches English and Art for Primary Education. Kirsty was a deputy head teacher in Newcastle and literacy consultant for the National Strategies. She is interested in a wide range of education matters including effective teaching for EAL pupils, and she has published in this area. Her research involves exploring and understanding mental well-being in the experiences of teachers.

Janet Degg is an Assistant Professor at Durham University where she leads and teaches on the Humanities modules on the BA Primary Education degree. Prior to working at Durham University, she was a leader and teacher in primary schools in London and North East England, including deputy head and head teacher posts and SENCo and Mathematics Leader positions. She is currently researching the use of children's own mathematical representation in RME problem-solving.

Angela Gill is an Assistant Professor at Durham University. She is part of the Primary English team working with undergraduate and postgraduate students. For more than twenty years, Angela taught in primary schools in Durham and Somerset, during which time she was the subject lead for English and phonics. She has written a number of books and articles, including several about teaching phonics.

Alan Gleaves is an Assistant Professor in Educational Computing at Durham University. He has also worked as a technology consultant for the Department for Education and as a regional adviser in schools for various programmes, including the National Grid for Learning, Building Future Schools and the new primary computing curriculum. He has published widely in the area of mobile technology use in informal learning.

Elaine Lopez is a Lecturer at Newcastle University in Applied Linguistics and TESOL. Previously, she taught Linguistics and TESOL at the University of Leeds. Her interest in Applied Linguistics developed while she was teaching EFL in private language institutions overseas, and on returning to the UK she spent a decade working and studying in Yorkshire. Her research area is formal linguistic approaches to Second Language Acquisition and the application of this research to the language classroom.

Kulwinder Maude is a Senior Lecturer in Primary English at Kingston University. Her background is in primary teaching and she worked as an EAL Coordinator and later as an Inclusion Manager in primary settings in London. Her main research interests are the development of early reading in children with English as an Additional Language and experiences of BME staff and students in higher education.

Sally Neaum is a Senior Lecturer in Education at Teesside University. She has worked as a nursery and primary school teacher, an early years and inclusion advisory teacher and an Ofsted inspector of early years provision. She currently teaches a number of undergraduate modules on early literacy and inclusion and diversity as well as supervising doctoral research in the areas of Inclusion and Early Years. Her current area of research is children's engagement with literacy practices.

Rosie Ridgway is an Assistant Professor in the School of Education at Durham University. Rosie was a teacher in mainstream and special schools in both primary and secondary phases. She now teaches Special Educational Needs and Disabilities (SEND) and teachers' inclusive practices. Her research interests are in education practices that support the learning and achievement of all pupils, developing innovative methodologies and using technologies to support a more inclusive pupil voice.

Catherine Stewart is a qualified psychologist, teacher and freelance researcher in special needs education and has over twenty years of teaching experience within mainstream and further education in psychology, special needs, sociology and research with individuals aged 6 to 60. As a parent of a child with severe learning difficulties, Catherine has spent the last ten years researching teachers' narratives' regarding the special needs curriculum for students with SLD and PMLD.

Introduction

This is a book for carers, parents, teachers, teaching assistants and other professionals working with children who face challenges in literacy and language development, and who are experiencing language and literacy difficulties.

Although the title of the book is focused upon literacy, it will be, and is, immediately clear to all teachers, parents, carers and many professionals working with young children that both language and literacy occupy a critical space in the development of children and, furthermore, they are inextricably linked. Language skill stands behind the ability of a child to be literate, and in turn the capacity to communicate is augmented or impeded by the propensity and capability of a child to keep on developing their language. So although there are clear definitions of language and literacy in the literature – literacy referring to the reading and writing skills that allow children to communicate with the world around them, while language focuses on the oral aspects of communication: listening, speaking and interpreting non-verbal cues to communication – in reality, the two experience a spiralling and entwined relationship. As a teacher, one only has to watch the extent to which a child may or may not enjoy stories and poems and achieve what is expected of them at school to realise that for literacy skills to emerge, language repeatedly affects children's ability to be more literate.

Previous emphasis among educators had principally been on the development of language in very young children. However, over the last decade, there has been a much bigger emphasis on reinforcing and developing a foundation for literacy in very young children. For most children, their language and literacy development is a coherent and progressive journey in which formal teaching in school is supported and informed by informal and nurturing approaches at home. But there are many children for whom this doesn't happen: children may be struggling readers, disrupted writers or speakers with significant impediments to expression. The reasons that stand behind such language and literacy difficulties are diverse and often complex: forms of trauma, early neglect causing developmental delay, abuse causing affective impediments to learning, second language difficulties, specific learning difficulties, particular disabilities, transience within schooling and lack of supportive reading environment within the home life. Children who grow up with language and literacy difficulties, unless they become a focus of educational effort, grow into young people and adults for whom deep engagement with the world around them is intensely difficult.

This book explores issues in and ways of supporting children with their literacy and language, specifically the reading, writing and spoken language development of children within primary school and beyond. It does so, however, in a very different way to most other books in similar areas: it takes a whole-child approach, setting literacy and language in context in a wide variety of learning and subject settings, including phonics, early years, the digital and the mathematical, for example. This book also explores what such strategies and concepts mean in the lives of children who are often absent from more mainstream accounts of learning, and looks at the language and literacy experiences of children with, for example, Foetal Alcohol Syndrome, children who have Profound and Multiple Learning Difficulties, and children who are or have been looked after or adopted, among others. Furthermore, it examines what beliefs, practices and strategies teachers develop and reflect on as they often struggle both to understand the complexity of learning and development and the need to critically engage with the literature, but to do so in an informed, insightful and ultimately responsive and caring way. Drawing on the latest research in education, psychology, neurology and sociology, this book illustrates how such children's progress in literacy may often be mapped against difficulties in other areas of their lives, which lead to cognitive, emotional and social difficulties. These in turn impact upon educational progress, leading to lasting impacts on their lives as they grow. Focusing upon literacy gives an opportunity for critical interventions in these children's lives, and this is what this book aims to do. As well as explaining the connections between literacy development, emotional regulation, behaviour management and social progress, the book describes in detail particular activities for specific aspects of the major areas of literacy and language-related difficulty for these children.

Acknowledgements

There are many people to thank for their assistance with this book. We are indebted to the teachers, trainee teachers, parents, carers, guardians and families who have given us the opportunity to teach their children and to continually learn and develop our teaching. We would like to thank them for helping us to question our practices and our ideas, and who have provided, and given us permission to use, the material for the case studies throughout the book. We appreciate the advice and encouragement of a wide range of professionals with whom we work and have worked, in the areas of Educational Psychology, Social Work, Speech and Language Pathology, and Play, Music, and Physical Therapy. Special thanks are due to Amy Thornton, who has been a wonderful commissioning editor to work with. But our biggest thanks are to the thousands of children with whom we have all worked and from whom we have learned so much about persisting, progressing and prevailing all while encountering sometimes almost insurmountable difficulties.

List of abbreviations

ADHD	Attention Deficit Hyperactivity Disorder
ARC	Additionally Resourced Centre
BMA	British Medical Association
BSL	British Sign Language
CALP	Cognitive and Academic Language Proficiency
CD	Conduct Disorder
CPH	Critical Period Hypothesis
CRIDE	Consortium for Research in Deaf Education
DfE	Department for Education
DfES	Department for Education and Skills
EAL	English as an Additional Language
eFSM	Entitled to Free School Meals
EHCP	Education, Health and Care Plan
EP	Educational Psychologist
ESL	English as a Second Language
ESW	Educational Social Worker
EYFS	Early Years Foundation Stage
FAS	Foetal Alcohol Syndrome
FASD	Foetal Alcohol Spectrum Disorders
FL	Foreign Language
FP	Foundation Phase
FSM	Free School Meals
HI	Hearing Impairment
ICE	Identity Construction Environment
ITE	Initial Teacher Education
ITS	Intelligent Tutor System
KS2	Key Stage 2: Educational provision for 8–11 year old learners
KS3	Key Stage 3: Educational provision for 12–14 year old learners
KS4	Key Stage 4: Educational provision for 15–16 year old learners
KS5	Key Stage 5: Educational provision for 17–18 year old learners

L1	First Langauge
L2	Second Language
LAC	Looked After Children
LDA	Learning Difficulty Assessment
MLD	Moderate Learning Difficulty
NQT	Newly Qualified Teacher
OCD	Obsessive Compulsive Disorder
ODD	Oppositional Defiant Disorder
Ofcom	Office of Communications
Ofsted	Office for Standards in Education
PCK	Pedagogical Content Knowledge
PECS	Picture Exchange Communication System
PMLD	Profound and Multiple Learning Difficulties
RME	Realistic Mathematics Education
SAGE	Storytelling Agent Generation Environment
SALT	Speech and Language Therapy
SEN	Special Educational Needs
SENCo	Special Educational Needs Coordinator
SEND	Special Educational Needs and Disabilities
SES	Socio-Economic Status
SLCN	Speech Language and Communication Needs
SLD	Severe Learning Difficulty/Disability
SLT	Speech and Language Therapist
SPaG	Separate Spelling and Grammar
SSE	Sign-Supported English
TCKs	Third Culture Kids
UNHCR	United Nations High Commissioner for Refugees

1

Becoming a reader and writer: looking after literacy in the early years

Sally Neaum

 This chapter

This chapter will explore what we know about the early experiences that enable children to become readers and writers. Becoming a reader and writer starts in children's earliest days as they are held and spoken to and the adults around them respond sensitively and with consistency to their needs. In addition, children need a range of early experiences in their play and in their family life that enable them to come to literacy learning with a high chance of success. In this chapter these early relationships and experiences are illustrated through case studies of one child, Imogen, as she grows and learns in her family. Through these case studies and exploration of the significance of her experiences a picture is built of the relationships and everyday activities and interactions that look after young children's literacy.

Case study

Understanding children's reading 'biographies'

Imogen is now five years old and has just begun Year 1. She loves school. She is able to read and enjoy early chapter books, although sometimes prefers to share the reading, reading alternate pages with an adult. Today she got 8/8 in her first spelling test. At the end of her reception she had made wonderful progress with phonics and was able to apply her knowledge and skills from this in her reading and writing. She was always delighted to read to her teacher who commented that it was a pleasure to listen to her reading as she was developing fluency and would share her thoughts on what she had read. Imogen had lots of ideas for her writing and thought carefully about the presentation of her work. She was able to use some punctuation and make good phonetically plausible attempts at more complex words, for example 'orinj joos' (orange juice), 'rais' (race) and 'enjen' (engine).

At home Imogen has a range of favourite books, rhymes and songs that she knows off by heart. She looks at her books on her own and is able to read some of the text. She sits engrossed, sucking her fingers, as books are read to her. She finishes each day with a bedtime story. Her current favourite book, *Maps* (Mizielinska and Mizielinski, 2013), produces discussion about animals and plants, geographical features, cultural events and places of interest around the world. Imogen is very chatty. She can initiate conversation and respond in discussion, recall things that have happened, recount incidents, and joke and play with language and words. She asks myriad questions, and answers questions fully and with interest, often including her own ideas and opinions. Imogen loves role-play and uses her emerging writing skills in her play, for example, writing down appointments and prescriptions at the opticians, taking orders in a cafe, and writing numerals and number words as a judge while watching *Strictly Come Dancing* on the TV.

It is clear that Imogen has moved into school with ease, and is becoming literate with success. She is able to confidently leave her parents at the start of the day, to manage her needs in school and to regulate her behaviour so that she is able to meet the school's expectations. So what has enabled this to happen? What early experiences have enabled Imogen to start school and learn with confidence? And how has her literacy been looked after in her early years so that she has moved into becoming literate with ease, enjoyment and success?

Ready to learn

Research shows us that there are a number of important relationships and experiences that contribute to children being able to learn at school. These happen in children's families and communities long before they start school. These necessary early experiences include the development of:

- bonding and attachment;

- executive function skills;

- physical skills: balance, proprioception, crossing the midline and sensory awareness and integration.

Bonding and attachment

School readiness has as much to do with social and emotional development as cognitive development. (Moullin et al., 2014, p.7)

John Bowlby (1953, p.13), author of the original report from which the concepts of bonding and attachment emerged, describes it thus:

An infant and young child should experience a warm intimate and continuous relationship with his mother (or permanent mother substitute) in whom both find satisfaction and enjoyment.

Bonding and attachment are fundamental to a child's flourishing. They create a secure base from which a child can explore, learn and relate to others. The security that they bring enables children to learn how to manage their own feelings and behaviour, and develop confidence and self-reliance. Bonding and attachment develop in a child's earliest years from warm, sensitive and consistent care from adults. This includes everyday interactions such as holding the child, making eye contact, smiling, singing, laughing, talking and playing, as well as anticipating their physical needs to be warm, clean, fed and safe. This 'tuning into' a child and responding to their needs provides the child with a dependable source of comfort, and reassures them that they are lovable and their needs will be met (Moullin et al., 2014). This warm, responsive care is internalised by the child and forms the basis of their ability to regulate their feelings and guide their behaviour as they grow and learn.

There is strong international evidence that secure bonds and attachment have a positive impact on children's learning at school (Moullin et al., 2014). This security fosters the development of skills that enable children to move out into the world with confidence in skills such as self-reliance, autonomy and resilience. It has also been shown to have a positive impact on children's language development that is fundamental to learning. It is thought that the reason for this is the adult's interest and enjoyment in interaction with the child, and the child's receptiveness and motivation to learn from the adult. In addition a secure bond has an impact on the development of executive function and self-regulation skills (Moullin et al., 2014): the mental processes that enable us to plan, focus attention, remember instructions and juggle multiple tasks successfully (Harvard University, 2016).

Executive function skills

Executive functioning skills are necessary for learning, and are a strong predictor of children's readiness and ability to learn at school (Whitebread and Bingham, 2014; Blair and Diamond, 2008). School-based learning requires the ability to filter distractions, prioritise tasks, set and achieve goals, and control impulses (Harvard University, 2016). It is the development of executive function skills that enable children to achieve this. Executive function has a number of aspects:

- Working memory: this governs our ability to retain and manipulate distinct pieces of information over short periods of time.

- Mental flexibility: this helps us to sustain or shift attention in response to different demands or to apply different rules in different settings.

- Self-control: this enables us to set priorities and resist impulsive actions or responses.

Young children learn these skills in everyday interactions in the home and at pre-school (Bernier et al., 2010; Whitebread and Basilio, 2012). They develop through reliable, supportive and responsive interaction that establishes daily routines, scaffolds a child's growing independence and models appropriate social interaction. The development of these skills is closely aligned with bonding and attachment as it requires adults who are 'tuned in' and responsive to a child's needs to scaffold and mediate tasks and experiences, so that a child can become increasingly independent and able to self-regulate, plan, focus and persist.

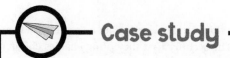 **Case study**

Developing executive function skills

Imogen, aged 18 months, has decided that she wants to choose her own clothes and dress herself. She has a clear idea about what she wants to wear and is adamant that she is going to do it 'on my own'. At times this works well. At other times it doesn't: Imogen chooses clothes that are not suitable for the weather or the day's activities, and she finds some aspects of dressing herself, such as pulling things over her head, buttons and zips, frustrating. Helen, Imogen's mum, supports Imogen's desire to become more independent in dressing herself in a number of ways.

- With a routine of talking about what they are going to do that day and looking out of the window at the weather to decide what sort of clothing is needed, Imogen then chooses which clothes to wear within some boundaries.

- Initially Helen chooses two or three things for Imogen to put on herself and is helped with the others. Helen guided Imogen towards the simpler items of clothing so she can practise and gain confidence in her ability to dress herself. As Imogen has become more skilled and confident she can now put more of the items on without help.

- For the tricky aspects such as buttons and zips Helen uses opportunities that arise to model how she manages these on her own clothes, and Imogen helps her. When dressing herself Imogen started by doing one button or finishing fastening a zip that Helen had started, and now does more as her confidence and fine motor skills have developed.

- When Imogen becomes frustrated by not being able to do something, they have agreed that she will have three goes on her own before they do it together.

Through these interactions Helen scaffolds Imogen's learning. She acknowledges Imogen's desire to do things independently and adapts her interaction to facilitate this. She focuses Imogen's attention on making appropriate choices, supports her in using her fine and gross motor skills in new ways, and encourages Imogen to focus on the task and persist when it is frustrating. These 'tuned-in' interactions enable Imogen to complete tasks successfully, engender confidence in her ability and increase her level of autonomy and independence. This mediated learning enables Imogen to become increasingly independent, able to plan, focus, persist and self-regulate, all of which are important early executive function skills.

Physical skills that support learning

Learning is not all in the mind but requires a range of physical skills, and evidence suggests that a number of these are highly significant in children's ability to engage in learning (Reeves and Bailey, 2014; Pagini, 2012; Goddard Blythe, 2000, 2011, 2012).

Balance

Children need to have a strong sense of balance both when moving and sitting still. Balance is controlled through our vestibular system that provides sensory information about motion, equilibrium and spatial orientation. Therefore we learn to balance by moving, by getting a sense of our body in space and gaining control over it. Gaining balance is important as once we have balance we can move more freely. This enables us to move and stay still without having to exercise conscious control over our bodies: our body is mind-free (Johnson, 2014). When children have had insufficient experiences for their body to be well balanced they will need to think and concentrate on maintaining balance and uprightness; their bodies are not yet mind-free, and this can inhibit focusing on, and attending to, other things.

Crossing the midline

The midline is an imaginary line that runs horizontally down the middle of our body, and 'crossing the midline' refers to any motor action that involves looking, reaching or stepping across this imaginary midline. Crossing the midline emerges as babies and young children develop bilateral integration: good communication between the left- and right-hand side of the brain. Children's ability to cross their midline is central to self-help skills such as getting dressed, physical activity that requires looking, reaching or stepping across the midline, and the development of a dominant side of the body. This leads into becoming literate as it is necessary to cross the midline when tracking left to right to read and write (O'Connor and Daly, 2016).

Sensory awareness and integration

Sensory awareness and integration refer to children's ability to receive and respond to information gathered through their senses. It includes the five external senses – touch, taste, sight, hearing and smell – and the internal vestibular and proprioceptive senses (O'Connor and Daly, 2016). Proprioception is the awareness of your body in space. When our proprioceptive system is adequately developed our proprioceptors (sensory nerve endings located in muscles, tendons, joints and the vestibular system) are constantly providing our brain with important spatial information that enables us to sit still, pay attention and engage visually with text-based information (Johnson, 2014; Neaum, 2017). This sensory engagement with the world shapes neural pathways and we build our understanding of the world around us as we make ever more complex connections based on previous experiences and sensations. Thus babies and young children need rich sensory-motor experiences to build a strong foundation for later learning; they need to move-to-learn, to have the time, space and opportunities to take in information through their senses and piece it together. As Connell and McCarthy (2014, p.53) observe, sensory integration 'greatly affects not only what a child perceives but also how he interprets, understands and responds to sensory information – in other words, how he learns.'

These physical skills that support learning begin in children's earliest days. Babies need 'tummy time' – time spend in a prone position lying on their tummy on the floor – they need to crawl, and have opportunities to stand and fall, spin, roll and be upside down. They also need rich sensory experiences to stimulate their senses, such as skin-to-skin contact through holding, stroking and massaging, quiet singing and eye contact while feeding and dressing. Then, as they grow and develop, young children need wide ranging opportunities for vigorous activity and movement to develop physical foundations for learning (Neaum, 2017). This should include opportunities for jumping, hopping, dancing, swinging, spinning, mixing, scanning, building, reaching, placing, pushing and pulling, filling and stacking, hanging, balancing, climbing, crawling and being upside down.

Case study

Developing physical skills that support learning

Imogen has always loved being in the garden at home and at her grandparents' house. When she goes outside she often just runs into the space. She spends time looking, running, stopping and running again. She climbs on the rockery and plays on the swing. She has a trampoline and can drop, sit and twirl in the air when jumping. She laughs and laughs when her older brother, Joe, jumps next to her and she is bounced about and has to work hard to stay upright. She has her own set of gardening tools and helps, in short bursts, with the gardening, digging, planting, cutting, and using the hose to water the plants. She enjoys doing running races with her dad, collecting leaves in the wheelbarrow with her Poppa, and putting the washing out with Granny. When they have a barbeque or a picnic in the garden she helps by fetching and carrying things up and down the steps to the kitchen and setting them out carefully.

In these everyday activities Imogen is developing a range of important physical skills that support her in being ready to learn. Through moving and stopping, bouncing, swinging, spinning, climbing, reaching, pushing and pulling she is learning about her body in space. She is moving to learn to balance, control her body and cross her midline. She is engaged in rich sensory experiences with the time and space to build her understanding of the world around her. All of which enables her to be ready to learn at school, to sit and focus on tasks, and have the skills necessary to becoming a reader and a writer; tracking left to right and across her midline, spatial awareness and bilaterality (Neaum, 2017). Imogen has *not* learned to sit still and focus by sitting still: she has accomplished this by engaging in vigorous activity and movement in her early years.

Becoming a reader and writer

In addition to important relationships and experiences that lead into learning, there are some more specific interactions and experiences that enable us to look after children's early literacy. Becoming literate begins in children's earliest days as they are held and talked to, and develops through interaction and engagement with meaningful literacy practices in their everyday lives and play (Edwards, 2014). Shea (2011) refers to these interactions and experiences in the home as *soft teaching*, in which parents encourage, respond, coach and answer questions, and children watch, reflect and ask as their curiosity is sparked by the behaviours of others, and replicate observed reading and writing behaviours in their play and interactions.

These important early interactions and experiences include:

- talking, enjoying books, rhymes, songs and poems, and language play;
- the ability to symbolise;
- understanding forms and functions of print;
- metalinguistic awareness;
- phonological awareness.

(Neaum, 2017)

Talking, books, rhymes, songs and poems, and language play

The most important aspect of looking after young children's early literacy is talking. Spoken language is the basis of all literacy learning, and a strong predictor of children's later school attainment (Basit et al., 2015). Language acquisition begins in the earliest days of life in our communication with babies through smiling, gazing, singing and chatting. Parents instinctively enter into this social relationship with the assumption that the baby is interested in, and capable of, communication. Indeed parents often engage with babies as if they are participating in the interaction by anticipating and modelling their contribution in the interaction. Babies respond reciprocally to these communicative acts in various ways: through becoming still and listening, through eye contact and gazing, and, as they grow and develop, through whole-body movements and vocalisations. This is evidence of a strong internal drive for babies to engage in communication and enter into social interaction. These powerful social communicative interactions are the beginnings of language acquisition and, when nurtured, enable children to acquire and develop spoken language with ease. Then, to enable young children to acquire and develop language successfully, they need be alongside people who use language to explain, to discuss, to explore, to imagine, to express ideas and thoughts, who play with language though rhymes and jokes and word play. Put simply, they need to be alongside people who say more than is necessary (Neaum, 2012, 2017).

Case study

Talking with young children

Imogen, aged 13 months, and her granny are baking buns. They have gathered all the ingredients and set them out on the table. Before they begin they discuss what type of buns to make and agree on Imogen's favourites, vanilla buns with Nutella icing. They begin by gathering all the ingredients and equipment that they need. Throughout this process Imogen's granny talks out loud about what she is looking for, where they will find it, pondering whether they have everything that they need, pointing to and listing what they already have, and reading the recipe aloud to see what else they need. Finally, they have all they need and are ready to begin.

They begin by weighing the sugar. Imogen's granny asks her to get the bag of sugar and open it. Once opened they carefully pour the sugar onto the scales. Again, Imogen's granny talks through what they are doing and comments that they need to pour the sugar very carefully so that they don't spill it, and so that they can look carefully at the dial and weigh out the correct amount to put in the buns. As she pours the sugar onto the scales Imogen responds, 'Am am'.

Once the sugar has been weighed they do the same with the other ingredients. As Imogen points to and picks up each ingredient her granny tells her what it is and talks through what they are doing with it, this commentary includes articulating her own thought processes.

Eventually they get to the making and mixing. In the final stages they add the flour to the soft mixture and Imogen's granny comments that they need to use a metal spoon and fold it in very carefully to keep the air in the mixture so that the buns rise. Imogen tries to copy her granny's gentle folding in of the flour commenting, 'I are'.

In this short interaction there is a wealth of language experience. Imogen is listening and responding to questions, responding to what she hears and understands, expressing preferences and using non-verbal communication and her developing language to make herself understood. She is listening to commentary that involves a range of linguistic uses and structures as well as building her understanding of the world. Imogen and her granny are using language to interact and to create meaning together in the activity.

This is part of Imogen's ongoing experience with language in her family. From being a tiny baby Imogen was involved in interaction with others, initially through touch, eye contact, facial expressions, repeating of her noises and expressions, and gentle, soft talk to her. This became more animated and reciprocal as she became able to use simple gestures, vocalisations and facial expressions to communicate. With daily rich language experiences including talk, listening to language, practising her emerging skills, books, singing, rhymes and music, she rapidly became able to use words to communicate. At 13 months she is able to mediate her experiences through language and use language to communicate. We can anticipate that her language will become increasingly sophisticated as she grows and learns while immersed in language.

Halliday (1973) identifies seven functions of language. These describe a hierarchy in the ways that children use language. Initially, children learn and use language to meet their needs and get along with others. Halliday refers to this as pragmatic use: language that enables us to meet our material needs ('I want . . .'), control the behaviour of others ('don't do that – mine') and interact socially with others. However, in addition to these pragmatic uses of language children need to be able to express their thoughts and ideas, and ask questions to elicit information about the world around them. Halliday (1973) refers to this as mathetic language and argues that these aspects of language are crucial to success in school, both to learn and to be taught successfully. This requires that children are involved in a range of rich language experiences, at home and in pre-school settings, that include opportunities to ask and answer questions, to ponder, discuss, describe and seek explanations. It requires that we go beyond a functional use of language to using language as a tool to extend and enrich young children's experiences.

In addition to immersion in talk in daily routines and in their play, an excellent way for young children to hear, use, practise and manipulate language is through books, songs, rhymes, poems and language play. These activities are a rich source of enjoyment that open up a child's experiences and offer authentic ways for them to hear and use language. They extend and enhance children's language capability by encouraging focused listening and responding, alerting children to rhyme and rhythm in language, introducing vocabulary, engaging children in playing with words and syntax, and providing opportunities for children to develop their pronunciation and fluency in speech (Neaum, 2017).

Therefore, looking after very young children's language acquisition and development requires that children are alongside adults who are tuned into their early communication and gestures, say more than is necessary and adapt their interaction to the child's abilities and needs. Children need opportunities to enjoy books, rhymes, songs and poems, and to play with language through jokes, riddles and language play, and, to engage in talking and interaction to practise and refine their developing language.

Symbolising and representation

Alongside the acquisition and development of spoken language, looking after young children's literacy requires that they have opportunities to become aware of literacy and what it means to read and write. One important aspect of this is the ability to symbolise. In anticipation of becoming literate children need to be able recognise and represent things symbolically.

The ability to use one thing to represent another is fundamental to literacy learning: writing is the symbolic representation of spoken language, and reading is understanding and decoding symbols that represent speech. Vygotsky (in Rieber and Hall, 1997) makes a distinction between first-order and second-order symbolism. First-order symbols can be understood directly: the symbols directly signify the objects or actions. For example, when we see a line drawing of a dog we recognise it as a dog. It clearly isn't a real dog but we can 'read' and understand this symbol for a dog. This is because there is a direct relationship between what we see and the object that it represents.

Second-order symbolism is more complex. Second-order symbols are more indirect and opaque. In terms of literacy they consist of 'written signs for oral symbols of words' (Vygotsky, in Rieber and Hall, 1997, p.142). For example, we use the symbols d /o / g to represent the object of a dog, and when we see this combination of symbols we recognise it as representing a dog. In contrast if we were presented with the symbols σκύλος it would have no meaning for us as English speakers and readers because we cannot understand this combination of symbols. This is because writing uses second-order symbols, which means that they bear no resemblance to the object that they represent: the symbols are indirect. Young children need to develop this ability to use symbols to represent the world to enable them to come to reading and writing with a good chance of success (Neaum, 2017). This ability develops through the early use of gesture, through learning to talk, through concrete experiences in play that require symbolic use of props and equipment, and through early mark-making and drawing.

Case study

Symbolising in play, gesture and language

Last summer, when Imogen was four years old, her favourite game was doctors. She was the doctor and everyone else became a patient and was called in to her surgery for their appointment. Firstly Imogen set up a room. She set up a chair behind a table, and put a notepad, pen and a piece of card as a computer keyboard, on the table. At the side of the table was the chair for the patient. She found whatever was to hand (depending on where she was playing) to act as a stethoscope, syringe, medicine bottle and spoon.

Once the room was set up Imogen called out 'Next' from inside the room and someone had to go in to see the doctor. Patients were greeted by her standing straight and tall, then gesturing toward the chair with a sweep of her hand before she sat down herself. The consultation began with Imogen asking 'How can I help you?' in a slow, serious voice, her head tilted slightly to one side and a short nod as she spoke.

Once the problem had been explained Imogen tapped on the 'keyboard' with two fingers, made her diagnosis and treated the patient. This involved using the props that she had to give an injection or medicine or listen to the patient's chest. This was completed in silence with knowing looks and nods of the head.

Finally, she made a series of strokes on a sheet of paper and handed it to the patient with the words 'Here is your prescription.' She then called the next patient with a shout of 'Next'. This was repeated tens, perhaps hundreds, of times over the summer. In this repeated play sequence Imogen demonstrated her developing ability to symbolise. She used gesture, voice, body position and movement to represent being the doctor. She used what was to hand to represent the doctor's instruments and engage in medical procedures. She recorded her diagnosis by representing it in writing, entering it into the computer, and using her emergent writing on the prescription. In these ways she showed that she was able to use one thing to represent another. This ability will support Imogen's later literacy learning as she is increasingly able engage with the symbolic representation of speech in the form of reading and writing.

Learning about forms and functions of print

Their developing ability to symbolise enables children to be become increasingly aware of the use of symbols, including print, in environmental print, story books and in the digital environment. These symbols, including print, become increasingly meaningful to children as they interact with them in meaningful ways in their everyday lives. Young children's engagement with print enables them to come to know why, and where, reading and writing are used. At this early stage this is about coming to know what print is, what it is used for and, broadly, how it works. This is often referred to as the functions and forms of print. An early understanding of these functions and forms is important so that emergent literacy in children's play, and later more formal literacy learning, is set in a meaningful context.

Children are exposed to a wealth of environmental print, for example on packaging, as advertising, on household appliances and controls, as print on clothing, through digital technology on phones, computers and other hand-held devices, as shop signs and logos. Neumann et al.'s (2011) review of evidence on the role of environmental print in emergent literacy suggests that environmental print can play an important role in literacy development. They conclude that interaction with environmental print will develop children's logographic reading skills, which in turn will promote emergent literacy skills and conventional reading skills.

Engagement with books is another vital aspect of children's earliest engagement with print. Reading books to children contributes to them becoming aware of print. Through exposure to books children can, among other things, come to differentiate between drawing, writing and pictures, understand that print is a transcript of oral language, become aware that print carries a story and recognise the intonation, patterns and gestures involved in reading.

In addition, to be fully literate children need to be digitally literate. As digital technology is increasingly part of young children's lives, they need opportunities to develop this aspect of their literacy. At home and in their community it is highly likely that children will have opportunities to become aware of print in the digital environment through the use of telephones, computers, tablets, game consoles and other electronic devices. This more inclusive definition of literacy also needs to be a feature of their experience in pre-school settings, to enable children to develop the necessary breadth of print awareness. Beschorner and Hutchinson (2013), in their study which investigated the use of iPads in two pre-school classrooms, concluded that providing iPads in addition to traditional print enabled the children to extend their print awareness, interacting with, organising, and analysing meanings of the print in this situational context. They found that the children created varying forms of writing in the digital environment of the iPad:

> For example, children were able to write using letters or symbols and/or write drawings using several apps. The Doodle Buddy and Drawing Pad apps were both frequently used by students to write messages using letters and/or drawings formed on the screen using their finger, typed text using the keyboard, digital stickers or stamps, and photographs taken with the iPad. (Beschorner and Hutchinson, 2013, p.6)

Metalinguistic awareness and knowledge

Another important aspect of looking after very young children's literacy is the development of metalinguistic knowledge. Metalinguistic awareness is the early stage of metalinguistic knowledge. It is the ability to think and talk about language. Initially children learn and use language in functional ways – to communicate with others, to get things that they want and to manage others. Language in these instances is used in an implicit, unanalysed way. Metalinguistic awareness is children's growing ability to 'see' language beyond this functional use, to switch attention from the functional use of language, and focus on the language itself. It requires that children learn to think about and manipulate the structural features of language (Lightsey and Frye, 2004). Young children therefore need opportunities to enable them to become aware of aspects of language and then to use this knowledge as they move into becoming literate.

Case study

Developing metalinguistic awareness

Imogen has chosen *The Toy Hospital* (Mills, 1998) as a bedtime story. She loves this book and knows it well. As Imogen passes the book to Helen, her mum, she reads the title out loud tracking her finger along the text on the cover. Helen points out the letter / i / in the word hospital and says,

'There is the letter / i / in the word hospital – /h / o /s/ p / i /t /a /l / – / l / just like / l / for Imogen.'

Helen reads through the book and Imogen listens intently, occasionally joining in under her breath 'TWANNNNNG', 'OWWWWW', 'BLAH-blah BLAH-blah'. At the end of the book Imogen joins in loudly with the final sentence, 'a super-duper, extra bouncy, BRAND NEW TRAMPOLINE', then says, 'I've got a trampoline, but mine is blue.'

Helen replies that, yes she has, and perhaps the story is secretly about Imogen, not a squirrel. Imogen's eyes widen and she laughs as she agrees. Helen then turns back to the beginning of the book and begins again, substituting the word 'squirrel' with 'Imogen'. As they read through the story Helen also substitutes other words, 'She ran upstairs to phone for an ambulance' becomes 'She ran upstairs to phone for a yacht' and 'You'd better see a doctor straight away' becomes 'You'd better see an astronaut straight away'. Initially Imogen laughs at the substitutions and corrects her, but soon she joins in adding her own implausible substitutions.

At the point in the story when Squirrel/Imogen is in the hospital Imogen joins in with the story, taking on the voice of the squirrel. And, copying her mum, she changes the text, so instead of telling the doctor 'My leg is hurting' she changes it to 'My foot is broken'.

Helen finishes reading the book by extending the final sentence to 'a super duper, extra boingy, bouncy, brilliant, blue trampoline', and Imogen copies and repeats the sentence over and over again. They chat briefly about how bouncy and boingy Imogen's trampoline is as she snuggles down to sleep.

In this interaction Imogen is learning about language. Helen alerts Imogen to details of language, such as the particular words chosen to describe the squirrel and the trampoline, and they play with language in her substitution of other words and creation of alliterative strings. Helen draws Imogen's attention to letters and words in a concrete and meaningful way. She models the constituent parts of words (phonemes, graphemes), and how we build up and break down words to read (segment and blend). The awareness of language that comes from this engagement alerts Imogen to structure and meaning in language: that it consists of words, and that words have meaning and that these words and meanings can be analysed and discussed (Neaum, 2017). This supports Imogen's knowledge about language, her metalinguistic awareness, which is vital to becoming literate with ease and success.

Phonological awareness

Phonological awareness is another important aspect of looking after young children's literacy. Phonological awareness refers to the ability to identify and manipulate units of oral language. This includes the ability to identify and make oral rhymes, and awareness of aspects of language such as words, syllables and onsets-rimes. Children's ability to identify and manipulate oral language in these ways demonstrates a developing awareness of the detail within spoken language and the ability to focus on aspects of language beyond meaning.

Therefore to look after young children's early literacy development they need to be involved in interaction and experiences that provide opportunities to develop phonological awareness. In their early years this involves opportunities to listen and respond to a wide range of sound, to tune into sounds, to develop sensitivity to what they hear, to begin to discriminate between sounds, and to respond to, and talk about, what they hear. All of this anticipates phonological awareness. This may include listening to and making music, physical movement and dance in response to sound and music, attending to environmental sounds, and creating and listening to stories and poems with sound effects. In addition, young children need to develop sensitivity to rhyme and alliteration through engagement with stories, rhymes, riddles, songs and poems and in language play to 'tune' their ear into the sound of rhyme and alliteration. This needs to continue and increase in complexity through early childhood and children need to be encouraged to think and talk about the rhymes and alliteration.

Finally, and only when they are capable of achieving this, to look after young children's literacy and enable them to become literate, children need to acquire phonemic awareness. Phonemic awareness is the 'the ability to focus on and manipulate sounds (phonemes) in spoken words' (National Reading Panel (NRP), 2000: 2.1). It is one part of the broader knowledge and skills that constitute phonological awareness, and usually appears after children are able to detect rhyme and identify and manipulate other aspects of language such as words, syllables and onset-rime.

The evidence for the importance of phonemic awareness in becoming literate is compelling. Indeed phonemic awareness has been shown to be the most important prerequisite for learning to read (Melby-Lervåg et al., 2012; Adams, 1990). Adams (1990) observes that the extent to which children have learned to hear phonemes as individual and separate speech sounds will strengthen their ability to see individual letters and spelling patterns. And, conversely, the extent to which they have not learned to hear the phonemes will limit their ability. Adams refers to this as a 'double or nothing return'. Melby-Lervåg et al. (2012) conclude similarly: that the relationship between phonemic awareness and learning to read may be a causal one, in that adequate phonemic skill may be a prerequisite for learning to read effectively. To achieve this young children will need some explicit teaching. However, this more explicit teaching should be play based and enjoyable as children need to experience a significant degree of success in these early attempts with oral recognition of phonemes prior to the introduction of phonics. This could include games focused on hearing and identifying particular phonemes, such as feely bags, parachute games and ring games; tablet-, whiteboard- and electronic toy-based activities and games focused on oral recognition of phonemes; books, rhymes and songs that use alliteration; sound walks, indoors and outdoors; identifying, collecting or taking photos of items indoors and out that begin with a particular phoneme; treasure hunts where children have to find items and orally identify the initial sound; treasure boxes in which children collect items that begin with an identified phoneme (Neaum, 2017).

The Matthew effect in literacy

Stanovich (1986) writes of the 'Matthew effect' in literacy. The Matthew effect references the biblical verse Matthew 25: 29, 'The Parable of the Talents':

> For unto every one that hath shall be given, and he shall have abundance: but from him that hath not shall be taken even that which he hath.

Stanovich (1986) uses this as an analogy for becoming literate: the rich get richer and the poor get poorer. He observes that there are accumulated advantages for children whose early experiences are rich in talking and listening and engagement with print. These children tend to move into becoming literate with relative ease and find it engaging and enjoyable. This means that they remain involved and interested in literacy practices and so their literacy skills grow and improve – the rich get richer. In contrast, children whose early experiences are more limited are more likely to find becoming literate more difficult. They are therefore less likely to engage with literacy for enjoyment and with interest, and, consequently, less likely to develop fluent, effective literacy skills – the poor get poorer (Neaum, 2017).

So, if we are to look after young children's early literacy acquisition and development we need to look beyond the obvious explicit teaching of literacy skills and knowledge and towards what we know about what enables young children to come to school-based learning – and literacy learning – with a high chance of success. Our understanding of how we look after young children's literacy needs to recognise that becoming literate is not a discrete set of disconnected skills, but starts in a child's earliest years, in the quality of their relationships and in early experiences that are vital in anticipation of later literacy learning.

 Concluding thoughts

This chapter has outlined some of the vital relationships and experiences that lead into becoming literate and has emphasised the importance of these in enabling young children to come to school-based learning, including literacy learning, with a high chance of success. It argues that it is in these ways that we look after young children's literacy.

References

Adams, M.J. (1990) *Beginning to Read. Thinking and Learning about Print.* London: MIT Press.

Basit, T., Hughes, A., Iqbal, Z. and Cooper, J. (2015) The influence of socio-economic status and ethnicity on speech and language development. *International Journal of Early Years Education*, 23(1): 115–33.

Bernier, A., Carlson, S.M. and Whipple, N. (2010) From external regulation to self-regulation: early parenting precursors of young children's executive function. *Child Development*, 81(1): 326–39.

Beschorner, B. and Hutchison, A. (2013) iPads as a literacy teaching tool in early childhood. *International Journal of Education in Mathematics, Science and Technology*, 1(1): 16–24.

Blair, C. and Diamond, A. (2008) Biological processes in prevention and intervention: the promotion of self-regulation as a means of preventing school failure. *Development and Psychopathology*, 20(3): 899–911.

Bowlby, J. (1953) *Child Care and the Growth of Love*. London: Penguin.

Connell, G. and McCarthy, C. (2014) *A Moving Child Is a Learning Child*. Minneapolis, MN: Free Spirit.

Edwards, C. (2014) Maternal literacy practices and toddlers' emergent literacy skills. *Journal of Early Childhood Literacy*, 14(1): 53–79.

Goddard Blythe, S. (2000) Early learning in the balance: priming the first ABC. *Support for Learning*, 15(4): 154–8.

Goddard Blythe, S. (2011) Physical foundations for learning. In R. House (ed.) *Too Much Too Soon*. Stroud: Hawthorne Press.

Goddard Blythe, S. (2012) *Assessing Neuromotor Readiness for Learning*. London: Wiley-Blackwell.

Halliday, M. (1973) *Explorations in the Functions of Language*. London: Edward Arnold.

Harvard University (2016) *Executive Function and Self-regulation*. Centre for the Developing Child. **http://developingchild.harvard.edu/science/key-concepts/executive-function/**.

Johnson, S. (2014) *A Developmental Approach Looking at the Relationship of Children's Foundational Neurological Pathways to Their Higher Capacities for Learning*. Available at: **www.youandyourchildshealth.org/ youandyourchildshealth/articles/teaching%20our%20children.html**.

Lightsey, G. E. and Frye, B. J. (2004) Teaching metalinguistic skills to enhance early reading instruction. *Reading Horizons*, 45 (1): 27–35.

Melby-Lervåg, M., Lyster, S.A.H. and Hulme, C. (2012) Phonological skills and their role in learning to read: a meta-analytic review. *Psychological Bulletin*, 138: 322–52.

Mills, E. (1998) *The Toy Hospital*. London: Heinemann Young Books.

Mizielinska, A. and Mizielinski, D. (2013) *Maps*. London: Big Picture Press

Moullin, S., Waldfogel, J. and Washbrook, E. (2014) *Baby Bonds. Parenting Attachment and a Secure Base for Children*. London: Sutton Trust.

National Reading Panel (2000) *Teaching Children to Read*. Available at: https://www.nichd.nih.gov/ publications/pubs/nrp/documents/report.pdf.

Neaum, S. (2012) *Language and Literacy for the Early Years*. London: Sage.

Neaum, S. (2017) *What Comes Before Phonics?* London: Sage.

Neumann, M.M., Hood, M., Ford, R.M. and Neumann, D.L. (2011) The role of environmental print in emergent literacy. *Journal of Early Childhood Literacy*, 12(3): 231–58.

O'Connor, A. and Daly, A. (2016) *Understanding Physical Development in the Early Years. Linking Bodies and Minds*. London: Routledge.

Pagini, L. (2012) Links between motor skills and indicators of school readiness at kindergarten entry in urban disadvantaged children. *Journal of Educational and Developmental Psychology*, 2(1): 95–107.

Reeves, M.J. and Bailey, R.P. (2014) The effects of physical activity on children diagnosed with attention deficit hyperactivity disorder: a review. *Education 3–13: International Journal of Primary, Elementary and Early Years Education*, 1–13.

Rieber, R. and Hall, M.J. (1997) *The Collected Works of L.S. Vygotsky: The History of the Development of Higher Mental Functions*. London: Plenum Press.

Shea, M. (2011) *Parallel Learning of Reading and Writing in Early Childhood*. London: Routledge.

Stanovich, K. (1986) Matthew Effects in Reading: Some Consequences of Individual Differences in the acquisition of literacy. Available at: **http://people.uncw.edu/kozloffm/mattheweffect.pdf**.

Whitebread, D. and Basilio, M. (2012) The emergence and early development of self-regulation in young children. *Profesorado. Revisita de curriculum y formacion del profesorado*. **www.ugr.es/~recfpro/rev161ART2en.pdf**.

Whitebread, D. and Bingham, S. (2014) School readiness: starting age, cohorts and transitions in the early years. In J. Moyles, J. Georgeson and J. Payler (eds) *Early Years Foundations: Critical Issues*, 2nd edn. Berkshire: Open University Press.

2
Language, literacy and the learning environment

Caroline Walker-Gleaves and Alan Gleaves

 This chapter

This chapter explores the importance of the places and spaces in which we choose to learn. It examines the assumptions that have been held about learning environments for many years and challenges the thinking behind these. The chapter develops your understanding of the importance of the environment for learning and helps you to rethink what might work best for the children whom you teach. It will explore three themes in relation to the learning environment and that overlap in the examination of distance, proximity and language – they are, in turn, the significance of proximity in the development of child language and identity development; the nature of teacher and child relationships, attachment and learning; and finally the wider environment, that is the spatial and ecological structure and nature of the classroom as a place for language to flourish.

Introduction

For all people, including children, the places and spaces in which we learn and choose to learn are critically important (Klatte et al., 2013). For example, some people learn best when they are in low lighting, sitting in comfortable sofas and on cosy rugs, and in close proximity to other people. Some people learn best when they are in very high and daylight illumination, in perfect silence and distant to people. Some people learn best when they have music to accompany them, and others when they study to the beat of a bass. There are very many assumptions around what works best for individuals trying to learn. For example, for many hundreds of years, there was a general belief that limited aesthetics and harshness were the necessary prerequisites for people to learn, the hard wooden chairs, the upright backs and the bare classrooms testament to a tradition that considered suffering and discipline a rite of passage to higher and purer learning and achievement. Not only that, the individual chairs, the central and elevated position of the teacher in the classroom and the hard reflective surfaces, all conspired to a view of learning that is individual, silent and to be endured, rather than social, dialogic and about empowerment. For people, and especially children, who are facing difficulty with learning, and for whom language is an impediment to their educational and personal development, not least their literacy, it is very clear that such environments, rather than encouraging development, may well become a terrifying hurdle which, rather than unlocking their potential, firmly shuts the door on any possibility of creating the spark of opening up the prison that language and literacy may have become, or may well become if it is not noticed or addressed.

Why are the places and spaces in which children learn so significant?

The ideas that learning ecology, proximity and environment may contribute to the quality of what is learned, as well as paving the way for a longer-term development of a more enjoyable and positive view of learning, is now beginning to be established in education, albeit it is still an area that needs more research and more research evidence (Walker-Gleaves, 2011). However, it is an area that is also complex and very wide-ranging, since it covers the areas of relationships, atmosphere, ergonomics, design, architecture, noise, physical ecology and attachment (Kyriakides et al., 2009). In other words, the area has implications for learning across all three of the emotional, social and physical domains, and so is demanding and complex to research and to disseminate and make an impact in practice. But it is a critically important area though – and may contribute to children's ability to become not only more literate learners, but also more assured and self-sufficient ones. This chapter will explore three themes in relation to the learning environment and that overlap in the examination of distance and proximity and language – they are, in turn, the significance of proximity in the development of child language and identity development; the nature of teacher and child relationships, attachment and learning; and, finally, the wider environment, that is the spatial and ecological structure and nature of the classroom as a place for language to flourish.

Case study

Using movement and touch to help develop writing skill

Freddie was seven years old and adopted, after being in foster care for three years. He had been severely and chronically physically abused and neglected, and had not attended school regularly for at least three years. As a result, he could neither read nor write and had very limited language. His adoptive mother read stories to him every night and he loved to hear in particular stories about animals. As a result, he started to become interested in wildlife, and developed a love of birds through repeated visits to a wildfowl sanctuary. At the sanctuary, Freddie liked to walk through the many ponds and grassed areas, filling in the birds that he had seen on little competition quiz sheets that the sanctuary ran, with little bird fridge magnets for the neatest ones. But over the course of many visits, Freddie would return home very angry because he wanted to write the names of the birds and he could neither write quickly enough to be able to do this, nor neatly enough to be able to submit his sheet for a possible prize. As a result, Freddie oscillated between being angry and heartbroken that he could not write properly. His mother decided on a course of action combining writing and physical closeness based on attachment.

Like many children who have been in public care, Freddie had been diagnosed as having an attachment disorder. In Freddie's case, he was diagnosed as having 'disordered attachment' (Sroufe, 1986), that is demanding affection and attention on some occasions out of proportion with the particular context or activity, and at other times raging at caregivers without warning and for no apparent reason. Freddie seemed to love doing literacy activities with his mum, however – ones where he was physically close, had time completely devoted just to him with no distractions, and where he could feel that he was doing well with something that was out of his reach yet meant so much to him – the ability to be part of the whole experience of the birds to which he was so attached. So this is exactly what happened, every single night for a whole year. Freddie and his mum would sit in a warm and cosy room, with hundreds of sheets of blank white paper, a range of brightly coloured pens and pencils, and together, using tracing paper over nature books, they would carefully trace out the letters of all the birds that Freddie had seen at the sanctuary. Then Freddie and his mum would stand up and make the letters in the air, using their arms to wave out the letters and words. Then they would go back to the sofa, and sitting closely together, Freddie would write all the bird names on his iPad using a drawing app.

The process was often difficult, Freddie being angry and tired and his mum also impatient that there was so much to do and that maybe being able to write some birds was good enough to earn a prize at the bird sanctuary. But no ... Freddie wanted to be able to write them all, and anyway, sometimes, often, it was lovely to sit in a warm and inviting little room, cocooned together, seeing little hands making shapes and then laughing at the flapping of arms, or the little games together when Freddie's mum made mistakes and Freddie pretended to be the teacher and tell her off for her messy writing. No, neither Freddie nor his mum could stop, or wanted to stop.

Closeness, attunement and the deliciousness of proximity

Vygotsky (1978, p.57) asserted that learning was socially mediated: he claimed that the child's development was in effect a double helix and that each element of a child's cultural development appears twice: first, on the social, or interpsychological, level, and later, on the individual, or intrapsychological, level. He went on to argue that, therefore, and logically, the later and higher cognitive, linguistic and behavioural functions originate primarily as relational qualities, and that they arise out of relationships between humans. All the higher functions originate as actual relations between human individuals. Although Vygotsky's work on learning has become central to how most teachers construct and enact their teaching practices, the premise upon which Vygotsky based his social learning and constructivist theory, the quality and extent of close relationships, has been largely marginalised in educational literature, and this has occurred within all domains of educational practice, from very early years through compulsory schooling up to technical, vocational and higher education (Walker-Gleaves, 2011).

The reasons for this are partly to do with the complex nature of learning and the factors that might motivate children to learn at one particular time, in one particular environment, but not in others. For example, researchers investigating child–teacher attachment systems (Dogruoz and Rogow, 2009; Kochanska, 1993) in early learning environments have mixed findings: there is some evidence for suggesting the longevity of child–teacher attachments, in some cases lasting for the whole of childhood into adulthood; but in other research, there is doubt about the potency of relationships as antecedents to effective and successful learning, and the validity of separating out the influence of child–teacher relationships from other developmental factors.

Yet parallel research in language and child development, from a developmental psychological, rather than a relational and pedagogic perspective, shows that the Vygotskian preoccupation with relationships in learning was and is exactly correct, and indeed is critical to understanding interventions in language and literacy. In fact, while it is language that is the hallmark of human relationships, the reverse is also true, that it is relationships that are the hallmark of successful language, and in turn literacy. Indeed, language is one of the main tools we have to make bonds, share ideas, air our emotions and narrate our experiences. And as such, it is the foundation of all learning, problem-solving and literacy development, and therefore the predicate and predictor of all life chances and opportunities.

How are closeness and language linked?

The case study with Freddie highlights the manifestation and inextricable relationship between proximity, language and its cyclic nature, that is the more interaction, the greater the degree of possibility of language use and development, and as a result the better fostering of opportunities for the application of language to literacy. What this case study shows is the gradualism and naturalism of physical and proximal approaches to learning literacy, or in other words the lack of rigid barriers between different elements of literacy activity. This is an important principle because, typically, language is learned through our everyday interactions with the world – children talk to caregivers and they talk back. People communicate with others, and they communicate back in turn. Overall, there is little direct instruction or conscious thought about the process and it happens very naturally, unselfconsciously and almost unconsciously. However, by the same token then, it is possible to see that when children struggle to learn language, alongside they frequently experience problems with making friends, they have behaviour difficulties and academic success becomes difficult and elusive. Through a process of iteration and recycling, communication becomes more and more difficult when children's confidence is compromised, and this begins to affect self-esteem, the ways in which children see themselves, and this in turn frequently causes children to disengage with peers and the opportunities for socialisation that would otherwise cement communication. In short, language, interaction and learning become a negative and downward spiral in which they ultimately lead to compromised learning outcomes (Schore, 2000). This process of developing the conditions necessary for Vygotskian relationships is premised on the notion of attachment developed by Bowlby (1952).

The theory of attachment and its links to later relationships

John Bowlby first outlined his theory of attachment and its central role in child development more than 50 years ago. Attachment theory is a theory of personality development in the context of close relationships that has become the most dominant and paradigmatic framework for understanding relationships and bonds, across all social and human sciences. Bowlby (1953) asserted that although attachment is significant throughout the life span, the unique bond that develops between an infant and primary caregiver in the first year of life not only forms the imprint for all future relationships, but also serves as a guiding architecture as to how individuals conduct their relational behaviour and its make-up, including, for example, trust, loyalty, respect and fidelity. Bowlby argued that the pre-language experience of bonding is so strong since it relates to the most existential aspects of life, including safety, comfort, sustenance and contentment, and as a result, relationships without these vital elements are characterised by acute distress. Children experiencing these, argued Bowlby, are so traumatised that they develop haphazard and often counterproductive means both to acquire them, or to keep them when they reappear. They do this on the basis that they may not experience such care with regularity, so their behaviour may become disordered and disorganised. Conversely, effective caregivers provide these and act to confirm and cement their care and attachment, with caregiver and cared for in a cycle of continual provision and reception.

In evolutionary terms attachment is very important for survival as it ensures that young children remain close to their caregivers, particularly when they are under threat. However, such attachment is not simple nor unconditional – the precise nature of children's attachments is strongly influenced by the behaviours and emotional characteristics of their carers (Bowlby, 1952). The more responsive, careful and gentle the caregiver is, then the greater the chances that a longer term and stronger attachment will take place. However, this is not automatic, and the development of attachment is a dynamic process, being augmented and attenuated constantly through processes of, for example, attunement (picking up and responding to micro-level behaviours), and motivational displacement (knowing when to place one's needs aside to respond solely to the needs of the child). It is also very important to recognise that young children are capable of having different types of attachments to different people and, for example, may have a secure attachment to their grandmother and an anxious attachment to their mother. But attachments to genetic-biological family are neither automatic nor necessarily the most secure or long-lasting, and Bowlby himself emphasised the role of kinship attachments on secure and safe caring (Bifulco et al., 1992). Furthermore, research (Kyriakides et al., 2009) suggests many vulnerable children may have developed important attachments to older siblings, neighbours or educational professionals who provided more reliable care than their parents.

Attachment and language learning

Educational impacts on children and young people that development secure and reliable relationships are well supported in the literature (Schore, 2000) and these are particularly important in relation to language and subsequent literacy development. For example, children who are sure of attunement and that teachers will be responsive at all levels are more likely to take risks, whether this might be with embarking on something that they find difficult, like writing a story, or trying a new reading book; in addition, such children may be more sure of their own worth and have a more secure identity, and as such feel as though they do not need to act to please teachers, peers or others. This is also particularly important for children's capacity to understand the minds of others and their own minds (to mentalise) and, related to this, to place themselves in the position of empathising and changing perspective. These facets of a child's development are linked in complex and changing ways, and may be reinforced through attachment and the emotions that result through being able to carry out cognitive tasks as a result of attachments. Nevertheless, such stages and the progress of children's learning is complex, and attachment as an overarching theory and predictor of learning is currently being questioned in psychological terms, on the basis that it is very conditional, fluctuating with the individual caregiver, and also positions the cared for as having no 'agency', or capacity to decide to act, for themselves (Fearon and Roisman, 2017).

Nevertheless, as Vygotsky (1987) has pointed out, and as we discussed earlier, an individual's experience of relationships is bound up with associated emotions and vice versa, and if we assume that a child's experience of learning is based on both these, then we can see quite clearly that the whole process of attachment, emotional development, relationships and learning development are linked in a never ending cycle. As such, and in consequence, then, if a child has not developed a strong foundation of emotional competence in these areas by the time they enter school, they will struggle to manage the learning and social environment of school as successfully as their peers. Those children who have been seriously abused or neglected in their earliest years, however, are particularly at risk of developing a disorganised attachment to their caregiver (Fearon and Roisman, 2017). It is a profound irony that the caregiver to whom they are programmed to be attached is the carer who is unreliable and thus further compounds their problematic attachment. In learning terms, it is akin to a pupil continually returning to the teacher who repeatedly undermines their confidence, but they have only one teacher, so no other option but to return to them. However, although around half of all children have some degree of haphazard attachment to carers, it is only around 5 per cent of the population that present as having much more substantial bonding difficulties, and this would almost certainly include the number of children who have also been subject to a care order for reasons of abuse and neglect (Walker-Gleaves, 2015). Many other difficulties are associated with this group of children, including problems with language, literacy, engaging with education, progressing onto training and jobs, wider health and social difficulties, and indeed many childhood mental health disorders are associated with this type of attachment and there is evidence that such difficulties may continue into adulthood (Edwards, 1995).

Who decides what is acceptable in terms of relationships?

The idea of close physical relationships as being central to the ways in which children's learning and language and ultimately literacy are promoted and fostered is enshrined in the concept of 'parenting capacity' (Lewis, 2005), and parental reading with children is cited as an important element of how such capacity is developed in practice in familial settings. Indeed, social workers and other practitioners continue to assess families, using an ecological model, in relation to three key dimensions:

- the developmental needs of individual children;

- the capacity of the parents to meet the child's needs;

- the family and environmental situation in which the family live.

The dimensions relating to parenting capacity are:

- basic care

- ensuring safety

- emotional warmth

- stimulation

- guidance and boundaries

- stability.

What is clear from statutory guidelines into parenting assessments is that the notion of parents doing all that they can to promote and support the physical, emotional, social and intellectual development of a child from infancy to adulthood is assumed to be obvious and desirable for all parents and carers (Lewis, 2005), and further that such support is not assumed to be incidental nor voluntary, but as a clear mandate for parents to ensure the development of empathic understanding and giving priority to their children's needs. However, this may require a more nuanced and complex understanding of the creation and promotion of such aspects of parenting as the need for understanding and responding sensitively to the challenges which a particular child's temperament and development pose. The example of the Freddie case study is a case in point: being able to respond to considerably changeable and dynamic child development, and recognising one's own intrinsic characteristics which might impede each individual child's particular developmental needs, is complex and very difficult for many parents and carers. Being able to do this requires creativity, constant vigilance and 'response-ability', and great flexibility, especially since children experiencing difficulty have different needs which require the parental responses best suited to stimulate and further their development and well-being but which have traditionally been outside the scope of literature and support from other professionals or wider sources due to their uniqueness (Forehand and Kotchick, 1996). But there are problems with aspects of relationships and language- and literacy-related activity for another reason, and this is that reading and writing with a child is such an ordinary activity that there are often assumptions about its naturalness that parents, teachers and other professionals alike may take for granted when and how it is occurring. Nevertheless, consideration of the environment that adults can 'design' to promote and embed attachment, attunement and the precursors of language and literacy learning are central to the development in turn of 'relational zones' (Goldstein, 1999) and provide opportunities to:

- explore children's inner lives;

- empathise with others and understand others' views;

- stimulate the imagination but also be a useful prompt for direct and indirect communication on a range of issues.

Much research has shown that sharing a book with a child is a pleasurable experience and the literature in education and psychology illuminates how books are both a 'mirror to nature' and a way of adults and children exploring together the links between their own 'outer' and 'inner worlds' (Birch and Ladd, 1997). However, there is less literature on sharing writing together, and the notion that standing behind both are a need for the proximity of relationships and the detailed mechanics of contact and closeness is a less well developed theme in mainstream educational literature (Ziontis, 2005; Walker-Gleaves, 2011) and there are still considerable conceptual gaps in relation to how professionals for example could develop a much greater professional understanding of the practical and environmental ways in which literacy might be leveraged to improve a child's opportunities and life chances, especially when starting out from some disadvantage and/or vulnerability (Heneker, 2005; Brooks, 2013).

Teacher and child relationships, attachment and relational zones

Schools, classes, lessons, projects, experiments, all of them are based on language and literacy – indeed, language is the means by which all teachers teach and all children learn. But children with speech and language needs in the form of developmental language disorders are at a much higher risk of difficulties with reading, writing and spelling and these are compounded if they have early difficulties, and if there are no accommodations or interventions that help children to overcome problems as early as possible in their educational career. For example, in primary settings, if children can't say words, they will be more likely to have difficulties in 'sounding out' words for reading and spelling or writing them down. If children can't manipulate pens, pencils and other writing implements, then they will be more likely to have difficulties in basic letter development and so struggle to write more complex sentences and stories later on. Likewise, if children can't understand the words they hear, they will struggle to understand what they have read.

Literature suggests that children with communication difficulties are more likely to have behaviour difficulties (Eppi Centre meta review, 2010) and recent research shows that many children with identified behavioural needs have previously unidentified speech, language and communication needs (Cohen et al., 1998). The reasons for this are, however, complex and related to the earlier section on the relational and social nature of language and therefore of learning. First, as children's attempts at socialisation develop, friendships become increasingly important, for many reasons, including copying behaviour, trying out different behavioural strategies, exploring decision-making and basic moral frameworks, and so on. Much of this occurs at the stage of formative language development, where there are already difficulties in expressing meaning simply because of the smaller vocabularies that children possess in the early years and primary age groups (Bercow, 2008). But as a result, communication is all the more critical – imagine, for example, the frustration of not getting your message across, and the sadness at not being able to share in even basic socialisation with friends. Poor language and literacy skills act as barriers to all manner of social relationships and so children with difficulties are doubly disadvantaged (Brooks, 2013).

How widespread are language disorders?

Developmental language disorders are often hidden but relatively common: studies of the national distribution of problems demonstrate that currently around 7 per cent of all children had a severe enough language deficit to impact upon their learning ability and thus longer-term educational progress (Bercow, 2008). But what is significant about this figure is that although it is relatively high, it attracts far less attention in research, media and teacher education terms than other difficulties such as autism and dyslexia. The reasons for this relative obscurity and invisibility are, again, related to the areas that this chapter mentioned earlier, and that is attachment and relationships. But perversely, rather than research and policy to date acknowledging that language, literacy and behaviour are linked, and that poor language may be exacerbated by poor relationships which foster poor behaviour in the form of frustration and anger, the converse equation, suggesting that poor language skill may be enhanced by very high-quality relationships, particularly in the form of close and sustained bonds, is hitherto extremely under-researched and the literature suggests that the main responsibility for interventions thus lies in the work of adjunct professionals, such as speech and language therapists and educational psychologists (Lindsay and Dockrell, 2012). Emerging research (Dockrell et al., 2015) argues strongly for a much more balanced approach: it acknowledges the specialist knowledge and methodologies of such professionals, but is also calling for a far more sophisticated, nuanced and expert recognition of the unique pedagogic relationship that teachers may foster with children with language and literacy difficulties.

Language, literacy and policy shifts

The Green Paper *Every Child Matters* (DfES, 2003) and the Children's Act 2004 identified a need for health authorities, schools and social services to work together to support children's social and emotional development, and numerous policies and legislation since have identified strategies, interventions and frameworks all designed to address this aspect of children's learning, particularly in relation to children from adverse home environments. To this end a number of school programmes which have fostered and utilised 'positive' (Howes et al., 2003) child–teacher relationships have been implemented in the UK with the aim of reconceptualising the teacher–pupil relationship not solely as a cognitive 'dyad' but also as a precursor and a critical element of every child's cognitive *and* affective development – in fact, such programmes reflect an explicit attention to the theories that were covered in the first section of this chapter – those of attachment and relationships (Ziontis, 2005).

In pedagogic relationship terms then, teachers may play a key role in both identifying and supporting children with language disorder in the classroom. In 2008, the Bercow Review recommended explicitly that the 'standards for qualified teacher status ensure that students develop a better understanding of children and young people's speech, language and communication needs and of how to address those needs' (Recommendation 22). It also recommended that the Department for Children, Schools and Families (now the Department for Education) 'includes speech, language and communication, both as a core requirement and as an elective module, in the new Masters in Teaching and Learning' (Recommendation 23). However, like policy pronouncements in areas of teacher preparation and funding stream investment, such as the support for children with Profound and Multiple Learning Difficulties or Looked after, Fostered and Adopted Children, such changes have not been forthcoming and, indeed, training has not kept pace with research findings and funding has been withdrawn or capped in many areas that would otherwise support the knowledge development of teachers in these critically important areas (Law and Garrett, 2004). In fact, parents and professionals alike have expressed grave concerns that reviews such as the Carter review and subsequent initiatives in initial teacher training take little account of any of the foregoing areas mentioned, including language and literacy disorders and difficulties (Ziontis, 2005). Indeed, one of the very great impediments to current thinking in the area of teacher preparation is the rationale for this book – and that is that trainee teachers need to have enough understanding to be able to promote positive speech, language and communication strategies at a very informed, insightful and nuanced level, not with an exclusive focus on literacy. Such wide-ranging issues, knowledge and skills as are presented throughout this book are entwined and form a critical premise on which to develop high-level pedagogic practice as these skills impact effective access to the whole curriculum.

Developing language-promoting pedagogic relationships

So what evidence is there to suggest that this is worth researching, and what might such rich and valuable pedagogic relationships look like? Well, first, children with language disorders often lack verbal strategies to respond to instructions and to listen in the classroom and may only take in one or two words of what is said to them. They may well struggle with the speed of spoken language and in addition may not be able to remember the instructions given to them. This can lead to failure to follow instructions that can be perceived as 'naughty' behaviour by the class teacher (Charman et al., 2015). In other cases, children with language disorder are mistaken for being lazy or stupid, when in fact such children have difficulty understanding and expressing vocabulary, complex sentences and extended discourse, such as conversation or stories, all of which alienates children and makes them less likely to even embark on activities or social relationships in case they further expose their 'deficits' to others. Similarly, children with a language disorder may have difficulty following playground rules and often misinterpret jokes from peers as other children 'making fun'; as such, they may look like moody children, and be labelled by teachers as having problems with socialisation and in some cases conditions such as Oppositional Defiant Disorder or even Conduct Disorder. The labelling, frustration and inability to respond leads to more disruptive behaviour and increased risk for social, emotional and mental health problems in the longer term (Clegg et al., 2009).

However, although early research has recognised the salience of all of these concepts in successful learning, and emerging research is suggesting the pathways of causality between attachment, relationships and language, there is still a dearth of critical literature that seeks to explore in detail the impact of deliberate types of attachment relationships in schools and, second, whether these can, longer term, be used to facilitate more profound affordances in literacy. Perhaps the currently most interesting areas of literature that tangentially reflect the gains to be made as a result of 'deliberate relational pedagogy' are those where intensive interventions in one area, such as phonics, accelerated reading or nurture groups, have demonstrated significant gains in areas allied to the main purpose of the research but have not yet demonstrated causality. In general, these programmes in addition reflect an increased recognition of the importance in child development of relationships with non-parental adults and growing interest in the potential of preventative interventions in the early years (Axford et al., 2015). Indeed, like the most effective parents, teachers facilitate children's explorations of their environment while playing a significant role in developing their verbal ability to reflect on their own beliefs – in other words, they are critical agents in language and literacy development. In sum, then, the literature describing the actual and potential impact of teacher–pupil relationships on children's emotional development still has some way to go in terms of elucidating the actual mechanics of particular practices and in terms of ensuring that teachers, parents and professionals are aware of, and can critically reflect on, new developments in research. There is a long way to go.

The spatiality and ecology of the classroom

Our environment can affect behaviour, communication, emotional well-being, motivation and general engagement, and getting the environment right for learners contributes to their overall achievement. As adults, we are frequently acutely aware of the noise that surrounds us and how it affects our daily life and indeed our functioning. Noise can affect our mood, our ability to concentrate and our willingness to engage with activities as a group or as an individual (Ljung et al., 2009). We also often subconsciously block out surrounding noise that seems to exist as a backdrop to everyday life. For example, the quality and size of media devices in the twenty-first century, such as portable speakers and large commercially available bass-enhanced headphones, mean that the surrounding ambient noise levels are frequently very high. Not only that of course, but the increase in traffic, in the air and on the road, together with the frequent reduction in the quality of building materials and sound insulation, means that we are surrounded an insurmountably large amount of noise. Research shows that noise makes most human activity more difficult – it is harder to concentrate, it is harder to hear and it is more difficult to focus. Furthermore, in learning psychological terms, there is evidence to suggest that the cognitive load of multiple forms of media, far from contributing to a rich learning environment, acts to make the media richness become redundant at best and conflicting at worse (Klatte et al., 2010). However, there are many children for whom noise is not simply noise – it is a background to life, and a constant reminder for many that they come second to aural and oral stimulation when they are with the most significant others in their lives, as the case studies show clearly. For these children, the intelligibility of speech is severely compromised by the competing noises which they are surrounded by, as well as the emotional impacts of the noise, especially in relation to the fact that the significant individual involved in placing the children in these situations is the primary caregiver (Jamieson et al., 2004).

Case study

The importance of soundscapes in understanding children's experiences of ecology

Myriam

Myriam is a ten-year-old girl who lives with her parents in a large detached house not far from the school that she attends. She is an only child and her parents are both professional lawyers. Myriam has all the latest gadgets and mobile devices, including an iPhone, an Apple iPad and a rose gold laptop. She is often early to school since she is dropped off by her parents so that they can get into their office before the rush hour kicks off. Although Myriam has the latest Beats bass-enhanced headphones, she does not wear them. When I asked her why she said this:

> I don't like wearing headphones because it's the same as what my mum and dad are like in the car or when we go out for a run. My dad wears his all the time so he can listen to music and he doesn't talk to me or the dog. My mum wears them at home, but just has one bud in and she listens to Sky rolling news but I can tell that when I talk to her, she isn't listening to me.

Jared

Jared is eight years old and lives with his father in a bed and breakfast in the centre of the city. The school is located just off a ring road as it enters the built-up area. Jared's parents separated and Jared went to live with his father who had custody of him. Jared's father works long hours in a call centre to provide for them both, and leaves Jared alone in the shared room in the B&B. But the place is so noisy with so many comings and goings that Jared's father started to leave the TV on very loud to drown out the noise and the frequent fights that occur. Jared doesn't like the loud noise because he can't sleep and can't read the books that he brings home from school, but he likes the fights and constant din even less.

Changing the language and literacy environment for the better

Children's language development, as we have already explored in this and other chapters, is inextricably bound up both explicitly and implicitly with the relational and environmental and indeed intimate nature of the various ecologies in which they operate. In the case studies above, there are many strands of language development at work that necessitate an examination of the factors that may impede and enhance the children's development in schools and classrooms. From the two case studies alone, it is possible to isolate several areas that necessitate a theoretical underpinning both to understand their origin and nature, and also how a teacher and school may make changes so that the language development of children, especially those with difficulties, may make progress. In particular, then, elements of importance include:

- motivation of adults to meaningfully listen and make space for communication;

- competing for adults' and others' concentration while talking and listening simultaneously;

- finding an appropriate place in which to listen comfortably and enjoyably;

- creating areas of different comfort, privacy and noise insulation so that children can adapt and choose their environment depending on their particular needs;

- feeling safe around different noise levels;

- having space to read and think within poor social environments;

- finding peace and quiet when there are learning difficulty and disability-related reasons for needing it.

In order to be able to adapt the classroom environment to the needs of children so that it is language- and communication-focused, there are several strategies that may be adopted to help evaluate both the quality of the existing environment and also understand what children might want and need to be able to accommodate their language and literacy development. Steps that might be taken therefore, include:

- auditing the starting points in terms of speech, language and communication development that children have on arrival at the school/class;

- examining the research base in learning environments in schools for particular purposes, including reading and writing, reading together, reading alone, reading in groups;

- interviewing children about what sort of 'spaces' they like and why, and recording their responses using research tools such as 'pupil view templates' (Wall et al., 2005);

- using photo-elicitation research methods when asking children to take photos of their favourite places so that you have precise knowledge of what it is that children like and the reasons (Mandleco, 2013);

- examining the structure and layout of classrooms, corridors and the gardens around the buildings, always focusing on questions such as: What are the interactions taking place here? How is children's attention altered in this space? Is this space distracting because of what is happening around it? Or providing focus because of the qualities of the space itself? What colours, materials and artifacts are being used around spaces and places where language and literacy are being taught and promoted?

- Thinking about the spaces and places within classrooms and schools in general: for example, for children with different needs, such as attachment and relational needs, are there spaces in the classroom and school that feel secure but not enclosed and threatening? Can children see a way out and feel safe if they want to leave particular areas? Do children actively want to stay in the space? Go to the space? Or never want to go there?

- considering the thoughts and feelings of others, including, for example asking what would parents/carers/guardians think about the spaces and places for learning? Would they want to sit and read/write with their children in these contexts?

Concluding thoughts

This chapter has examined the relationships between the characteristics of effective literacy- and language-promoting environments, physical relationships that promote effective language and literacy development and the spaces and places in which learning takes place, and considered the implications for children experiencing emotional, social and behavioural difficulties. It has also explored how these needs can be supported both by assessing and changing the nature of the learning environment, and also by giving teachers and others – professionals, parents and carers alike – the knowledge and tools with which to think more carefully about how the physical environment of the classroom and the relationships that they have with children may affect children's language and literacy development very significantly.

References

Axford, N. et al. (2015) *The Best Start at Home: What Works to Improve the Quality of Parent-Child Interactions from Conception to Age 5 Years? A Rapid Review of Interventions.* London: Early Intervention Foundation.

Bercow, J. (2008) *Bercow Review of Services for Children and Young People (0–19) with Speech, Language and Communication Needs.* London: Department for Children, Schools and Families (DCSF).

Bifulco, A., Harris, T. and Brown, G.W. (1992) Mourning or early inadequate care? Re-examining the relationship of maternal loss in childhood with adult depression and anxiety. *Development and Psychopathology,* 4(3): 433–49.

Birch, S.A. and Ladd, G.W. (1997) The teacher–child relationship and children's early school adjustment. *Journal of School Psychology,* 35: 61–79.

Bowlby, J. (1952) Maternal care and mental health. *Journal of Consulting Psychology,* 16(3): 232.

Bowlby, J. (1953) *Child Care and the Growth of Love.* London: Penguin Books.

Brooks, G. (2013) *What Works for Children and Young People with Literacy Difficulties?* London: Dyslexia-SpLD Trust Publications.

Charman, T., Ricketts, J., Lindsay, G., Dockrell, J.E. and Palikara, O. (2015) Emotional and behavioural problems in children with language impairments and children with autism spectrum disorders. *International Journal of Language and Communication Disorders,* 50(1): 84–93.

Clegg, J., Stackhouse, J., Finch, K., Murphy, C. and Nicholls, S. (2009) Language abilities of secondary age pupils at risk of school exclusion: a preliminary report. *Child Language Teaching and Therapy,* 25(1): 123–40.

Cohen, N.J., Barwick, M.A., Horodezky, N.B., Vallance, D.D. and Im, N. (1998) Language, achievement, and cognitive processing in psychiatrically disturbed children with previously identified and unsuspected language impairments. *Journal of Child Psychology and Psychiatry,* 39(6): 865–77.

Department for Education and Skills (DfES) (2003) *Green Paper: Every Child Matters*. London: DFES.

Dockrell, J., Lindsay, G., Law, J. and Roulstone, S. (2015) Supporting children with speech language and communication needs: an overview of the results of the Better Communication Research Programme. *International Journal of Language and Communication Disorders*, 49(5): 543–57.

Dogruoz, D. and Rogow, D. (2009) *And How Will You Remember Me, My Child? Redefining Fatherhood in Turkey*. New York: Population Council.

Edwards, J. (1995) 'Parenting skills': views of community health and social service providers about the needs of their 'clients'. *Journal of Social Policy*, 24: 237–59.

Eppi Centre (2010) *The Interaction Between Behaviour and Speech and Language Difficulties: Does Intervention for One Affect Outcomes in the Other?* London: Eppi Centre, Institute of Education.

Fearon, R.M. and Roisman, G.I. (2017) Attachment theory: progress and future directions. *Current Opinion in Pscyhology*, 15: 131–6.

Forehand, R. and Kotchick, B.A. (1996) Cultural diversity: a wake-up call for parent training. *Behaviour Therapy*, 27: 187–206.

Goldstein, L. (1999) The relational zone: the role of caring relationships in the co-construction of mind. *American Educational Research Journal*, 36(3): 647–73.

Heneker, S. (2005) Speech and language therapy support for pupils with behavioural, emotional and social difficulties (BESD): a pilot project. *British Journal of Special Education*, 32(2): 86–91.

Howes, C., James, J. and Ritchie, S. (2003) Pathways to effective teaching. *Early Childhood Research Quarterly*, 18: 104–20.

Jamieson, D.G., Kranjc, G., Yu, K. and Hodgetts, W.E. (2004) Speech intelligibility of young school-aged children in the presence of real-life classroom noise. *Journal of the American Academy of Audiology*, 15: 508–517.

Klatte, M., Bergström, K. and Lachmann, T. (2013) Does noise affect learning? A short review on noise effects on cognitive performance in children. *Frontiers in Psychology*, 4: 578.

Klatte, M., Lachmann, T., Schlittmeier, S. and Hellbrück, J. (2010) The irrelevant sound effect in short-term memory: is there developmental change? *European Journal of Cognitive Psychology*, 22: 1168–91.

Kochanska, G. (1993) Toward a synthesis of parental socialization and child temperament in early development of conscience. *Society for Research in Child Development*, 64: 325–47.

Kyriakides, L., Creemers, B. and Antoniou, P. (2009) Teacher behaviour and student outcomes: suggestions for research on teacher training and professional development. *Teaching and Teacher Education*, 25: 12–23.

Law, J. and Garrett, Z. (2004) The effectiveness of speech and language therapy and its potential role in child and mental health services. *Child and Adolescent Mental Health*, 9(2): 50–5.

Lewis, M. (2005) The child and its family: the social networks model. *Human Development*, 48: 8–27.

Lindsay, G. and Dockrell, J. (2000) The behaviour and self-esteem of children with specific speech and language difficulties. *British Journal of Educational Psychology*, 70(4): 583–601.

Lindsay, G. and Dockrell, J. E. (2012) Longitudinal patterns of behavioral, emotional and social difficulties and self-concept in adolescents with a history of specific language impairment. *Language, Speech, and Hearing Services in Schools*, 43(4): 445–60.

Ljung, R., Sörqvist, P., Kjellberg, A. and Green, A. (2009) Poor listening conditions impair memory for intelligible lectures: implications for acoustic classroom standards. *Building Acoustics*, 16: 257–26.

Mandleco, B. (2013) Research with children as participants: photo elicitation. *Journal for Specialists in Paediatric Nursing*, 18(1): 78–82.

Schore, A.N. (2000) Attachment and the regulation of the right brain. *Attachment and Human Development*, 2(1): 23–47.

Sroufe, L.A. (1986) *The Role of Infant Caregiver Attachment in Development. From Clinical Implication of Attachment*. Mahwah, NJ: Lawrence Erlbaum Associates.

Vygotsky, L.S. (1987) Thinking and speech. In R.W. Rieber and A.S. Carton (eds), *The Collected Works of L. S. Vygotsky, Volume 1: Problems of General Psychology*. New York: Plenum Press, pp. 39–285 (original work published 1934).

Walker-Gleaves, C. (2011) Invisible Threads of Pedagogic Care. Saarbrucken: Verlag.

Walker-Gleaves, C. (2015) Understanding the educational achievements and difficulties of looked after children. In S. Martin-Denham (ed.), *Making an Impact: Preparing to Teach in Specialist Provision*. London: Sage.

Wall, K., Higgins, S. and Smith, H. (2005) 'The visual helps me understand the complicated things': pupil views of teaching and learning with interactive whiteboards. *British Journal of Educational Technology*, 36(5): 851–67.

Ziontis, L.T. (2005) Examining relationships between students and teachers: a potential extension of attachment theory? In K.A. Kerns and R.A. Richardson (eds), *Attachment in Middle Childhood*. New York: Guilford Press, pp. 231–53.

3
Phonics and reading

Angela Gill and David Waugh

 This chapter

In this chapter, we will consider why some children learn to read successfully while others do not, and will explore some of the challenges children face when developing their literacy skills. Consideration will be given to strategies that can be used in school and in conjunction with parents and carers to support those children who need additional help if they are to succeed in literacy. Particular attention will be paid to phonics and other strategies used in early reading.

What are the factors that enable some children to succeed in literacy?

Scarborough (2009) sums up the key elements of reading in a similar way to the Simple View of Reading Model (Gough and Tunmer, 1986 – see Figure 3.1), which was brought to wide attention by the Rose Review (DfES 2006):

As recently as 20 years ago, learning to read was not thought to commence until formal instruction was provided in school. Accordingly, reading disabilities were largely considered problems with no known antecedents at earlier ages. It is now abundantly clear that reading acquisition is a process that begins early in the pre-school period, such that children arrive at school having acquired vastly differing degrees of knowledge and skill pertaining to literacy. (1986: 23)

Scarborough discusses the multifaceted nature of reading and its acquisition and illustrates this with a model that has strong similarities to the simple view of reading. Language comprehension and word recognition are two key elements which must ultimately be coordinated if a child is to read well.

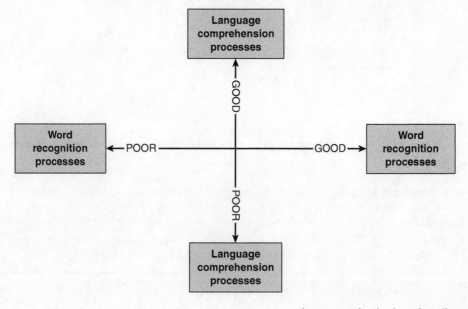

Figure 3.1   Simple view of reading model.

Source: DfES (2006) *Independent Review of the Teaching of Early Reading (Final Report by Jim Rose)*. Ref: 0201/2006 DOC-EN. Nottingham: DfES, p.77.

Word recognition

This involves phonological awareness, with the reader able to identify sounds and syllables individually and in words, as well as *decoding*, whereby sounds and symbols can be matched to read and spell. It also involves the sight recognition of familiar words.

Language comprehension

Background knowledge of facts and concepts, a wide vocabulary, an understanding of phrase and sentence construction, the ability to infer meaning and an understanding of the ways in which text can be presented all contribute to successful language comprehension.

Word recognition alone is insufficient, since it is possible to read words without understanding their meaning. Try reading a manual for a piece of machinery, for example: you may be able to read all the words, but do you understand what the text means? Similarly, language comprehension must be underpinned by word recognition, otherwise children will be unable to read some words and will lose the sense of the text.

Before considering the challenges young children face when acquiring the skills and knowledge needed to be literate, try the activity below.

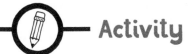 **Activity**

You as a language learner

Think of a time when you have been in a foreign country where you knew little or none of the native language, then answer the following questions:

- What was easy to understand and why?
- What was difficult to understand and why?
- How did your ability to read well in your native language help or hinder your understanding?
- What misunderstandings arose when you attempted to communicate with local people?
- What was your motivation to be able to understand some of the native language?

The essence of language acquisition

The essence of language acquisition, according to Krashen (2002, p.1), is that we get meaningful messages:

> Language *acquisition* is very similar to the process children use in acquiring first and second languages. It requires meaningful interaction in the target language - natural communication - in which speakers are concerned not with the form of their utterances but with the messages they are conveying and understanding.

When you thought about yourself as a foreigner in a land where you were unfamiliar with the language, you probably decided that you could hazard a guess at some words, especially if they were on shops or goods, or if they looked similar to English words. Perhaps you tried to speak to people, maybe using a phrase book for vocabulary, but tried to use an English-style word order that didn't work in the native language. You may have tried to say some words aloud, but found that you couldn't make yourself understood because you were not pronouncing them properly because the grapheme-phoneme correspondence was different from English. But all the time you were trying to read and to communicate, you were motivated to do so because you wanted to find things and places, make purchases and eat and drink.

One of the key things that could help you to communicate in another language is knowledge of the grapheme-phoneme correspondences in that language. In German, for example, we know that many letters have similar sounds to those we find in English, but that W is sounded in a similar way to how we sound V in English, while V sounds like the way we pronounce the /f/ sound (think of Volkswagen which Germans would pronounce 'Folksvagen'). Several researchers, including Lesaux and Siegel (2003), Vadasy and Sanders (2011) and Yeung et al. (2013) (in Jamaludin et al., 2016), suggest synthetic phonics (blending phonemes) may be effective in developing reading skills across languages.

Vadasy and Sanders (2011) (in Jamaludin et al., 2016) found that non-native English speakers benefited from being taught synthetic phonics at an early age. Yeung et al. (2013) (in Jamaludin et al., 2016) found that being taught synthetic phonics facilitated the acquisition of phonological awareness, expressive vocabulary, word reading and word spelling in young ESL readers. However, Yeung et al. (2013) (in Jamaludin et al., 2016) also point out that applying their findings across different ESL contexts could be problematic and doubtful, due to the complexities of different language structures.

A large-scale study into the effectiveness of synthetic phonics in the development of reading skills among struggling young ESL readers was recently carried out in rural Malaysia by academics from the University of Malaya (Jamaludin et al., 2016). In the context of Malaysia, Gomez and Reason (2002) (in Jamaludin et al., 2016) indicate that the processing skills gained in learning the Malay language have enabled the ESL readers to decode and read in English effectively. The research concluded that children who were taught using synthetic phonics methods made significant improvements in reading in comparison to those children who were not taught using synthetic phonics methods. In the study, the use of synthetic phonics improved children's mastery of decoding and comprehension skills. Jamaludin et al. (2016) concluded that synthetic phonics is beneficial for young ESL readers.

It would seem that there is an important role for phonics in reading development for both first and second language learners, but what other factors are involved? Think of young readers trying to come to terms with reading. What is their motivation to be able to read? What might they already know which can help them and what do they need to know if they are to be successful? In the next section, we will look at some of the challenges early readers face and some of the strategies we might deploy to support them.

Perceiving the value of reading

For some children (and adults) reading is not regarded as a valuable skill. For some, reading is simply associated with school and does not play an important part in their lives. If you struggle, there is little pleasure in reading, but there can still be pleasure in hearing stories and poems and song lyrics.

Often, children will attempt texts that are beyond their reading abilities once they have been engaged by hearing a story or watching a film or TV drama. The success of the Harry Potter stories was such that even children whose reading levels were well below what was needed to read the books fluently bought them and read them on the first day of publication.

Many children arrive at school with little experience of stories and rhymes. It is, therefore, important that teachers make extensive use of these and help them to understand the concept of stories and their structure. By engaging children with texts, we also help them to understand how to write their own. We can do this through shared reading, where we model reading a text as children follow and then join in, but there is also an important role for reading stories to children. This has now been enshrined within the National Curriculum (DfE, 2013), for example in the Y3–4 section (p.37):

> Pupils should continue to have opportunities to listen frequently to stories, poems, non-fiction and other writing, including whole books and not just extracts, so that they build on what was taught previously. In this way, they also meet books and authors that they might not choose themselves.

Finding things they 'want' to read

There is a particular challenge for teachers in findings texts that are both at an appropriate reading level and maturity level for struggling readers. Dull, repetitive texts or stories which involve younger children merely confirm for older strugglers that reading is unappealing. It is important to consider children's interests and to be able to expose them to texts that address these. Having a good knowledge of a range of texts, both fiction and non-fiction, is vital for teachers if they are to be able to identify those which might engage otherwise disinterested readers. As Merisuo-Storm (2006) has argued:

> It is crucial that the teacher gathers information about his or her pupils' interests. With interesting reading material it is possible to encourage even the most reluctant reader to read. (p.124)

Children need to know how stories work if they are to develop an ability to listen to and read them. Some may have had limited experience of stories before starting school and so it is vital that they gain lots of experience of stories and storytelling in school.

Some teachers write stories and other texts for their pupils in order both to model writing and to provide bespoke reading which they know incorporates children's interests. Some schools pair older children with younger ones so that they can read together and less experienced readers can benefit from more experienced readers' skills.

In addition to providing texts on paper, it is important to recognise that for most people much of their reading and writing is digital.

Digital texts

Levy (2009) suggests that the definitions of reading should be widened in order to embrace developments in technology and to acknowledge the fact that children access text in multi-modal formats. She goes on to argue that we now live in a world where printed text is not the dominant format. Bearne (2004) suggests that texts are now not limited to text and image, but can include moving images and sound too. Kress (2003) suggests that different texts demand different pathways to access meaning, and that we retrieve information from digital images differently to the still images commonly used in books.

Factors that inhibit reading development

For some children reading can be a tortuous process and their limitations are constantly exposed to others whenever they are involved in a reading activity, whether this be in guided reading, reading aloud to the class, reading to a teacher or teaching assistant or learning lines for a play or assembly. The case study below provides an example of how a little sensitivity from a teacher can help alleviate some of these problems.

 **Case study**

Group and individual reading

Nadya was concerned that some of her Year 4 class were very reluctant to read aloud, either to her or her teaching assistant or in-group reading. She discussed this with a friend who taught at another school, who made some suggestions that Nadya adopted:

- Avoid asking less able readers to read aloud when the rest of the class is engaged in independent, quiet reading, as this makes all of their errors public and reduces self-esteem.
- If children are going to read aloud to someone, tell them what they will be reading in advance and get them to practise first.
- In group reading don't ask children to read around the group but use guided reading techniques whereby children read independently and sometimes quietly to the teacher, and where the main focus is upon discussing the text.

Nadya found that getting children to practise reading first was very successful, but decided that it was best to hear individual readers when the rest of the class were involved in activities which were not done in silence. She found that guided reading led to a deeper understanding of texts and that all children were able to contribute to discussions. Teaching points could be made to the group and individuals' errors were less public.

The case study shows that there are simple strategies that can be deployed in order to raise children's self-esteem and reduce anxiety about reading. However, it is still very important that all children are taught the basics of reading if they are to progress into being fluent readers, and this means developing a good understanding of how letters and sounds are related. Systematic synthetic phonics has been regarded as so important by successive governments that it is enshrined within the Teaching Standards as the only aspect of the curriculum which all primary teachers must be able to teach effectively. Some educators (notably Wyse and Styles, 2007, and Davis, 2012) have questioned the emphasis on systematic synthetic phonics in carefully argued articles, while others have done so in rather less rigorous ways, two examples of which appear later in the chapter. However, phonics is a key part of the National Curriculum (DfE, 2013) and a key element of Ofsted inspections and of the testing regime in Key Stage 1 in England, and anyone teaching in an English primary school will be expected to be able to teach phonics effectively. Later in the chapter we examine other approaches to reading, but the next section focuses on phonics and some of the challenges teachers and children face.

Why children need to learn to sound out letters right through words

Intergrams

Before reading the next section, try reading each of the following words:

Aindcocrg

rraeches

That was probably very difficult. Now try reading them again in the knowledge that the words are anagrams of real words and that the first and last letters are the same in the real words as they are in their anagrams. Still difficult? Then try reading:

Aoccdrnig

rseearch

The words were probably easier to read once the letters were jumbled in a different way and you read them as *According* and *research*. The text below was circulated widely on the Internet from around 2003 and has been used to try to demonstrate that we don't actually sound every grapheme when we read. Try reading it:

Aoccdrnig to a rscheearch in the Lingutcs Dep at Cmabrigde Uinervtisy, it deosn't mttaer in waht oredr the ltteers in a wrod are, the olny iprmoetnt tihng is taht the frist and lsat ltteer be at the rghit pclae. The rset can be a toatl mses and you can sitll raed it wouthit porbelm. Tihs is bcuseae the huamn mnid deos not raed ervey lteter by istlef, but the wrod as a wlohe.

You probably found that you could read it as:

According to a researcher in the Linguistic Dep at Cambridge University, it doesn't matter in what order the letters in a word are, the only important thing is that the first and last letter be at the right place. The rest can be a total mess and you can still read it without problem. This is because the human mind does not read every letter by itself but the word as a whole.

Ask yourself the following questions:

- Did you spot that 'rscheearch' is not an anagram of researcher?

- Did you spot that 'iprmoetnt' is not an anagram of important?

- Did you notice that almost half (32 out of 69) of the words (the small words) are presented in the normal way?

- Why do you think you could read the text in its jumbled form? Was it because the words were not generally very jumbled? Was it because you used the meaning of the text to help you to make guesses?

The 'research' behind the assertion that we can read the text despite its jumbled presentation has been challenged by several researchers, including Mark Davies of the Cognition and Brain Sciences Unit in Cambridge, UK, a Medical Research Council unit that includes a large group investigating how the brain processes language. Davies maintained that if research on reading had been conducted in Cambridge, he would surely have heard about it. For an interesting dissection of the text and the claims made about it, see https://www.mrc-cbu.cam.ac.uk/personal/matt.davis/Cmabrigde/. For the purposes of this chapter, some simple word reading activities should illustrate why it is important that we *do* actually read through words sounding a phoneme for each grapheme, even if we do this rapidly and subconsciously because we are advanced readers. Try reading the words below aloud:

cavern except snipe craven gusty boredom expect form from clam gusty reserve dairy calm bedroom diary reverse spine

The words are all *intergrams* and each has a partner that is an anagram of itself with the first and last letters remaining the same. The words have different meanings. Did you misread any of them? It is clear that in order to read each word correctly without having any context for the words, you need to attribute a phoneme to each grapheme in the right order throughout the word. The example of jumbled text provides context for the words that help you to read them and the letters are not so jumbled that they cannot easily be deciphered. If it were true that only the first and last letters were necessary to read words, could we present the text as below and still be able to read it?

Ag to rh by te Lc Dt at Ce Uy, it dt mr in wt or te ls in a wd ae, te oy it tg is tt te ft ad lt lr be at te rt pe. Te rt cn be a tl ms ad yu cn sl rd it wt pm. Ts is be te hn md ds nt rd ey lr by if, bt te wd as a we.

One of the reasons why you probably found this difficult to read, even though you have already seen the words expanded, is that many of the small words are indistinguishable from the longer ones, so they don't provide guidance to help the text flow. Without these words and with less information in the other words, reading and understanding the text is virtually impossible. Far from showing that we only need the first and last letters to decode words, the examples of text above show that we actually need a combination of phonic knowledge, an ability to sound words all the way through (even if we are mentally swapping some sounds around to put them in the right order), and good language and reading comprehension to enable us to inform our attempts at word recognition.

Despite having an alphabetic code which is often described as *opaque* because so many graphemes can be sounded in different ways (think of *ch* in *school*, *chef* and *chip*) and so many phonemes can be represented by different graphemes (think of the /k/ sound in *chemistry, brick, account, cat, kid*, etc.), there are no 'un-phonetic' words. There are certainly many words that cannot easily be sounded out, especially by novice readers, but English spelling is 100 per cent phonetic because every letter or group of letters in every word represents a sound. Sometimes, however, the combination of letters is unusual or may be unfamiliar to a reader: think of words like *yacht* and *debt* which have unique grapheme representations of the /o/ and /t/ sounds. However, it is often the most common words in the language that present new readers and spellers with the greatest challenge.

 Activity

Look at the 100 most common words listed in Table 3.1 and decide which can be learned easily by sounding them out and which might present problems for inexperienced readers.

Table 3.1 The 100 most common words in the English language, in order of frequency

the	are	do	about	and
up	me	got	a	had
down	their	to	my	dad
people	said	her	big	your
in	what	when	put	he
there	it's	could	I	out
see	house	of	this	looked
old	it	have	very	too
was	went	look	by	you
be	don't	day	they	like
come	made	on	some	will
time	she	so	into	I'm

is	not	back	if	for
then	from	help	at	were
children	Mrs	his	go	him
called	but	little	Mr	here
that	as	get	off	with
no	just	asked	all	mum
now	saw	we	one	came
make	can	them	oh	an

Source: Masterson et al. (2003).

You probably decided that words like *about, and, up, got, had, down* and *dad* could be sounded out, but what about *said, do, their, one* and *people*? These words include 'tricky' parts for readers who don't know of other words with the same letter sound correspondences. The *ai* in *said* and the *eo* in *people* rarely make the vowel sounds found in those words, while *eir* in *their* can be found in a few words such as *heir*, but most of these may be unfamiliar to children. These words can cause frustration for early and struggling readers, especially as the words feature so frequently in texts.

The 2013 National Curriculum refers to *common exception words*, rather than *tricky words* and the programme of study for Year 1 includes

> read common exception words, noting unusual correspondences between spelling and sound and where these occur in the word. (DfE, 2013, p.20)

Very few words have more than one 'tricky' part once children have mastered basic grapheme-phoneme correspondences, so a focus on the unusual grapheme-correspondences can emphasise this and show children that a phonics approach is helpful. They can also be shown groups of words with common features so that they can focus on tricky parts and see that they can occur frequently.

Grouping by decodable and common exception words

The most common 100 words can be grouped into decodable or common exception words, as shown in Table 3.2.

Table 3.2   Decodable words

a	dad	but	look	time
an	had	put	too	house
as	back	will	went	about
at	and	that	it's	your
if	get	this	from	day
in	big	then	children	made
is	him	them	just	came
it	his	with	help	make
of	not	see	don't	here
off	got	for	old	saw
on	up	now	I'm	very
can	mum	down	by	

Source: DCFS (2007).

The words with tricky parts which only become easily decodable once children have learned more phonemes and phonic strategies are listed in Table 3.3.

Table 3.3   Tricky words

The	me	said	little	Mrs
To	be	have	one	looked
I	was	like	when	called
No	you	so	out	asked
Go	they	do	what	could
Into	all	some	oh	
He	are	come	their	
She	my	were	people	
We	her	there	Mr	

Source: DCFS (2007).

Grouping by phoneme and spelling pattern

Many of the most common words can be grouped with others which have similar features so that they can be learned together. Grouping might include:

he, she, we, me, be – with an *e* that makes the *ee* phoneme

no, go, so – with *o* that says its letter name

do, to – with *o* that makes the *oo* phoneme

of, off, on – initial *o* phoneme

can, dad, had, get, big, him, his, not, got, mum, but, put, was – CVC words

Mr, Mrs – titles that required capitalisation

time, made, came, make, here – containing split diagraphs

little, people – *le* final phoneme

some, come – rhyme

the, their, there, them, that, they, this, then – initial *th* phoneme

looked, called, asked – *ed* ending

it's, don't, I'm – containing apostrophes

when, what – initial *wh* phoneme

an, as, at, if, in, is, it, of, on, up – a vowel followed by a consonant

to, no, go, he, we, me, be, so, do (by, my) – consonant followed by a vowel, including the alternative *y*

Content words

Many of the 100 most common words' main purpose is to join other words in sentences, so they are called *function words*. Without them, we couldn't create sentences. *Content words* are those which name and describe things and actions. Think about your experiences in a land where you didn't speak the native language: it was probably the content words which were most help as you shopped, ordered food and drink and asked for directions. Similarly, children's first words tend to be content words like *mummy, daddy, drink* and *dog*, and when they first begin to recognise words around them it is usually the content words which they can first read in shops and signs. While it is important to teach the most common function words, it is also vital that the most commonly used nouns, verbs and adjectives are learned alongside them.

The most common content words are listed in Table 3.4.

If we supplement the common content words with proper nouns such as place names, people's names (including children and famous people), football teams, pop stars and sports stars, we can reinforce phonic understanding while providing children with the vocabulary they need to be able to create meaningful writing.

Table 3.4   *The most common content words*

Nouns		Verbs		Adjectives	
1	time	1	be	1	good
2	person	2	have	2	new
3	year	3	do	3	first
4	way	4	say	4	last
5	day	5	get	5	long
6	thing	6	make	6	great
7	man	7	go	7	little
8	world	8	know	8	own
9	life	9	take	9	other
10	hand	10	see	10	old
11	part	11	come	11	right
12	child	12	think	12	big
13	eye	13	look	13	high
14	woman	14	want	14	different
15	place	15	give	15	small
16	work	16	use	16	large
17	week	17	find	17	next
18	case	18	tell	18	early
19	point	19	ask	19	young
20	government	20	work	20	important
21	company	21	seem	21	few
22	number	22	feel	22	public
23	group	23	try	23	bad
24	problem	24	leave	24	same
25	fact	25	call	25	able

http://www.oxforddictionaries.com/words/the-oec-facts-about-the-language

Case study

Engaging struggling readers

Harriet's Year 5 class included a group of children who showed little inclination to read and it was clear that they were not making sufficient progress. Harriet decided to try to engage them by focusing on their areas of interest. For most, this was popular music, so Harriet made a display of pictures and printouts from websites for each of the following artistes: Justin Bieber, Justin Timberlake, DJ Snake, Ellie Goulding, Craig David, Adele, Olly Murs, Coldplay, Clean Bandit and Drake.

There were some groans from some children at the inclusion of musicians they didn't like and pleas for the inclusions of others whom they did. Harriet told the group that they could add to the display by finding information as she had done. She also encouraged them to draw from the information to write three-sentence biographies of as many of the stars as they wished.

Besides discussing music and the stars' lives, Harriet spent time looking at the spellings of names and asked children to focus on the tricky parts and learn these for a pop stars spelling test. This was very successful and the group were happy to learn the spellings of the artistes' names and then wanted to add more names and learn these too. Harriet took the opportunity to focus on some grapheme-phoneme correspondence and show how these occurred in other words.

The case study illustrates the importance of engaging reluctant readers through texts that interest them. Harriet used pop stars but could equally have used sports personalities, football teams, actors or TV programmes.

Self-sustaining word recognition

Stuart et al. (2009, p.57) show how early readers 'rapidly start to develop a 'self-teaching' system', whereby the application of phonics rules to decipher unfamiliar printed words results in storage of those unfamiliar items in sight vocabulary. This results in their increasing store of words becoming 'a database from which children can infer previously unknown phonic rules . . . Thus the word recognition system becomes self-sustaining: the child no longer needs be taught how to decipher words on the page' (Stuart et al., 2009, p.57).

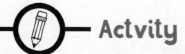 **Actvity**

Reading unfamiliar words

In order to see how we are able to draw upon our 'database' of phonic knowledge, try reading the words below. How do you know how to say them, if you had never seen them before?

hemiplegia   pharyngeal   serology   crural   bicameral

You probably looked at parts of the words, including clusters of letters, as well as at individual grapheme-phoneme correspondences. You have probably met some of these in other words, for example *hemi* in *hemisphere*, *ology* in *biology* and *bi* in *bicycle*, and this may have helped you. You probably read the *g* in *hemiplegia* as a soft *g* rather than a hard *g* because you know from other words which end with *gia* that *g* tends to be soft. If you look back at the pop stars' names earlier, you will see Timberlake, DJ Snake and Drake. If children only knew one of these names and how to say it, they would already have a head start when it came to pronouncing the others. Think back, too, to your experiences abroad: you probably learned to say some words you saw in shops and on menus because you had already learned others with similar sound symbol correspondences. In France, these might be *oeuf* and *boeuf*, *fin* and *vin*, *mouton* and *bouton*, for example. In a short time, we begin to develop our own phonic database and we can help children to do the same by exposing them to a wide range of vocabulary and by discussing words and how they are constructed.

Morphology

Morphology is the study of forms of words and the National Curriculum has placed increased emphasis upon children's understanding of morphemes, in recognition of the importance of being able to see how words are constructed when reading and writing. To et al. (2014, p.13) argue that:

> Because many English words are morphologically related, learning one base word might increase the total vocabulary by a count of several words, if the student learns word formation processes of English. For example, if a person learns the word 'love', then morphologically related words (i.e., loveable, lovely) can also be acquired.

Johnston and Watson (2007), too, maintain that 'Children's reading will become more fluent if they recognise these familiar chunks, and thus sound and blend them at the syllable level' (2007, p.44).

What is a morpheme?

Morphemes are the smallest units of meaning in words, so *hope* is a single morpheme and *hopeful* has two morphemes: *hope* is the *root word* and *-ful* is a suffix which modifies the meaning of the root word. Similarly, *usual* is a single morpheme and *unusual* has two morphemes: *un-* and *usual*, with the prefix *un-* modifying the meaning of the root word *usual*.

Prefixes and suffixes cannot usually stand alone as words and need to be attached to root words to give meaning, so they are known as *bound morphemes*. Morphemes that can stand alone and have meaning are called *free morphemes*. Often, in English, we put two free morphemes together to create a *compound word*, for example *toothbrush*, *shoelace*, *football* and *workbook*.

 **Activity**

Modifying words using prefixes and suffixes

Look at the spelling list in Table 3.5 for Year 5-6 from the National Curriculum (DfE, 2013) and decide which words can be modified by adding prefixes and/or suffixes. For example, accommodate could become *unaccommodating, unaccommodated, accommodated, accommodates, accommodating, accommodation*, etc.

Table 3.5   Spelling list for Years 5–6 from the National Curriculum

accommodate	conscience	existence	neighbour	secretary
accompany	conscious	explanation	nuisance	shoulder
according	controversy	familiar	occupy	signature
achieve	convenience	foreign	occur	sincere
aggressive	correspond	forty	opportunity	soldier
amateur	criticise	frequently	parliament	stomach
ancient	curiosity	government	persuade	sufficient
apparent	definite	guarantee	physical	suggest
appreciate	desperate	harass	prejudice	symbol
attached	determined	hindrance	privilege	system
available	develop	identity	profession	temperature
average	dictionary	immediate	programme	thorough
awkward	disastrous	individual	pronunciation	twelfth
bargain	embarrass	interfere	queue	variety
bruise	environment	interrupt	recognise	vegetable
category	equip	language	recommend	vehicle
cemetery	especially	leisure	relevant	yacht
committee	exaggerate	lightning	restaurant	
communicate	excellent	marvellous	rhyme	
community		muscle	rhythm	
competition		necessary	sacrifice	

You probably found it harder to find words that could *not* take a prefix or suffix than to find those which can. In fact, only *lightning* cannot take either. Some of the words could also become compound words if another free morpheme was added; for example, *bargain-hunter, forty-five, muscle-bound* and *underachieve* (compound words can be hyphenated).

Here, again, we can see the potential for developing children's database of word knowledge. Once they learn how to add prefixes and suffixes to some words, they begin to find them in others and understand how they modify meaning. When we teach children to spell, we should take time to look at the words that can be derived from those in our lists and talk about the effect of adding morphemes as well as exploring what different morphemes mean.

What is important in teaching phonics?

We can summarise the important elements in successful phonics teaching by drawing upon a range of research (Ehri et al., 2001; Brooks, 2003; DfES, 2006; Johnston and Watson, 2005; Torgerson et al., 2006). These include:

- providing a broad rich diet of meaningful texts so that children engage with them and want to learn how to read them successfully;

- teaching phonemes in the context of words so that children see them as meaningful;

- teaching common exception words so that children can gain access to texts even when some of the most common words have unfamiliar grapheme-phoneme-correspondences (GPCs);

- teaching about morphology, so that children understand how words work, what different prefixes and suffixes mean and the effect they can have upon root words;

- systematic incremental teaching of discrete lessons which have a structured plan (review, teach, apply, practise) and build upon prior learning;

- a focus on clear enunciation so that children learn an accurate representation of sounds and do not add additional *schwa* sounds to phones, e.g. *shh* not *shuh*, *mmm* not *muh*;

- an awareness of and sensitivity to accents and the impact these can have upon learning, especially where the teacher's accent differs from many of the children's;

- providing lively and interactive lessons which engage and involve children, using visual aids and a multi-sensory approach (see Jolliffe and Waugh with Carss, 2015, chapter 8);

- using names of things children know as examples, including their own names and names of things which interest them;

- celebrating success;

- working with carers/parents so that they understand your approach and back it up at home.

A fish called 'ghoti'

There have been many attempts to show that the English alphabetic system is so complex that it is impossible to teach it phonetically, including George Bernard Shaw's suggestion that fish could be spelled as ghoti, since gh makes a /f/ sound in laugh, o makes an /i/ sound in women, and ti makes a /sh/ sound in station. It is, however, a rather implausible suggestion since gh never makes an /f/ sound at the beginning of English words, no other words have o representing an /i/ sound apart from *women* and in no words which end with ti is the sound /sh/. So while this provides an amusing example of the varied grapheme-phoneme correspondences in English, it does nothing to support an anti-phonics stance. However, a more coherent case against synthetic phonics is made by supporters of analytic phonics. After reading about the two approaches, consider which you, as a skilled reader, use and when.

Analytic phonics

Analytic phonics relies on a problem-solving approach in which knowledge of the sound patterns in words helps the reader to read other words with similar patterns; for example, if we can read *sing* we should also be able to read *bring*, *think*, *king*, *wing* and *swing* because we can apply our knowledge of the sound pattern -ing to other words. This is an approach 'in which the phonemes associated with particular graphemes are not pronounced in isolation. Children identify (analyse) the common phoneme in a set of words in which each word contains the phonemes under study' (Brooks, 2003, p.11).

Synthetic phonics

Washtell (2010, p.44) maintains that synthetic phonics is 'an approach to the teaching of phonics which works by isolating the phonemes in a word. The phonemes are then blended together in sequence to decode the word.' It is argued that this is a more systematic method of teaching of phonics than the analytical approach. Grapheme-phoneme correspondences are introduced to children in a planned sequence and children are taught to *synthesise* the sounds to form words. It should be noted that although we tend to associate the word synthetic with artificiality (synthetic fibres, etc.), it actually means to bring together.

What about children who don't 'get' phonics?

English is a complex language and is different from many other alphabetic languages. This is due to the complexity of syllable structure and inconsistent spelling systems (Wyse and Goswami, 2008). This means that teaching reading in English using a phonics approach may not be as effective as other methods.

When we reflect on syllable structure it is important to consider that in countries such as Greece, Finland, Italy and Spain syllable structure is simple and there is 1:1 mapping between phonemes and graphemes. Words in these languages are often longer than words in English, but they are easier to segment into phonemes. De Cara and Goswami (2002) explain that many of the world's languages have words made up of syllables with a simple consonant-vowel (CV) structure, but that in English only 5 per cent of monosyllables are CV, and that the primary syllable type in English is CVC (43 per cent of monosyllables).

English is also different from many other languages because of the inconsistency in spelling. In English one grapheme can represent more than one phoneme, and one phoneme can be represented by several graphemes. Many of the most frequently used words in the English language have unusual grapheme-phoneme correspondences in them. This is evident in the list of 100 most commons words used in English (Masterson et al., 2003), which includes *people*, *would* and *said*. Seymour et al. (2003) suggest that English is exceptionally inconsistent in both reading and spelling, and that this inconsistency inhibits the rapid acquisition of grapheme-phoneme recoding skills. However, Crystal (2005) points out that there are only around 400 irregular spellings in the English language, and that 84 per cent of words conform to a general pattern.

Spencer and Hanley (2003) carried out research in primary schools in Wales, where children are taught in both Welsh and English. The Welsh language has a consistent spelling pattern; mapping from grapheme to phoneme is simple. However, Welsh has a more complex syllable structure. So Welsh and English differed greatly in terms of spelling consistencies, but are similar in terms of complexity of word structure. Spencer and Hanley (2003) found that Welsh-speaking children were significantly more accurate in reading than English-speaking children, and that the Welsh speakers had developed superior phonemic awareness. Spencer and Hanley (2003) concluded that there is strong evidence that reading acquisition is influenced by the complexity of the language system, and that the rapid development of phonic awareness is reflected where 1:1 grapheme-phoneme correspondences are present.

So, for children who speak languages such as Greek, Finnish, Italian, Spanish or Welsh, the teaching of reading using phonics can be effective, and children in these countries are often fluent readers before the end of their first year of instruction (Seymour et al., 2003).

However, as the research suggests, the teaching of phonics alone may not be as effective for children who use the English language. Wyse and Goswami (2008) suggest that the complexity of reading acquisition in English means that direct instruction at levels other than the phoneme may be required, and that it is unlikely that one method of teaching reading will be entirely effective. Sousa (2005) and Farrington-Flint et al. (2008) (in Watts and Gardner, 2013) agree that, due to the presence of words that do not conform to regular grapho-phonic correspondences in English, exclusively using a phonic method of teaching reading would be problematic and would impair word recognition skills. Smith and Robertson (2007) (in Watts and Gardner, 2013) suggest that a multi-method approach to the teaching of reading is required to ensure inclusion and achievement of all pupils, based on their differing learning needs and styles. Blevins (2006) (in Watts and Gardener, 2013) notes that knowledge of alphabetic principles enriches phonemic awareness, but that this alone it not enough. He argues that children also need to develop knowledge-based competencies for developing comprehension skills. The United Kingdom Literacy Association (UKLA, 2006) stress that 'phonics are necessary' but that it is 'not in itself sufficient to develop effective and enthusiastic readers'.

Ehri (1995) (in Watts and Gardner, 2013) identified four stages in the reading process that require children learning to read to use strategies in addition to phonics. In the first stage, the *pre-alphabetic* stage, the reader uses visual features of words to read them. In the second stage, the *partial-alphabetic* phase, the reader uses recognised letters to attempt unknown words. The *full-alphabetic phase*, which is the third stage, is the point at which children learning to read are able to accurately recognise words and use familiar words to help them read unfamiliar ones. In the final stage, the *consolidated alphabetic phase*, readers are able to recognise words instantly. Ehri (2005), among others, suggests that children rely less on phonological strategies as they move through reading stages, and that they retrieve words from memory and identify features of words in order to read them.

Willingham (2015) notes that those who support a whole-word approach argue that it removes the need for 'drilling' children in letters, and means they can be engaged in reading that is pleasurable and authentic. The ability to instantly recognise words enables fluency. Many whole-word approach supporters advocate that a child should be given reading that makes sense and that has a clear point, and in doing so the child will be motivated to engage with the text. Clay (1991) (in Watts and Gardner, 2013) discovered that children rarely applied phonic methods when reading independently unless asked to do so.

Paulescu et al. (2000) (in Watts and Gardner, 2013) suggest that 'reading in English requires patterns of brain activity that conform to whole word recognition rather than grapho-phonic correspondences.' Using a whole-word approach involves learning large numbers of words. It is suggested that children will need to know something like 50,000 words by the time they complete school (Willingham, 2015). Of course, not all of these words need to be read immediately. Willingham (2015) suggests that readers can often make sensible guesses about words by using other words in the sentence. They use words that they already know to help them read unfamiliar ones. Children also use other clues, such as pictures and punctuation.

Concluding thoughts

Children struggle with reading for a variety of reasons, which may include systemic learning difficulties or English being an additional language and not the one they hear at home. However, there are strategies available which can help all children to improve their reading, including sharing texts, engaging their interest, and developing their word recognition skills and understanding of morphemes. In addition, it is important to work in partnership with parents and carers so that they understand the school's approach and support their children's learning wherever possible. Many schools provide leaflets which offer guidance on supporting children's reading, but given that some parents and carers may have limited literacy skills or have English as an additional language, it is also important to offer personal and face-to-face guidance.

References

Bearne, E. (2004) *Rethinking Literacy*. London: QCA.

Blevins, J. (2006) Word-based morphology. *Journal of Linguistics*, 4(3): 5313.

Brooks, G. (2003) *Sound Sense: The Phonics Element of the NLS: A Report to the DfES*. London: DfES.

Crystal, D. (2005) *How Language Works*. London: Penguin.

Davis, A. (2012) A monstrous regimen of synthetic phonics: fantasies of research-based teaching 'methods' versus real teaching. *Journal of Philosophy of Education*, 46(4): 560–73.

De Cara, B. and Goswami, U. (2002) Similarity relations among spoken words: the special status of rimes in English. *Behavior Research Methods, Instruments and Computers*, 34(3): 416–23.

Department for Education (2013) *The National Curriculum*. London: DfE.

Department for Education and Skills (DfES) (2006) *The Independent Review of the Teaching of Early Reading* (Rose Reviews). London: DCSF.

DCFS (2007) Letters and Sounds: Principles and Practice of High Quality Phonics. Phase One Teaching Programme of the National Strategies, Primary. London: DCFS.

Ehri, L., Nunes, S.R., Stahl, S.A. and Willows, D.M. (2001) Systematic phonics instruction helps students learn to read: evidence from the National Reading Panel's meta-analysis. *Review of Education*, 17(3): 393–447.

Gomez, C. and Reason, R. (2002) Cross-linguistic transfer of phonological skills: a Malaysian perspective. *Dyslexia*, 8: 22–33.

Gough, P.B. and Tunmer, W.E. (1986) Decoding, reading and reading disability. *Remedial and Special Education*, 7: 6–10.

Jamaludin, K., Alias, N., Khir, R., DeWitt, D. and Kenayathulka, B. (2016) The effectiveness of synthetic phonics in the development of early reading skills amongst struggling young ESL readers. *School Effectiveness and School Improvement*, 27(3): 455–70.

Johnston, R. and Watson, J. (2005) The effects of synthetic phonics teaching of reading and spelling attainment: a seven year longitudinal study. Available online at **www.scotland.gov.uk/Resource/ Doc/36496/0023582.pdf** (accessed 2 January 2015).

Johnston, R. and Watson, J. (2007) *Teaching Synthetic Phonics*. Exeter: Learning Matters.

Jolliffe, W. and Waugh, D. with Carss, A. (2015) *Teaching Systematic Synthetic Phonics in Primary Schools*, 2nd edn. London: Sage.

Krashen, S. (2002) *Second Language Acquisition and Second Language Learning*. Los Angeles: University of Southern California. Available at **http://testing.greenlitex.com/sites/mmea.greenlitestaging. com/files/Second%20Language%20Acquisition%20%26%20Learning%20by%20S.%20 Krashen.pdf** (accessed 29 August 2016).

Kress, G. (2003) *Literacy in the New Media Age*. London: Routledge.

Lesaux, N.K. and Siegel, L.S. (2003). The development of reading in children who speak English as a second language. *Developmental Psychology*, 39: 1005–19.

Levy, R. (2009) 'You have to understand words . . . but not read them': young children becoming readers in a digital age. *Journal of Research in Reading*, 32(1): 75–91.

Masterson, J., Stuart, M., Dixon, M. and Lovejoy, S. (2003) *Children's Printed Word Database*. Economic and Social Research Council funded project (ref. R00023406). Nottingham: DCSF.

Merisuo-Storm, T. (2006) Girls and boys like to read and write different texts. *Journal of Educational Research*, 50(2): 11–25.

Oxford Dictionaries website: **www.oxforddictionaries.com/words/the-oec-facts-about-the- language** (accessed 31 August 2016).

Scarborough, H.S. (2009) Connecting early language and literacy to later reading (dis)abilities: evidence, theory and practice. In F. Fletcher-Campbell, J. Soler and G. Reid (eds), *Approaching Difficulties in Literacy Development: Assessment, Pedagogy and Programmes*. London: Sage, pp. 3–38.

Seymour, P., Aro, M. and Erskine, J. (2003) Foundation literacy acquisition in European orthographies. *British Journal of Psychology*, 94: 143–7.

Spencer, L. and Hanley, J. (2003) Effects of orthographic transparency on reading and phoneme awareness in children learning to read in Wales. *British Journal of Psychology*, 94(1): 1–28.

Stuart, M., Stainthorp, R. and Snowling, M. (2009) Literacy as a complex activity: deconstructing the simple view of reading. In J. Soler, F. Fletcher-Campbell and G. Reid (eds), *Understanding Difficulties in Literacy Development: Issues and Concepts*. London: Sage.

To, N., Tighe, J. and Binder, K. (2014) 'Investigating morphological awareness and the processing of transparent and opaque words in adults with low literacy skills and in skilled readers'. *Journal of Research in Reading*, 14(2): 1–18.

Torgerson, C. J., Brooks, G. and Hall, J. (2006) *A Systematic Review of the Research Literature on the Use of Phonics in the Teaching of Reading and Spelling*. London: Department for Education and Skills.

United Kingdom Literacy Association (2006) *Submission to the Review of Best Practice in the Teaching of Early Reading*. Royston: UKLA.

Vadasy, P.F. and Sanders, E.A. (2011) Efficacy of supplemental phonics-based instruction for low-skilled first graders: how language minority status and pretest characteristics moderate treatment response. *Scientific Studies of Reading*, 15: 471–97.

Washtell, A. (2010) Getting to grips with phonics. In J. Graham and A. Kelly (eds), *Reading under Control: Teaching Reading in the Primary School*. Abingdon: Routledge.

Watts, Z. and Gardner, P. (2013) Is systematic synthetic phonics enough? Examining the benefits of intensive teaching of high frequency words (HFW) in a Year One class. *Education 3–13*, 41(1): 100–9.

Willingham, D. (2015) *Raising Kids Who Read: What Teachers and Parents Can Do*. San Francisco: Jossey-Bass.

Wyse, D. and Goswami, U. (2008) Synthetic phonics and the teaching of reading. *British Education Research Journal*, 34(6): 691–710.

Wyse, D. and Styles, M. (2007) Synthetic phonics and the teaching of reading: the debate surrounding England's 'Rose Report'. *Literacy*, 41(1): 35–42.

Yeung, S.S.S., Siegel, L.S. and Chan, C.K.K. (2013) The effects of a phonological awareness program on English reading and spelling among Hong Kong Chinese ESL children. *Reading and Writing*, 26: 681–704.

4
Communication and the spoken word

Kate Allott

 This chapter

This chapter will explore the unique language environment of the classroom and the implications for children with speech, language and communication needs. It will then go on to consider how these needs can be supported within school, and will look in particular at how poetry and drama can provide opportunities for children to develop their language and communication skills in enjoyable and non-threatening contexts. It should be noted that the focus will be on language and communication rather than speech, taking speech to mean the ability to articulate the sounds that make up language clearly and accurately. Language will be taken to mean understanding and using words and putting them together to make meaning, while communication refers to the appropriate use of language to facilitate effective interaction (Afasic, n.d.).

The language environment of the classroom

For all children school can be a difficult environment for communication, but for children with speech, language and communication needs (SLCN) the challenges of the classroom are likely be much more difficult to meet than for their classmates. Speech, language and communication needs are sometimes referred to as a 'hidden disability', and may not be recognised, with children instead being seen as difficult, shy, uncooperative or inattentive. Yet along with emotional and behavioural difficulties they are the most common category of special need found in schools (Department for Education, 2014). They include both receptive difficulties (hearing and understanding) and also expressive language difficulties. They may be short term or long term, and range from mild to severe. They include difficulties understanding and using language, and also difficulties communicating appropriately in different social contexts. They have major implications for learning, so much of which is language based, but they also often have close links with emotions, social relationships and behaviour. The links may work in either direction so that, for example, difficulties with behaviour may well affect children's language learning and self-esteem problems may affect children's communication skills (Bercow, 2008).

> I always hope I won't get picked to answer a question. (Jake, aged 7)
>
> When I'm talking in my group I think the others might laugh if I say something silly. (Marnie, aged 10)

These comments suggest that the classroom can be a daunting environment for communication for some children. Recognition of this has led in recent years to initiatives such as 'Communication Friendly Settings' (Elklan, 2016), but even so there are features of classrooms and classroom interaction that make classroom communication very different from, say, communication at home. To begin with, there are the numbers involved. Managing talk between thirty or so individuals is difficult. Sound levels can be a constant issue, and allowing everyone enough time to talk is another challenge. In many conversations there may be participants who dominate and others who withdraw, but in the classroom this cannot be allowed to happen, apart, of course, from the teacher's domination of talk, which is a consequence of the teacher's managerial role and pedagogic purpose. Teachers have to organise the life of the classroom and teach their pupils, and they do these things largely through talk. Beyond these fairly practical considerations there is a host of more complex issues.

In many social settings any participant in talk can propose topics; these may not be taken up, or not for long, and participants may not always be interested in topics which are chosen, but they can then try to move the talk on to something else – in other words, topic choice is open to everyone. In school, topic choice during lessons is largely determined by the teacher. This is so during whole-class teaching, but even when children are working in small groups or pairs they are expected to be 'on task' and not talking about topics of their own choice. For children who can talk at length about their own interests and preoccupations, but who find it difficult to tune in to other people's expectations in conversation, this can be very difficult.

Questions are a key feature of classroom interaction, but unlike in other contexts they are very largely asked by one participant – the teacher. And while some of them are 'real' questions ('Have you all finished?' 'Who's been to France?') many are not: the prevalent form is the 'teacher-question' or 'pseudo-question', where the questioner already knows the answer or knows what kind of answer is being looked for. Questions are used for assessment, and children are well aware from very early on that judgements are being made of their answers. Indeed, the characteristic three-part IRF (initiation-response-feedback) exchange of the classroom (Lee, 2007) builds in the judgement: every response from a child is likely to be evaluated by the teacher in some way, either with a non-verbal response such as a nod, a smile or a puzzled look, or with a non-specific response such as 'fantastic' or 'good try', or with more specific feedback such as 'Well done, you remembered the three key points' or 'Yes, you've explained to us how you worked it out.' While praise is intended to reassure children and build confidence, it can have the opposite effect. Children may stop noticing the regular comments such as 'brilliant' but be acutely aware of the occasions when what they say does not generate these comments or generates a comment such as 'interesting idea', which they may find quite unsettling.

Taking a more detailed look at the language demands of the classroom, we will consider first the demands on receptive language and then expressive language. Children in school have to do a lot of listening. Listening takes up a high proportion of their time, and they may be expected to listen for lengthy periods of time. Teachers sometimes comment on children's difficulties with attention and concentration, without recognising what demands are made on these children in the classroom. Apart from the sheer volume of talk children listen to in school, there are comprehension demands that may be very unlike those they meet in talk outside school. The content of the talk may be unfamiliar, so they are unable to make links to their own experience. The content may be challenging; teachers may be explaining complex mathematical concepts or abstract moral principles. The language itself may cause difficulties, with more complicated grammatical expressions than children are used to, and often with vocabulary they are unfamiliar with. The concept of CALP – cognitive and academic language proficiency (Cummins, 1984) – is relevant here: although it was introduced in the context of children learning English as an additional language, all children need to acquire this proficiency.

All of this can make listening hard work and unrewarding. Children who may have had real difficulty attending to and understanding what is being said then find themselves being expected to follow instructions and carry out activities that demonstrate their understanding. It is worth noting that teachers can support children with receptive language difficulties in a number of simple ways, such as:

- avoiding speaking at length – for example, introductions and explanations can be broken into chunks interspersed with activities;

- speaking more slowly;

- simplifying language, for example speaking in shorter sentences;

- monitoring vocabulary carefully and giving clear explanations of words children may not be familiar with;

- using visual aids;

- alerting children to key points and repeating them.

Moving on to expressive language, for some children the challenge is that participation in talk in the classroom is compulsory. While at home children can often retreat to their bedroom or a quiet corner, and parents may be quite happy not to have their conversations interrupted, at school there is usually a clear expectation that everyone joins in. Teachers are also very familiar with the phenomenon of children who are quiet at school but never stop talking at home, according to their parents.

Of course there are reasons for this: it is often much easier to talk in smaller groups where you are very well known and where you have many shared reference points. Also, children at home are much more likely to be able to select the topic for talk, and finally they are much less likely to feel that what they say is being judged and evaluated. There is an interesting parallel to a study of children's attitudes to writing (Grainger et al., 2003) which discovered that children often preferred writing at home to writing at school because of the increased ownership and freedom.

In addition to the issue of lack of topic choice for children (except in informal talk, which may be very strictly curtailed in the classroom), there is the question of the audience. While children may be comfortable talking in pairs and small groups, the wider audience of the class, or possibly the whole school, can be frightening. Even teachers may find the sea of faces in front of them during school assemblies, including staff as well as children of all ages, can cause a degree of stage fright. Another issue is that children are often expected to speak in a more formal register at school than they would at home or in the playground. As with receptive language, both content and the language itself can be challenging. Children may be talking about unfamiliar or complex topics, and may be quite anxious about getting the right answer or making a contribution that will be evaluated as acceptable. The linguistic challenge accompanies the cognitive: at the same time as doing the thinking they have to find the right words and put them together effectively.

Although school presents challenges for children with speech, language and communication needs, there are many ways in which these children can be supported within the classroom. Firstly, it is important to note that teachers are likely to recognise the importance of language: they know that it allows children to express their emotions and establish and develop good social relationships, as well as being an essential learning tool. They understand the need to provide a secure and positive environment for talk, so that children can develop confidence as well as skills. This may involve reviewing the physical environment as well as the learning environment, and reviewing teacher–pupil interaction. Dockrell et al. (2012) found that while behaviours such as use of children's names, gestures, use of open questions, and pacing and pausing talk were seen regularly, other strategies such as modelling and extending language, encouraging the use of new vocabulary and supporting listening skills, were less frequently seen.

Dockrell et al. also found that interactions with children with speech and language needs were usually of good quality but that more needed to be done in terms of planning structured opportunities for language development. Jolliffe (2014) describes strategies such as dialogic teaching and Philosophy for Children which develop talk for learning. Teachers do have at their disposal an increasing range of strategies for facilitating talk: for example, many now use paired talk as a way of involving all children in discussion, maximising talking time and also providing less confident children with an audience of one and a peer rather than an adult. Small-group talk needs to be carefully developed and supported (Jolliffe, 2007) if it is to work for all children, including those with language and communication needs. Strategies such as 'wait time' give all children some thinking time before responses are called for, which particularly helps those children who need more time to process their ideas and think through how they will present them – while also being of benefit to quick but superficial thinkers. A 'no hands up' policy, as implemented by increasing numbers of teachers, means that children no longer have to decide whether or not to volunteer to respond, which can be quite stressful. Strategies such as having all the children's names on lollipop sticks in a jar, and simply drawing names out to choose respondents, demonstrate to the class that selection is random and the child chosen simply represents the class as a whole.

High-quality teaching involves many varied opportunities for talk for a wide variety of purposes. In any one day children might, for example, discuss a piece of writing they are working on in guided writing groups, listen to explanations of how other children have worked out a mathematics problem, talk in pairs to plan and carry out a science experiment, and listen to the latest instalment of their class novel read by the teacher. Such talk is focused and purposeful, and the routines involved can be very supportive. For example, in guided writing children may take it in turns to evaluate their own work and discuss any difficulties they have had with it; the rest of the group may then take it in turn to give both a positive comment and a suggestion for improving the writing. For children with language difficulties the many opportunities for talk in the classroom provide invaluable models, both from adults and peers.

Poetry in the classroom

Some classroom activities have very specific benefits for children with language and communication needs. For example, the Primary National Curriculum (DfE, 2013) has the following statutory requirements for different ages:

- Year 1: recite poems by heart.

- Year 2: continue to build up a repertoire of poems learned by heart, appreciating these and reciting some, with appropriate intonation to make the meaning clear.

- Lower Key Stage 2: preparing poems and playscripts to read aloud and to perform, showing understanding through intonation, tone, volume and action.

- Upper Key Stage 2: prepare poems and plays to read aloud and to perform, showing understanding through intonation, tone and volume so that the meaning is clear to an audience.

Choral speaking and recitation give children opportunities to use their voices without needing to think about what to say. The case study that follows shows how one teacher used choral speaking to support children with language and communication needs.

 **Case study**

Poetry in performance

Eloise's Year 5 class included three children who were shy and who were reluctant to participate in whole-class or even small-group discussion or to read aloud, even in guided reading. George and Emily still struggled to read fluently, accurately and with expression, while Jamie was a keen reader who became almost inaudible when asked to read aloud. Eloise felt that it was important to address these issues in order to give them a voice in the class.

Eloise had chosen the classic poem *The Inchcape Rock* by Robert Southey for her class to study and to prepare for performance. Choice of poems is crucial to success in teaching poetry: Waugh et al. (2016) give many recommendations for high-quality poems of every kind. The poem tells the story of a bell placed on a dangerous rock in the sea by the Abbot of Aberbrothok to warn sailors. This deed gains the Abbot much gratitude. The villain of the poem, Sir Ralph, becalmed near the rock, has his sailors row him out so he can cut the bell from its buoy to spite the Abbot. However, on his return from his travels, laden with the spoils of his plundering, it is his ship that hits the rock and sinks. The poem consists of 16 four-line stanzas: Eloise organised her class into five groups, with George, Jamie and Emily in different groups, and gave each group three stanzas to work on, saving the last verse for the whole class. Eloise asked the groups to decide how to perform their stanzas, thinking of their voices as musical instruments that could be varied in terms of pitch (high to low), tempo (fast to slow) and dynamics (soft to loud). In previous years, Eloise had allowed groups to vary the number of voices used for different parts of a poem, but in this case she felt it was important that the children knew that everyone would be expected to read or recite every line, in order that her reluctant speakers could not opt out of as much as possible of the performance while keen performers stole the lime-light. Eloise encouraged the groups to learn their stanzas but allowed children the option of keeping the text in front of them so that worries about forgetting the lines did not cause anxiety.

Eloise noted that as the children worked on the text they spontaneously talked about what effects Southey was trying to create and what the significance of particular words and phrases was. They discussed the character and motivation of Sir Ralph. She had decided not to begin with a discussion of the text, hoping that consideration of the meaning of the poem and its impact would be more purposeful when linked to the performance. The children worked well rehearsing their verses, and when they were ready performed their sections in sequence. They clearly relished the language of the poem: the strong rhythm and rhyming couplets, along with effects such as alliteration and the drama of the narrative, made it a good choice for performance. Eloise observed that George, Emily and Jamie joined in enthusiastically; reading the verses so many times had made them completely fluent, and the choral speaking approach gave them security and confidence. Eloise then asked the children to work in their groups to evaluate their own performances and give other groups feed-back. The groups then considered and decided on any changes, practised again and finally as a class planned and rehearsed the final stanza, to be recited by all the children together.

The performance took place in assembly. Eloise projected images of the sea and old ships on to a screen to accompany it, but decided against any music or sound effects so that the children's voices could be heard clearly. She placed the children in two rows, with George, Jamie and Emily on the second row so that they did not feel too conspicuous. She had emphasised to the class that everyone needed to join in, for the groups to be heard clearly and to get the best effect. Eloise was delighted to see that the three children joined in with gusto, and afterwards appeared elated that they had been part of a performance that the rest of the school had clearly enjoyed.

Poetry has benefits beyond allowing children to use their voices. For children who struggle to read, the texts are relatively short, and yet the language is often rich, allowing children to enjoy the feel of the words on their tongues and explore new vocabulary. For children with language comprehension difficulties, then, poetry can be enjoyed without necessarily having a full under-standing of the text. Faulkner (2014, p.144) explains that language play has a positive impact on language development. However, because poetry is often open to a range of interpretations, it can be valuable in helping those children with language difficulties explore the possible meanings of the text. For children whose communication difficulties include a very literal under-standing of language and difficulties with abstract concepts, poetry can be of enormous benefit, as the case study that follows demonstrates.

Case study

Working on similes

Sarah, a trainee teacher in a Year 3 class, had been asked to teach a lesson on similes. She knew that this could be difficult for George, a pupil with Asperger syndrome. Sarah planned to use Roger McGough's poem *The Writer of This Poem*, which is a list of similes describing the author in some-what exaggerated terms. She decided to use visual prompts as much as possible, either objects (such as the pen nib and boxing glove referred to) or pictures (the tree, scaffolding and chemist's). She then asked the children to consider each simile in turn, having explained that there was only likely to be one point of comparison between the object and the author, and to evaluate the simi-les – which did the children think worked best and why, which were the most surprising, which did not work well and why not. Children disputed their favourites with some energy: was *As strong as scaffolding* better than *As smooth as a lolly-ice*? Did everyone have the same image in mind in response to *As clever as a tick*? The children then worked in pairs to produce similes to describe a character in their class novel, and again Sarah provided some visual prompts for children who found this difficult. In a subsequent lesson, Sarah introduced a 'Happiness is ...' poem, and then asked the children to compose their own. She modelled the process and ideas in shared writing, structuring the poem by using the five senses. George was able to make the link between the abstract concept and concrete objects that he could see, hear, smell, touch and taste. Sarah's care-ful planning ensured that the class had plenty of time to analyse models before they moved on to writing their own poems, and that they were well supported both by her and by their peers.

Drama in the classroom

Drama has a great deal to offer children with language and communication needs. It can play a significant part in helping them to communicate more successfully and become more effective language users. It often focuses on ways of communicating without words, showing children how much can be communicated by expression, gesture and movement. In drama activities children can become deeply absorbed in their roles, the situation they have been placed in and the problems they need to solve. Language becomes an essential tool for describing, explaining, reasoning and persuad-ing. Children need to cooperate to make the drama work: Freebody (2013) explains that drama is created through interaction and talk – in planning beforehand to establish what the work will be, during the drama work itself and in reflection afterwards.

Carroll (1978) suggested that talk in drama is very different from typical classroom talk. He argued that drama allows participants to engage in real-life situations but in a slower, more considered way, which gives more time for considered language choices. He also argued that in drama we are both partici-pant and spectator, and therefore more aware of our own language use and more able to reflect on it (Carroll, 1980). Another benefit of drama is that content is less important than in other classroom talk, and there is less emphasis on facts (Carroll, 1988). Very significantly, the generally accepted power relationship of the classroom is disrupted because in drama teacher and children engage together with the organisation, characters and context of the work (Carroll, 1996). Freebody (2013) proposed that 'in role' talk gives pupils opportunities to produce language matched to both the role and the scenario, and her research showed that they were able to do this even when exploring controversial issues.

Drama is likely to have particular benefits for those children with communication difficulties who find it hard to use and interpret language in different social contexts. They may not find it easy to distinguish between the surface meaning of what is said and what is actually intended, or between words and non-verbal communication when there is a discrepancy between them. Drama allows children not only to experiment with using language in different social situations, but also to analyse it and make different interpretations of the same scenario (Winston, 2004). It also helps them to see the benefits of planning for, rehearsing and evaluating their language use in different situations, just as adults may plan how to present themselves in an interview situation, rehearse possible answers to questions they think they may be asked, and afterwards reflect on the responses they made and consider how they might have been improved. Learning to take on a role allows children to see a different point of view and also develop a repertoire of registers, from the formal style of an official to the language of a character from the past or the strange way of speaking of a fantasy character. Early role-play tends to focus on plot: as children grow older, the focus tends to shift to character, relationships and motivation (Hendy and Toon, 2001).

Drama meets many of the speaking and listening requirements of the Primary National Curriculum (DfE, 2013, p.17). It allows children to:

- listen and respond appropriately to adults and their peers;

- articulate and justify answers, arguments and opinions;

- give well-structured descriptions, explanations and narratives for different purposes, including for expressing feelings;

- use spoken language to develop understanding through speculating, hypothesising, imagining and exploring ideas;

- speak audibly and fluently;

- gain, maintain and monitor the interest of the listener(s);

- select and use appropriate registers for effective communication.

There are many drama conventions that offer opportunities to support language and communication needs. Mime, of course, and freeze frame, in which a tableau or still image is created, allow children to communicate through facial expression, posture and movement. This enables children with language difficulties to participate on an equal basis with other pupils. For children with communication difficulties, mime and freeze frame give opportunities to understand and practise non-verbal communication. They may, for example, need to think about appropriate expressions and gestures in different situations, and will benefit from seeing other children's responses and using them as models. Paired or small-group improvisations allow children to discuss, plan and prepare their work. This provides the security of a known structure and a rough script to follow. The convention of teacher in role, where the teacher is engaged fully as a character in the drama, leading and prompting children's participation, reduces the pressure of being watched as all the class is participating, and the teacher is skilfully supporting, extending and challenging children's thinking and language.

The 'mantle of the expert' approach involves children taking on roles that have particular skills, expertise or knowledge. This can be real expertise, gained from classroom research, or assumed as part of the drama, with children in role as, for example, scientists, archaeologists or town planners. The status this gives them can be reassuring to children with communication needs, and where the expertise is real, children are given confidence in what they are speaking about. Forum theatre, in which a few pupils perform an improvisation and this is then discussed by the whole class and developed, either afterwards or even during the improvisation, allows children with speech and language needs to see how language is used to negotiate situations, and to understand how speech and action are grounded in emotions and thoughts.

'Hot seating' is another well-known drama strategy. It involves one participant taking on a role, commonly of a fictional character or a character from history. Other participants then question the character. It has the potential to be a highly engaging activity that challenges all participants to use the knowledge they have of the character and situation and to explore both in more depth. For the participant in the hot seat, there is a significant challenge in thinking and talking as the character, particularly as they have no idea what questions might be asked. However, for children with language and communication difficulties the activity may be problematic. For some children, simply being the focus of everyone's attention is overwhelming. For others, the need to formulate a response without any thinking time means that they are unable to give articulate or considered responses. There are, too, the children for whom social aspects of language are a challenge, and so understanding the point of view of someone else may be very difficult. Teachers therefore have a problem to solve. Do they give children who are likely to produce incoherent or inappropriate responses a chance to sit in the hot seat? Do they allow children to opt out because they find being centre stage too threatening? Do they find themselves always picking the same children – the confident, articulate children who have a good understanding of the subject? This may seem the safest and kindest solution, but it does nothing to support children with language and communication needs, and may even entrench their perceptions of their own difficulties; children are often acutely conscious of who 'gets picked' and who does not, and why.

 **Case study**

Making the hot seat safe

Alex, a trainee teacher in a whole Key Stage 2 class in a very small village school, planned to use drama to enhance his history teaching. He was aware from previous experience in school of the dangers of picking children who would find it difficult to answer the questions, but did not want to rule them out (or allow them to rule themselves out). As part of a thematic study of crime and punishment, the class had been learning about the prison reformer Elizabeth Fry. Alex began by putting the children into threes, and asking them to generate questions they would like to ask Elizabeth Fry. He had prepared some questions himself, but in the event the children produced some good questions that were likely to prompt extended and thoughtful responses.

He then selected a group of three, including one child who was always keen to participate in any activity but who found it difficult to express himself clearly and fluently. Alex explained that Elizabeth Fry was accompanied by two members of her committee, and the other two children stood immediately behind the hot seat. Alex asked a child to pose the first question, but then said that before Elizabeth Fry gave her response, all the threes should discuss what they thought her view might be. This gave the group at the front time to formulate and effectively rehearse a response. When 'Elizabeth' spoke, Alex was pleased to note that the ideas and language of the other two were drawn on quite heavily. He also asked other groups to describe what they had expected 'Elizabeth' to say.

Alex was delighted not only that a child with language difficulties had been able to be successful in the hot seat role, but also that his strategy had meant that all the children were involved in the activity rather than most being simply an audience. In a later drama session, he selected a child who found it very difficult to speak in front of an audience. He used the same strategies as before, but at one or two points Alex felt that she was beginning to find the situation overwhelming, and he referred the question to one of the other two in her group for a response. It was evident at the end of the session that surviving the hot seat had provided an enormous boost to her confidence and self-esteem.

 Concluding thoughts

This chapter has suggested that while the classroom can pose significant challenges for children with language and communication needs, it also offers skilled support and a range of opportunities for language development. These include opportunities for talk with peers as well as adults, varied contexts for purposeful talk, and different roles in talk. We have considered the particular benefits offered by poetry and drama. The increased focus on the importance of speaking and listening in education means that there has been a corresponding focus on children's language and communication needs and how they can best be met. This focus should have a positive impact not only on their language but also on their social and emotional development, helping to ensure that they are not, in the words of ICAN (n.d.), the children's communication charity, 'left out or left behind', but are instead given the communication skills they need to fulfil their potential.

References

Afasic Speech, Language and Communication [Internet]. Available from **www.afasic.org.uk/recognising-a-problem/speech-language-and-communication/** (accessed 3 August 2016).

Bercow, J. (2008) *The Bercow Report: A Review of Services for Children and Young People (0–19) with Speech, Language and Communication Needs*. Nottingham: DCSF Publications.

Carroll, J. (1978) A language functions approach to learning areas in drama in education. *National Association for Drama in Education*, 3: 19–27.

Carroll, J. (1980) Language, the role of the teacher, and drama in education. *English in Australia*, 53: 35–43.

Carroll, J. (1988) Terra incognita: mapping drama talk. *National Association for Drama in Education*, 12(2): 13–21.

Carroll, J. (1996) Escaping the information abattoir: critical and transformative research in drama classrooms. In P. Taylor (ed.), *Researching Drama and Arts Education: Paradigms and Possibilities*. London: Falmer Press, pp.72–84.

Cummins, J. (1984) *Bilingual Education and Special Education: Issues in Assessment and Pedagogy*. San Diego, CA: College Hill.

Department for Education (2013) *The 2014 Primary National Curriculum in England: Key Stage 1 and 2 Framework*. London: Shurville Publishing.

Department for Education (2014) *Statistical Release: Children with Special Educational Needs 2014: An Analysis*. London: Department for Education.

Dockrell, J., Bakopoulou, I., Law, J., Spencer, S. and Lindsay, G. (2012) *Developing a Communication Supporting Classrooms Observation Tool*. London: Department for Education.

Elklan (2016) Communication Friendly Settings [Internet]. Available from **www.elklan.co.uk/information/cfs** (accessed 19 September 2016).

Faulkner, H. (2014) Poetry. In D. Waugh, W. Jolliffe and K. Allott (eds), *Primary English for Trainee Teachers*. London: Learning Matters, pp.42–157.

Freebody, K. (2013) Discourse in drama: talk, role and learning in drama education. *NJ-Drama Australia National Journal*, 37: 65–76.

Grainger, T., Goouch, K. and Lambirth, A. (2003) Playing the game called writing: children's views and voices. *English in Education*, 37 (2): 4–15.

Hendy, L. and Toon, L. (2001) *Supporting Drama and Imaginative Play in the Early Years*. Buckingham: Open University Press.

ICAN Mission Statement [Internet]. Available from **www.ican.org.uk/** (accessed 10 August 2016).

Jolliffe, W. (2014) Speaking and listening: spoken language. In D. Waugh, W. Jolliffe and K. Allott (eds), *Primary English for Trainee Teachers*. London: Learning Matters, pp. 16–37.

Jolliffe, W. (2007) *Cooperative Learning in the Classroom: Putting It into Practice*. London: Paul Chapman.

Lee, Y.A. (2007) Third turn position in teacher talk: contingency and the work of teaching. *Journal of Pragmatics*, 39: 180–206.

Waugh, D., Neaum, S. and Waugh, R. (2016) *Children's Literature in Primary Schools*. London: Learning Matters.

Winston, J. (2004) *Drama and English at the Heart of the Curriculum: Primary and Middle Years*. London: David Fulton.

5
Supporting struggling learners: teachers, learners and labels of SEN

Rosie Ridgway

 This chapter

This chapter will discuss aspects of the practices and philosophies of supporting struggling learners. It will discuss and enquire into reasons why children struggle with literacy in particular, and seek to cover the following questions:

- Who are the children struggling with literacy?
- How does a child get a label of 'Special Educational Need' (SEN)?
- What do the labels mean? Do they help?
- What strategies can teachers use to support struggling learners?

Who are the children struggling with literacy?

Children can struggle with literacy for a range of reasons. The difficulties they experience may affect particular areas of literacy (such as decoding) or have a more general impact across reading, writing and understanding of text. Children might struggle with literacy because of lack of experience or exposure to reading and writing, or because they have hearing, visual or motor difficulties which haven't been identified. Children might struggle with literacy because they are easily distracted and find it hard to focus their attention, or they might have difficulties with their long-term or working memory that makes it difficult to identify phonemes or recall words and hold them in mind while working out what a sentence means. Learners can experience such a variety of difficulties with literacy that it can be challenging for teachers to know which strategies to adopt in order to support them.

In this chapter, we will cover some of the controversies around labelling and understanding the difficulties that some learners face. The first areas we will examine are the challenges of categorisation and the problems that arise in how we try to describe and understand learners with SENs by exploring how the labelling process works. Then we will look at the relative risks and rewards associated with identifying and labelling the challenges that particular learners face by asking questions about what labels mean and whether they help. Several cases will be introduced to support our reflection on the dilemmas of labelling. Finally we will explore practical strategies for supporting learners in difficulty and reflect on these processes at a practitioner level. The biggest priority for teachers working with learners facing difficulties is to provide effective support which allows the learner to overcome challenges and make progress, whether they have a label of SEN or not.

Learners can experience difficulties with literacy that present in a variety of ways and are associated with different learning challenges. Labelling and diagnosis of SEN is controversial. Teachers need to be sensitive in understanding and responding to learners in difficulty. Teachers can evaluate the relative strengths and weaknesses of approaches to supporting learners in difficulty and make choices about their suitability based on the individual learner and the context. Effective practical support for students facing difficulties with their learning is a more important outcome than whether or not the learner is assigned a label of SEN.

 **Case study**

Understanding how children become struggling literacy learners

Sami was a seven-year-old having difficulties with literacy. His reading ability was similar to what you would expect for a much younger child and he seemed to be finding a number of issues difficult. He found matching letter sounds (phonemes) to written letters (graphemes) very challenging and could do this correctly for about half the letter sounds. He couldn't identify middle (medial) sounds (like the 'a' sound in the word 'cat') or blended sounds (where letter sounds are blended together to make a distinct sound like the 'st' in the word 'star') correctly. He struggled with writing: his handwriting grip was poor, and his writing was often illegible and featuring letters that were backwards, missing letters and different sizes. He often only managed to record a sentence after lots of adult prompting, and the attempts to sound out and spell words were inconsistent. Sami was disengaged, easily upset and frustrated and often refused to attempt written work; sometimes he stormed out of the room and occasionally threw his book on to the floor. Sami's mother was concerned about this and has spoken about how difficult it was to get him to do homework, she wanted to keep the peace and not upset him further and create a 'scene' at home.

 Activity

How could you support this pupil?

- What do you think is the main difficulty that Sami was facing?
- What interventions could you put in place at school to support Sami?
- What could you suggest to support Sami's mother to help him overcome these challenges?

Supporting Sami

Sami's weak literacy skills were beginning to get in the way of his enjoyment of school. It was important to identify the central difficulty he was facing and put in place some support to allow him to overcome these challenges. The main issue Sami was facing were the 'gaps' in his phonological awareness. Without a good understanding of how sounds and written forms (phonemes and graphemes) matched up, it was difficult for Sami to make sense of reading and writing tasks. The difficulties he was having with blending and medial sounds were less of a priority as this is a more sophisticated literacy skill (which can be addressed after basic phonic awareness has been established). The issues Sami was facing with his writing and letter reversals were also skills that could be focused on a little later so teaching would be continued as usual while focusing on the phonics intervention – for example, offering a wide variety of opportunities in class to practise writing and develop fine motor skills, like drawing, colouring, pattern-making, threading, etc. The behaviours Sami exhibited (frustration and acting out) reflected that he was beginning to give up on learning and feel like a 'failure'. This was a critical issue – it is important that Sami is not made to feel ashamed and engage in self-worth protecting behaviours (see Covington, 1984). For the teacher of this seven-year-old, a caring but boundaried response (Brown, 2012) was needed. A boundaried response kindly acknowledges that the child is distressed and offers to help them with that (empathy), but without excusing the inappropriate behaviour (because that will not help the child in the long term), for example: 'I can see you are upset, but we don't treat our books like that. Can you tell me what's wrong? How can we make that better?'

For Sami, a structured phonics intervention to extend and consolidate his phonic awareness was appropriate. This can be approached by offering specific taught time on a regular basis with a suitably qualified teacher (D'Agostino and Harmey, 2016; Slavin et al., 2011) or an individually tailored computer-based intervention to support Sami – for example a program such as ABRA or Lexia would work well (Higgins et al., 2012; McNally et al., 2016). These interventions are individually paced, and offer lots of opportunities for rehearsal, recall and extension. The significant advantages of targeted technology-based interventions are that they make progress explicit to the learner, they give instant feedback (with opportunities to self-correct) and they reward effort. It is argued by Mayer (2014) that such approaches are also more engaging for learners as they 'gamify' skill development, reducing the threat of failure by making skill acquisition a fun and integral part of the game. There is a significant body of evidence to support the implementation of these programs. For further information see the Education Endowment Foundation's evaluation of Online Reading Support programs (https://educationendowmentfoundation.org.uk).

What was very positive here was that Sami's mum was concerned and wanted to help her son, and she wanted the school to support her in doing so. Sami's mum would need to be reassured that a specific phonics intervention was in place at the school, that Sami was being supported and that she would be updated regularly on his progress. Homework and reading are not supposed to be negative experiences so it would be necessary to work with Sami's mum to make literacy activities fun again. This could be encouraged by offering phonics games and simple quizzes for Sami to share with his family as homework, for example playing I-spy together. This is a reminder that learning to enjoy reading and writing should be fun!

How does a child get a label of SEN?

Some children with physical disabilities are identified fairly early (often by a medical professional) before they reach school. Other children with less obvious challenges may not be identified as having difficulties until they reach school. Because these experiences may be quite different from each other, we will look first at what definitions of SEN and disability are, and then the organisation of the SEN identification system which aims to provide a coherent process for all learners experiencing difficulties.

What are SEN?

In England the current legal definition in the Children and Families act 2014 of Special Educational Needs (SEN) is that:

---

(1) A child or young person has special educational needs if he or she has a learning difficulty or disability which calls for special educational provision to be made for him or her.

(2) A child of compulsory school age or a young person has a learning difficulty or disability if he or she -

    (a) has a significantly greater difficulty in learning than the majority of others of the same age, or

    (b) has a disability which prevents or hinders him or her from making use of facilities of a kind generally provided for others of the same age in mainstream schools.

(Children and Families Act 2014)

SEN and disabilities are not the same thing, but they sometimes overlap. Disability is defined in the Equality Act 2010 as '. . . a physical or mental impairment that has a long-term and substantial adverse effect on their ability to carry out normal day-to-day activities'. So some children with disabilities may have SEN and some may not.

Why are SEN categories (or labels) important?

The system of SEN assessment and support in the English education system has made categorisation an important feature (Warnock, 2005). There are two tiers of response in the reformed SEN support system in education in England following the Children and Families Act 2014 (legislation) and the SEN Code of Practice 2014 (DfE/DoH, 2014, statutory guidance for local authorities, schools and practitioners).

The first tier is *SEN support*. This happens within school and includes the reasonable adjustments and additional activities a school offers in order to support the learner with SEN. Examples of SEN support in practice include: extra help from an adult to understand and complete their work in class, tasks broken down into smaller manageable chunks, extra sessions to help build up skills needed with learning, help to communicate with others and work with an adult to develop and meet learning targets.

The second tier is *Add-on intervention*. If further support is needed as the child or young person is still not making progress as would be expected for someone of their age, then an assessment process is triggered so that an *Education, Health and Care (EHC) plan* can be created. The assessment can be requested from the local authority by a young person (if they are age 16), their parent, health professional, teacher, social worker or family friend. The assessment involves collecting evidence about the learner from the child or young person themselves, their parents or carers, as well as from school, health professionals and social care professionals. This information is used to create an EHC plan that sets out the support needs that the individual has (what) and the way these needs should be supported (how). It is intended that this process take 20 weeks, though there is a discrepancy between local authority timelines and parental reports (Adams et al., 2017). One complicating factor in this process is that because these SEN reforms are so recent (2014), a lot of children and young people who were already receiving support through a learning difficulty assessment (LDA) or through a 'statement of special educational need' now need to have this reviewed and translated into an EHC plan – it seems likely that this will be a significant challenge until the transition period is over in spring 2018. Examples of support available through an EHC plan might be: access to specialist therapists, behavioural intervention, psychological intervention with the support of educational psychologists, access to a specialist education setting through change of placement. The SEN Code of Practice (2014) requires that SEN are identified by a 'primary' need and these can fall under the domains of:

- *communication and interaction* (for example, learners with speech, language and communication needs or those on the autism spectrum);

- *cognition and learning* (for example, those with moderate or severe learning difficulties, or specific learning difficulties such as dyslexia, dyscalculia and dyspraxia);

- *social emotional and mental health* (for example, learners with conduct disorders such as opposi-tional defiant disorder);

- *sensory and/or physical* (for example, learners who have a hearing, visual or multisensory impair-ment, or who require additional support because of a physical disability).

(See the SEN Code of Practice (DfE/DoH, 2014, p.97) for more detail.)

Which children have SEN?

The differences in rates of identification of Special Educational Needs and Disabilities (SENDs) can be overlooked at an individual practitioner level, but when we examine national statistics we can identify disproportional over-representation of some groups. In 2016 data from government statis-tics (DfE, 2016) recorded that 1,228,785 pupils in England have identified special educational needs (which is an estimated 14.4% of the school population). A small proportion (2.8%) of them have statements of SEN or an EHC plan (this figure has remained stable since 2007). Boys are more likely to be identified as having SEN than girls (SEN at school support: boys 14.7%, girls 8.2%; EHC/state-ment of SEN: boys 4%, girls 1.5%). This gender difference is particularly extreme in children with EHC/statement of SEN with a diagnosis of autism (boys 30%, girls 14.8%). Children with SEN are more likely to be eligible for free school meals (a proxy measure of socio-economic status) than those not eligible (no SEN + FSM 12.1%, with SEN + FSM 27.2%). Children in looked-after care (LAC) are more likely to be identified as having SEN (in 2015 66% children in LAC had SEN) and in particular these children are more likely to have social, emotional and mental health difficulties. Children from some ethnic groups are also more likely to be identified as having SEN, in particular Irish and Gypsy Roma Travellers and also Black Caribbean children.

The system for identifying and supporting learners with SEN depends on categorising learners by the challenges they have in communication and interaction, cognition and learning, social emo-tional and mental well-being, and physical and/or sensory difficulties. Learners facing difficulties with their learning can be supported at different levels of intensity of SEN support or through an EHC plan – this is known as a tiered approach. Boys from some ethnic and socio-economic status backgrounds and children in looked-after care are more likely to be identified as having SEN, and this is called disproportionality.

What do the labels mean? Do they help?

In order to access support and resources through the SEN system a learner is assessed (for an EHC plan) and the kind of educational, health and social care support required is identified under a par-ticular category (DfE/DoH, 2014). This practice of labelling is an inherent feature of the education system in England, yet we should approach such labels cautiously. Guidance for practitioners often suggests a simplified (often medicalised) account of SEN difficulties which learners face. This 'clarity' and simplification is not entirely helpful because it offers certainty where practitioners could ben-efit from critical awareness of the tensions at play. Classrooms are complex social environments and learning is a process which involves many components: cognitive, conative and affective (Sternberg, 2005); for this reason, the role of labels and diagnosis in education is complicated.

Let's consider the purpose of diagnosis in a clinical (non-educational) setting. A diagnosis describes and identifies a problematic issue and indicates a treatment or response outcome. Diagnosis is intended to identify what a problem is, its likely outcomes and appropriate treatments to remediate it. Many of the categorisations and labels used in special education provision have adopted medical diagnostic labels and language and applied them in educational settings. This has had some important (unintended) consequences for learners. Labels of SEN are associated with the broad categories discussed earlier, and these general labels may be used in ways that are not helpful to the learner (MacMahon, 2012). In education, diagnostic labels are used to categorise learners into particular groups to allow the system to support learner needs. Hessels (1997) points out that this focus on academic outcomes pays little regard to the personal or social impact of labelling. One major criticism of categorical approaches to SENDs is that they adopt a deficit or medical model where the category label consists of a list of failures to conform to typical norms (Oliver, 1990). For example, the term 'disorder' is commonly used in psychological or psychiatric diagnosis and identifies *a pattern of symptoms that impact negatively on different areas of life and are distressing for the individual*. The purpose of diagnosis of a psychological disorder is not merely to apply a label, but to identify the kinds of difficulties being faced to find solutions, use shared language to communicate information, and find strategies to support the person and minimise distress. Inherent in the process of diagnosis is a comparison between symptoms that would occur typically, and those that are a-typical. What is problematic about this for education is that in order to identify something as a disorder (for example ADHD) we need to assume that 'norms' of behaviour apply equally to all learners at a particular age, and that those who exhibit behaviours which are different from our expected norm are 'deviant' from the norm (rather than assuming that the 'norm' includes a broad range of behaviours).

Developmental approaches are useful in understanding how children develop and function at different ages. However, if developmental progression is interpreted too rigidly (as gateways, or stages) we become less tolerant of difference, and our expectations become less flexible in responding to individual differences. The risk here is that we stop seeing differences as part of human experience, and instead view them as problematic and abnormal.

A challenge stemming from the 'diagnostic' approach to SENs is a 'pathologising' of learning which focuses on the underperforming learner in isolation (and their internal functioning) with little reference to environmental, social or other factors which can have a strong influence on learning. In some critiques of labelling we see this presented as scapegoating, often in relation to arguments about disproportionality (Dyson and Gallannaugh 2008). Gallagher (1976) points out that focusing on SEND categories can discourage seeing the learner holistically, and narrows our attention on one particular aspect of difficulty.

The use of broad labels implies that if learners have the 'same' label they face the same difficulty and they imply 'sameness' of response (with little regard to individual differences). The lack of sensitivity to the specific nature of the individual and context can render generic strategies ineffective and risk further creating a self-fulfilling prophesy or justifying low expectations. Here generic labels become excuses for weak teaching and poor learning outcomes. It is essential to note that co-occurrence of difficulties with learning can cluster in unique ways so an additional challenge associated with categorisations is that boundaries between categories imply separation of difficulties into different 'kinds' (primary type of need) when co-occurrence and complex patterns are common. Having one primary 'label' does not mean that a learner is only facing one issue in their learning. Teachers need to move away from treating categorisation by SEN as a way of 'dividing up' learners, and view it as a product of structuring the education system (an imperfect model) and respond instead to the learner in front of them.

It isn't just the words associated with labelling which are important here, but beliefs and actions. Jordan and Stanovich (1998) point out that teachers' beliefs are significant in shaping how effective their teaching practice is. They found those professionals with fixed mindsets (pathognomonic) towards inclusion and the teachers' ability to reach some kinds of learners (teacher efficacy) were less effective in practice than those with more flexible (interventionist) mindsets. Work by Foroni and Rothbart (2011), Jordan and Stanovich (1998), and Schwartz and Jordan (2011) corroborate these findings though the role that labels of SEN play within the domain of teacher beliefs are less clear.

Florian and Spratt (2013) identified some core beliefs which support effective inclusive practice, one of which is the view that everybody struggles with something, and that we are all more similar than different. The argument proposed by Florian and Spratt (2013) is that by focusing on 'special' or distinctive characteristics, we lose sight of the underlying similarities of learners and instead we should focus on what pedagogies and practices can work for 'most' learners alongside some additional support. This greater acceptance of diversity and positive inclusive teaching practices is to be supported, but the risks of cautions around label use should also be considered. In the current system of SEN provision, those without formal labels risk double jeopardy: informal labels (stigma) and no support. We discussed, earlier that the allocation of support and resources are linked to SEN categorisation – so those without formal labels identifying their difficulties cannot access the most intensive provision. In effect those without labels (in the current system) may miss out on support (though the emphasis on progress measures aims to avoid this).

A further challenge is about the 'significance' that a label can have. If we begin to identify the label before the person, we risk sliding into stigma and prejudice. If we view the person as part of a 'labelled' group before we view them as an individual, the likelihood for prejudice and unconscious bias is far greater than if we view them as a sympathetic person with a unique range of positive and negative attributes (Green et al., 2005). If we assume that we as teachers are capable of making prejudicial judgements about our pupils, and that these may blame, excuse or stigmatise learners (Barga, 1996) we need to be cautious about how we employ labels and diagnoses and stay aware of that risk.

Link and Phelan (2001) describe *stigma* as having the following features: labelling, stereotyping, separation, status loss and discrimination where those stigmatised have less power than those not stigmatised. While being sensitive to the potential social and emotional impacts of labelling we should also be clear that no (formal) label does not equate to no stigma – it means stigma is attached to informal judgements which may possibly be even worse. For example, Riddick's (1995, 1996) interviews with students tell us that before a formal label pupils experienced being identified as stupid, mad and bad. Reinders (2008) wisely states 'Negative connotations do not reside in words, but in the mind. Negative connotations are attached to words because of how people think' (Reinders, 2008, p.46). This reminder can help teachers to navigate these complex issues. If the system of labelling is supportive and constructive for learners, it should be used sensitively while also working to challenge stigma and prejudice.

In some cases, the diagnosis and labelling process allows us to understand difficulties better (which is the intention). For example, where a child has had negative experiences in education, where they struggle to achieve what others find easy, having a label for this can be a relief and tremendously important in supporting them in understanding themselves (Riddick, 2000). It is better to identify yourself as having a problem with a specific name, rather than self-blaming and assuming you are 'no good at learning' or just 'naughty'.

It is also evident that the more specific and accurate a diagnosis is, the more likely a specific outcome response can be identified. In the case of generic labels of SEN we see less positive attainment outcomes and personal outcomes than with more specific labels (Riddick, 2000) but a reluctance in education to label SENs specifically because of concerns about stigma. This is an example of the interface between people's beliefs about labels, stigma and learning and how these can shape practice.

Diagnoses of difficulties with learning are not a magic wand to 'fix' problems (or make them vanish) nor should they be a weapon (where stigma and assumptions about the diagnosis mean one's individuality is forgotten). Diagnosis and labels in education give us a general direction about the kinds of difficulties a learner is facing, and offer some suggestions about what may be suitable intervention approaches. How to put these into practice and monitor their impact on learning is both individual and context dependent; teachers need to be aware of the sensitive and controversial nature of responding to 'special educational needs' to support their individual learners effectively.

Labelling: a controversial issue

The labelling of special educational needs is a controversial issue. Controversies around labels involve concerns about medical language describing learners negatively in terms of deficits and the concern that these encourage a narrow view of what is 'normal' behaviour for learners. An additional concern is the focus on 'within learner' characteristics as explaining difficulties with learning, and that broad labels are vague and over-simple – in effect not helpful to the learner or teacher in terms of responding to difficulties identified. In education some professionals worry about the risks of stigma associated with the language of SEN and think they encourage negative attitudes and beliefs. Practically, however, labels are a core feature of the SEN provision system and without formal identification learners risk struggling undetected and unsupported. When using the language of diagnosis in relation to learners and learning teachers need to be cautious about using medical language and not making assumptions about individuals based on 'labels' the learner has. The main purpose of identifying a difficulty is to put in place strategies to support the learner in overcoming them and if labelling supports this, then it is pragmatic to continue. In order to do this, it may be very useful, then, to consider such reflection points as a teacher.

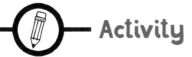

Activity

- What does a child's label of SEN mean in practice in your school?
- Do you recognise any points in the discussion about labelling from your own experiences?
- What challenges do you face in supporting struggling children's learning when they don't have a label of SEN?
- If you heard a child being referred to by their SEN label rather than by name, what would be your response?

 **Case study**

Should parents want a label for their children?

Ann, mother of Dominic (aged 9) who is on the autism spectrum, tells us:

> At first, I didn't want a diagnosis. I didn't want to know. I just wanted people to like my son how he was ... and autism is such a big label. It was scary. Like a life sentence (pause) but now, I know – I'm fine with it, we had such a long wait and things weren't improving and it was getting harder to explain his sounds and behaviours. Sometimes in meltdowns biting other children, and you know the diagnosis, you know – he wouldn't have been able to access extra support, and it's easier to explain to people. He's at a great school now. So if any parents are afraid, or don't want the label – I tell them. It will help. It will.

- What support could a school offer to a parent like Ann while she waits for diagnosis?
- What information could the teacher gather about Dominic's performance in school that would be helpful for Dominic and Ann?
- What do you think the 'great school' Ann mentions is doing for Dominic?
- What do you feel about Ann's decision?
- How do you think you would feel as a parent in her case?
- What do you think will be the educational implications of this decision as Dominic progresses through school?

Hornby (1995) and Dale (1996) likened the effect of getting a child's diagnosis to bereavement. They suggest that parents' expectations and hopes for their child have to be re-evaluated, and in this process they have a sense of loss. This is not to suggest that the autistic person is worth less than a typically developing one, rather that our expectations and reality are sometimes mismatched and evaluating this can be an emotionally painful process. On average in the UK, autistic spectrum diagnosis takes 3.5 years from a parent's approach to a health professional (Crane et al., 2016). This confirms that the process of acquiring a label is a very slow one and during this period of uncertainty the child will be in school. There is much to suggest that delays in the diagnostic process (Siklos and Kerns, 2007; Howlin and Moore, 1997) and negative experiences of delays, poor communication and bureaucracy are a source of dissatisfaction and stress for families (Crane et al., 2016; Mansell and Morris, 2004). Ann tells us that the label itself was 'scary', and in the process of getting used to her changes in expectation for Dominic, her views about using the term 'autism' changed. Ann felt that it was helpful to use the label 'autism' if it could allow her to communicate about the support Dominic needed, and to access additional help (in the form of a teaching assistant). Referring to the case study, it would be helpful for you to consider the sources of support for families:

- Council for Disabled Children: www.councilfordisabledchildren.org.uk

- Contact-a-Family: www.cafamily.org.uk

- National Network of Parent Carer Forums: www.nnpcf.org.uk

Some students require additional support to learn what others acquire with much less effort. These learners in difficulty require more opportunities to encounter subject matter and more intensive instruction that includes more structured opportunities for skill development and consolidation (repetition, recall and rehearsal).

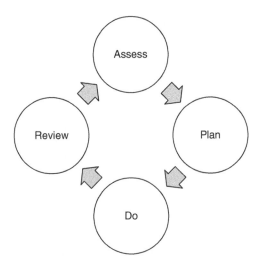

Figure 5.1   Reflective practice cycle for teachers supporting learners in difficulty.

Learners struggling with literacy may do so for a number of reasons, and identifying *what* the core challenges are is an intimidating task. Most teachers, however, have some awareness of where pupils 'should' be in their subject, and with a little further exploration gathering detailed information about learners' strengths and weaknesses we can get a better picture of what the source of the difficulties might be. (Is it solely a decoding problem or a broader processing issue to do with memory?) So it is appropriate as part of your classroom assessments to use some simple diagnostic activities to explore the challenges pupils are facing.

The reflective practice cycle offers steps towards developing and maintaining positive classroom support strategies for learners facing difficulties. This cycle should function in addition to positive whole-class strategies (to review these see Trussler and Robinson, 2015).

When working with pupils with an identified SEN, it is essential to find out not only about the 'label' but as much detail around the difficulties they face as possible. (If a child has a label of ADHD and you don't know what that is you need to find out!) Find official sources of information, get further training, read books and self-advocacy materials, join a CPD network and learn from specialist teachers. The more information and awareness you have about the nuances within a diagnostic label, the better support you will be able to offer.

Once you have some generic information, it is also important to use information relevant to the individual (personal and contextual) that is both formally and informally obtained – for example, prior assessments, generic school work, talk with previous teachers and most importantly parents/carers (or whoever is involved in direct care of the child, e.g. grandparents). The more information gathering you do to prepare yourself to understand and support this learner in their learning, the more effective your teaching and their learning will be. For example, if you have a generic descriptor of ADHD, it is useful to work out whether distractibility, hyperactivity, inattention or impulsivity are more dominant challenges faced by the learner. (This can be part of your observation focus when interacting with the learner.) It also follows that no one can be characterised in purely negative terms and that, just as a learner may face challenges in some ways, there are certainly areas of strength that the learner may have. These might be, for example, that they have good verbal and social skills, or they are very kind and supportive of younger children or peers when they are upset. They may be very imaginative and creative, they may be motivated by achievement and praise, or they may respond particularly well to having a 'responsibility' or classroom job to live up to. As a teacher, you can use these strengths to support the learner to overcome challenges – perhaps in a compensatory way or as a motivation to persevere. Importantly though, the recognition of a child's value, potential and strengths will improve the quality of your relationship as a teacher and learner (Tremmel, 1993). If there is a sense of care (Noddings, 2012) that you as a teacher like them, can see the good in them and want to help them to 'be the best they can be' it will be much easier for a child to risk more challenges (and potential failures) in their learning and this engagement is vital for learner perseverance and success (Rogers and Raider-Roth, 2006).

With older children it is worth asking them what strategies they use or other teachers have used effectively with them to overcome challenges (for example, it may be that a child needs some support in identifying when it is OK to fiddle and when they need to really focus and listen intently so the teacher might hand out and ask to hand back a fiddle toy to squeeze, or have a symbol or word that they show and use to 'sign post' when critical information (such as instructions) are being given. It is easy for us, as teachers, to slip into the idea that 'everything we say' is important, but if we reflect on this we know that, actually, much classroom talk is not 'key information' and for those who struggle to filter the 'essential' from the 'non-essential' (social talk not focused on a particular task or concept) then signposting can be a really useful strategy. Helpfully, it also reminds us to pay attention (Tremmel, 1993) to how much distraction and additional information we are offering and that this may well be contributing to problems in the learning environment. This acknowledges our own role in the complex social and educational environment that is the classroom.

There is persuasive research evidence that regular focused discussions on understanding and learning can be very helpful in creating constructive talk around classroom experiences (Higgins et al., 2005). It moves the focus away from what can be very painful, shaming experiences of learning failure and associated feelings of hopelessness towards targeted actions in response to learning challenges. These responses are not to be confused with telling a child to 'try harder' and take more responsibility for their own learning, but rather a shared interest between the teacher and child problematising learning. This discussion can include talking about what works for their learning, what is tricky and what they together can try next to overcome a challenge (Higgins et al., 2005, Schunk, 2008). These dialogues are also a good opportunity to reflect on positive experiences of learning and progress made – identifying success is a big factor in maintaining and strengthening learning relationships and fostering motivation (see Dweck, 2008, on mindset who argues that if my effort is paying off slowly over time and I see evidence of my progress, I am more likely to persevere in future). In addition there are whole-class strategies which support assessment for learning which reinforce this dialogue, because children don't just pay attention to what you say – it is what you do every day in your teaching that shows them what is important.

The adults who care for the child at home generally spend a lot of time with them and know them well, and so the discussions you have about the areas of difficulty and strength that a child has are a really good source of information to inform your teaching. Occasionally this may not be possible because people at home are busy and can't make time to come in to school for a discussion or talk on the phone – for example, if they work or have other commitments – but in my experience this is rare. Generally parents and carers are interested in how their children are progressing in school, and good communication with the people at home is generally advantageous for the child. Try to maintain a regular dialogue (about once per half term for a brief catch up, when all is progressing well), not just when things are challenging! Partnership with parents or carers is really useful for solution-finding and sharing when a child is struggling, and also as a means for sharing progress that the child is making. Collaboration is not always easy and partnership with parents should always remain professional and with a broad focus on the child. Key points should be summarised at the end of these 'catch-up sessions' and a record of this should be kept (again this is part of an ongoing monitoring process). Questions that you should consider in making sense of the issues discussed so far are given in Table 5.1.

Table 5.1   Supporting struggling learners: questions to consider

Assess	• *Learner focused observation:* What behaviours am I seeing? What does their work look like? What challenges is the learner having? What does the pupil say?
	• *Enquire:* What do the parents say? What do other professionals say (if involved)?
	• *Gather information:* What challenges are having most impact on the learner? What is the main issue that I can do something about? What do I need to find out more about?
Plan	• *Gather information:* What strategies are available to target support for this learner? How does the intervention align with the area of difficulty? What information is there concerning the relative effectiveness of these? What evaluation methods have been used to assess the outcome of intervention?
	• *Risks and benefits:* What are the risks/benefits of doing this? How will the intervention affect members of the class and the school?
	• *Implementation plan:* What will we measure? When will we review? How will I know the intervention is working? How can I make sure the quality of the intervention is high? Will this student miss out on something else during the time they are doing the intervention?
Do	• *Putting it into practice:* Who is responsible for doing the intervention? Can you describe the intervention activities to the learner and their parents? How long and how often are the intervention activities? Where and how will we keep and share records of this? Who is involved and have they given consent?
Review	• *Review:* Is there evidence to show that this intervention is working? What do the outcome measures show? Are there any other (unexpected) outcomes from the intervention? What are the next steps - continue, change, stop? What are parents' views about the intervention?

Case study

Supporting specific learners

Danny was a cheerful ten-year-old. He had a diagnosis of ADHD and struggled with both reading and writing. He had difficulty with settling down to a task, and in persisting with it (as he was easily distracted). When Danny did become more focused (with support), he found it difficult to identify what information was important to perform the task. He found it hard to distinguish relevant from irrelevant details when given instruction and it often required repetition. He often failed to complete tasks or produced so little written work it was hard to assess at the appropriate level. It may be that, given his difficulty with following instructions, Danny had a communication difficulty which wasn't diagnosed, so that rather than being cheeky, he simply didn't understand. The class teacher asked for a referral to speech and language therapy services for this to be assessed.

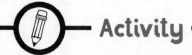

Activity

How could you support this pupil?

- What strategies could the class teacher use to support Danny's understanding of tasks?
- How could the teacher encourage him to persist with tasks?
- What do you think might happen to Danny when he reaches secondary school? What are the risks and opportunities? Will having a specific diagnosis help him access appropriate support?

We see in the case study that Danny needs support with two main issues: understanding tasks and persisting with them. The first challenge, understanding tasks, relates in particular to the issues he has in getting ready to work, identifying relevant details and knowing what to do and how. The second challenge, persisting with tasks, relates to 'keeping going' – this requires knowing how to manage learning and how to work on tasks for longer to develop persistence. Both of these issues of self-regulation (attention focus and persistence) are fairly common difficulties associated with ADHD and might also relate to Danny's working memory.

Danny needs support in establishing understanding of a task, so the teacher needs to offer additional scaffolding to help Danny organise and prioritise this essential information: what to do and how to do it. This can be in the form of learning objectives broken down with clear reference to the task, or in the form of a checklist of key steps which can be shared with the whole class, while a physical copy to refer to should support Danny's understanding more effectively. Using a checklist also allows the teacher to confirm understanding about the activity (identifying any misconceptions) and give a clear frame of reference if Danny needs redirecting back to the task during the activity.

For Danny, staying focused and persisting on a learning activity can be a challenge. Initially, while he is learning to focus for longer periods on task, he will require more support and direction from the adult (Elliott and Place, 2012). The support approach is called fading (or gradual release of responsibility) where adult directed activities gradually shift to self-directed activities, slowly allowing the pupil to develop self-management skills (Barry and Messer, 2003). This approach should be used to encourage Danny to think about how he is approaching and managing learning tasks, particularly with reference to literacy work. This can begin with helping Danny to monitor his 'on task' behaviour with reference to a visual organiser (Schunk and Rice, 1993). Initially this will be the teacher actively monitoring Danny's task focus and calmly and regularly redirecting the pupil back to the task, for example by reference to the bullet points in the checklist and the learner's work, or encouraging the pupil to review their progress and check off each step on the checklist as they complete sections of the activity. (Initially this will be modelled by the adult, with the eventual aim to develop learner independent self-regulation.) There are many ways teachers can check pupils' understanding, and where there are concerns about how much is being understood formative approaches may be used to assess understanding. For example, we can use visual inference tools such as pictures, sequence cards or mind maps.

Danny also needs support in approaching tasks strategically. It might be that his failure to perform well in extended writing tasks is due to poor organisation or lack of focus on the task. Either way teaching him how to approach such activities and make choices about which strategies to adopt is strongly recommended (Teaching and Learning Toolkit, 2015). This involves explicitly teaching what the strategy is and when it should be used (teacher led). The teacher then demonstrates how to use the strategy, acting as a model for its employment (teacher model). The activities should then be organised so the group can use the strategy (guided group model).

 Concluding thoughts

There are some challenging issues that arise when we approach labelling and special educational needs. There are conceptual challenges that labels may have stigmatising effects that shape the expectations of learners. In addition to the practical challenges labels and diagnoses may be so broad as not to indicate clear responses to them. There are also systemic challenges that arise from diagnosis and labelling with major delays to processes that ignore the voices of parents and learners. There have recently been moves to address these challenges (in the new EHCP framework and SEND code of practice as well as teaching standards) to protect the educational rights of all children, though many of the familiar challenges remain.

Given these obstacles, is it better to avoid SEN labels as such and aim for more personalised, inclusive approaches to support in education? Some would argue so, that this would encourage a more holistic and person-centred approach in educational provision. Pragmatically, given the limitations with the given educational provision structure, it seems likely that this would further disadvantage learners in difficulty ... with increasing focus on performance and attainment, many scholars suggest that we see a narrowing of expectations and a homogenisation of what it looks like to be a 'learner'. For those learners in difficulty, having an identified exceptionality, and thus officially creating an entitlement to a protected source of funding, means that support is more accessible than without such a label. Learners (and parents) have a formal name for the difficulties being experienced. For teachers, labels indicate the 'ball park' area of challenge a learner is facing, and allow some additional support to be offered. Having a label of SEN does not prevent learner-centred, high-quality teaching in inclusive classrooms and in many cases can be helpful. It is not ideal to be using general labels of SEN (rather than more specific ones), since it is probable that such learners are vulnerable to stigma. Critical awareness of these issues and advocacy for learners and their families are productive ways forward for practitioners working with learners in difficulty right now and in the future.

▬ References ▬

Adams, L., Tindle, A., Basran, S., Dobie, S., Thomson, D., Robinson, D. and Shepherd, C. (2017) *Experiences of Education, Health and Care Plans: A Survey of Parents and Young People*, DFE-RR657). Retrieved from: **https://www.gov.uk/government/uploads/system/uploads/attachment_data/file/604384/Education__health_and_care_plans_parents_and_young_people_survey.pdf**.

Barga, N.K. (1996) Students with learning disabilities in education: managing a disability. *Journal of Learning Disabilities*, 29: 413–21.

Barry, L.M. and Messer, J.J. (2003) A practical application of self-management for students diagnosed with attention-deficit/hyperactivity disorder. *Journal of Positive Behavior Interventions*, 5(4): 238–48.

Brown, B. (2012) *Daring Greatly: How the Courage to be Vulnerable Transforms the Way We Live, Love, Parent and Lead*. Harmondsworth: Penguin.

Children and Families Act 2014: **https://www.gov.uk/government/publications/young-persons-guide-to-the-children-and-families-act-2014**.

Clark, R.C. and Mayer, R.E. (2016) E-learning and the Science of Instruction: Proven Guidelines for Consumers and Designers of Multimedia Learning, 4th edn. London: John Wiley & Sons.

Covington, M.V. (1984) The self-worth theory of achievement motivation: findings and implications. *Elementary School Journal*, 85(1): 5–-20.

Crane, L., Chester, J.W., Goddard, L., Henry, L. and Hill, E. (2016) Experiences of autism diagnosis: a survey of over 1000 parents in the United Kingdom. *Autism*, 20(2): 153–62.

D'Agostino, J.V. and Harmey, S.J. (2016) An international meta-analysis of reading recovery. *Journal of Education for Students Placed at Risk (JESPAR)*, 21(1): 29–46.

Dale, P.S. (1996) Parent report assessment of language and communication. In K. Cole, P.S. Dale and D.J. Thal (eds), *Assessment of Communication and Language*. Baltimore, MD: Paul H. Brookes, pp. 161–82.

Department for Education (2016) *Special Educational Needs in England: January 2016*, SFR 29/2016. Retrieved from **https://www.gov.uk/government/organisations/department-for-education/about/statistics**.

Department for Education and Department of Health (2014) *Special Educational Needs and Disability Code of Practice: 0–25*, DFE-00205-2013. Retrieved from **https://www.gov.uk/government/publications/send-code-of-practice-0-to-25**.

Dweck, C. (2008) *Mindset: The New Psychology of Success*. New York: Ballantine.

Dyson, A. and Gallannaugh, F. (2008) Disproportionality in Special Needs Education in England. *Journal of Special Education*, 42(1): 36–46.

Elliott, J. and Place, M. (2012) *Children in Difficulty: A Guide to Understanding and Helping*, 3rd edn. New York: Routledge.

Florian, L. and Spratt, J. (2013) Enacting inclusion: a framework for interrogating inclusive practice. *European Journal of Special Needs Education*, 28(2): 119–35.

Foroni, F. and Rothbart, M. (2011) Category boundaries and category labels: when does a category name influence the perceived similarity of category members? *Social Cognition*, 29(5): 547–76.

Gallagher, J.J. (1976) The sacred and profane uses of labelling. *Mental Retardation*, 4(6): 3–7.

Green, S., Davis, C., Karshmer, E., Marsh, P. and Straight, B. (2005) Living stigma: the impact of labelling, stereotyping, separation, status loss, and discrimination in the lives of individuals with disabilities and their families. *Sociological Inquiry*, 75(2): 197–215.

Hessels, M. G. P. (1997) Low IQ but high learning potential: why Zeyneb and Moussa do not belong in special education. *Educational and Child Psychology*, 14: 121–36.

Higgins, S., Hall, E., Baumfield, V. and Moseley, D. (2005) *A Meta-analysis of the Impact of the Implementation of Thinking Skills Approaches on Pupils*, CFlat Working Paper. Newcastle University.

Higgins, S., Xiao, Z. and Katsipataki, M. (2012) *The Impact of Digital Technology on Learning: A Summary for the Education Endowment Foundation*. Retrieved from London: **https://educationendowmentfoundation.org.uk/public/files/Publications/The_Impact_of_Digital_Technologies_on_Learning_(2012).pdf**.

Hornby, G. (1995) *Working with Parents of Children with Special Needs*. London: Cassell.

Howlin, P. and Moore, A. (1997) Diagnosis in autism: a survey of over 1200 patients in the UK. *Autism*, 1(2): 135–62.

Jordan, A. and Stanovich, P. (1998) Teachers' personal epistemological beliefs about students with disabilities as indicators of effective teaching practices. *Journal of Research in Special Educational Needs*, 3(1). DOI:10.1111/j.1471-3802.2003.00184.x.

Link, B. and Phelan, J. (2001) Conceptualizing stigma. *Annual Review of Sociology*, 27: 363–85.

McMahon, S.E. (2012) Doctors diagnose, teachers label: the unexpected in pre-service teachers' talk about labelling children with ADHD. *International Journal of Inclusive Education*, 16(3): 249–64.

McNally, S., Ruiz-Valenzuela, J. and Rolfe, H. (2016) *ABRA: Online Reading Support*. Retrieved from London: **https:educationendowmentfoundation.org.uk/public/files/Projects/Evaluation_Reports/EEF_Project_report_ABRA.pdf**.

Mansell, W. and Morris, K. (2004) A survey of parents' reactions to the diagnosis of an autistic spectrum disorder by a local service: access to information and use of services. *Autism*, 8(4): 387–407.

Mayer, R.E. (2014) *Computer Games for Learning: An Evidence Based Approach*. London: MIT Press.

Noddings, N. (2012) The caring relation in teaching. *Oxford Review of Education*, 38: 771–81.

Oliver, M. (1990) *The Politics of Disablement*. Basingstoke: Macmillan.

Reinders, H. (2008) *Receiving the Gift of Friendship: Profound Disability, Theological Anthropology and Ethics*. Cambridge, UK: Eerdmans.

Riddick, B. (1995) Dyslexia: dispelling the myths. *Disability and Society*, 10(4): 457–73.

Riddick, B. (1996) *Living with Dyslexia: The Social and Emotional Consequences of Specific Learning Difficulties*. London: Routledge.

Riddick, B. (2000) An examination of the relationship between labelling and stigmatisation with special reference to dyslexia. *Disability and Society*, 15(4): 653–67.

Rogers, C.R., and Raider-Roth, M.B. (2006) Presence in teaching. *Teachers and Teaching*, 12(3): 265–87.

Schunk, D.H. (2008) Metacognition, self-regulation and self-regulated learning research recommendations. *Educational Psychology Review*, 20(4): 463–7.

Schunk, D.H. and Rice, J.M. (1993) Strategy fading and progress feedback: effects on self-efficacy and comprehension among students receiving remedial reading services. *Journal of Special Education*, 27(3): 257–76.

Schwartz, E. and Jordan, A. (2011) Teachers' epistemological beliefs and practices with students with disabilities and at-risk in inclusive classrooms. In J. Brownlee, G. Schraw and D. Bertelson (eds), *Personal Epistemology and Teacher Education*, pp. 210-272. Thousand Oaks, CA: Sage, pp. 210–72.

Siklos, S. and Kerns, K.A. (2007) Assessing the diagnostic experiences of a small sample of parents of children with autism spectrum disorders. *Research in Developmental Disabilities*, 28(1): 9–22.

Slavin, R.E., Lake, C., Davis, S. and Madden, N.A. (2011) Effective programs for struggling readers: a best-evidence synthesis. *Educational Research Review*, 6(1): 1–26.

Sternberg, R. (2005) The theory of successful intelligence. *Revista Interamericana de Psicología/ Interamerican Journal of Psychology*, 39(2): 189–202.

Teaching and Learning Toolkit (2015) *Meta-cognition and Self-regulation*. London: Sutton Trust.

Tremmel, R. (1993) Zen and the art of reflective practice. *Harvard Educational Review*, 63(4): 434–58.

Trussler, S. and Robinson, D. (2015) *Inclusive Practice in the Primary School: A Guide for Teachers*. London: Sage.

Warnock, M. (2005) *Special Educational Needs: A New Look*. Online at: **www.batod.org.uk/index.php?id=/resources/inclusion/archive-inclusion/Warnock2005.htm**.

Sources of information:

- Advanced Training materials: **www.advanced-training.org.uk**

- Communication Trust: **www.talkingpoint.org.uk**

- Council for Disabled Children: **www.councilfordisabledchildren.org.uk**

- Disability Matters resources and training: **www.disabilitymatters.org.uk**

- Dyslexia SpLD Trust: **www.thedyslexia-spldtrust.org.uk**

- Inclusion Development Programme: **www.idponline.org.uk**

- NASEN's SEND Gateway: **www.sendgateway.org**

6

Severe learning difficulties and children's language development

Catherine Stewart

 This chapter

This chapter aims to explore the idea in theory and practice that a teacher's identity and ecology shape the delivery of objectives and practical wisdom enables the learner to stay engaged. However, the focus this time is upon language, communication and the literacy curriculum delivered to students with SLD (severe learning difficulty). This is a complex world where teachers must seek to understand and allow students to engage in multiple mediums, to guide appropriate expression of thought and to achieve their full literal potential. Such pedagogy is beset with complications, where language is a complex phenomenon covering many levels of 'knowledge' and concepts; often unspoken through a sensory medium or verbalised in an non-universal and unique way by students who struggle to express feelings, knowledge and often appropriate responses. Here, language can mean communication (verbal and non-verbal, pictorial, mark-making and the written word) and engagement (social, emotional, verbal and non-verbal, written and other expressive forms of thought). The inability to articulate any of these factors can lead to frustration, disharmony and socially isolating states for the student and trepidation and melancholy for the teacher who seeks to aid students to be heard and understood (Stewart, 2016).

Spatial worlds and language obstacles

To begin, one must note the vast array and complexities of the ability to define students with SLD. They are all exceptional, presenting a large range of difficulties that can be neurological, physical and social. Indeed such differences mean a wealth of divergent linguistic and literary obstacles, many of which render the student unable to adapt to social situations, communicate effectively and engage in an unforgiving world. Such concerns necessitate an acknowledgement that how teachers and society define children, alongside their understandings of SEN, is directly related to the degree, intensity and multiplicity of disabilities thought present in an individual and which consequently imply the levels of support needed for that person to function in society (Jones, 2005).

Unsurprisingly then there is a superfluity of ways in which schools and teachers interpret the nature and prescriptions of the literacy national curriculum objectives to each particular assessment of need and ability within the pupil diversity of each school. Teachers across the world are encountering students from increasingly disparate ability and needs backgrounds. But while the student population is rapidly becoming diverse, teachers themselves are increasingly unprepared to teach them (Almog and Schectman, 2007) and are rarely exposed to deep and sustained inclusive pedagogical theory and practice during their initial preparation that would prepare them adequately for such contexts (Stowitschek et al., 2000; Hodkinson, 2009; Ekins and Grimes, 2009; SALT Review, 2009; Richards, 2010).

Teachers in SEN schools are 'special' teachers whose identity, practice and thought are subject to discourse and contextual practice in a more nuanced way than in mainstream schools (Buell et al., 1999; Jones, 2004). Not only that, there are tangible physical and psycho-social considerations at work in such schools that are not prepared for in regular ITE (initial teacher education) programmes; here literacy, communication and language take on a more sensory and pictorial connotation. Classrooms are spatially different, learning does not take part in a top-down hierarchy as in the mainstream, and often sensory overloads dictate the flow of sessions. More often than not the sensory experience within the classroom can serve as both a barrier and an aid to delivering any literacy or communication of knowledge. It is essential teachers and assistants work as a team to ensure support.

 **Case study**

The complex language-learning environment in SLD schools

Last year was a challenge. Two students clashed: one girl needed calm to concentrate that meant a lot of soothing music and soft cushions to enable focus and for her to begin her phonics practice. However, another girl communicated with loud uncontrollable outbursts, and she often had anxious moments if she could not verbalise or make herself known which manifested as physical disturbances. This often meant that pens and phonics cards were thrown into the air, half the class would go into meltdown, some would remove themselves from the teaching table, others would join in the chaos and some would retreat. Language acquisition here would move from specific literacy-related curriculum objectives to appropriate expression of frustration, sensory dampening and showing the vocalising student how to communicate her concerns differently.

The team that supports this student was offered PECS symbols and Makaton language to enable her to understand more positive ways to ask for things. In this way she could independently (at some point) tell us when she was upset or frustrated and in doing so extend her non-verbal vocabulary and also enable others to carry on with their daily targets. According to Jane, the class teacher: 'These students need understanding, patience and time to allow sensations to be expressed alongside guidance around the art of positive non-verbal communication; a sense of empathy, humour and tenacity to empower is a must.'

The teachers' beliefs and identities, and the art of language as emotive intervention

The linguistic style, ability and complexities of students mean that the way teachers perceive themselves is transactional with classroom behaviours and practice (Cross and Hong, 2012). Overall, teachers' professional identities are fluid with personal ones where practitioners are 'affected by the worlds they try to affect' (Britzman, 2003, p.5). We formulate our beliefs and values and how we interact with others based on what we experience throughout our life. We assimilate, differentiate and classify people into separate groups because it is more cognitively efficient (Porter, 2002, p.28).

There is an argument that SEN teachers have a more 'deliberate' role than those within mainstream curriculum roles, having to become pedagogical and cognitive experts in their students' progress and understand very personal nuances of communication and literacy barriers. They often have had to exercise far more strategic and inter-professional power than similar colleagues in mainstream schools as many students are frustrated, anxious and unable to make their needs, concerns and understanding known when viewed through the 'normal' lens of speech and the written word. Pajares (1992) rightly contends that attention to the beliefs of teachers informs educational practice, where beliefs are indicators of the decisions teachers make throughout their lives (Nisbett and Ross 1980; Rokeach, 1968) and their ability to transcend normal language and literacy education.

To understand how teachers within SLD settings enable their students to engage in a world that often denies them an existence entails the need to expand current conceptions of teachers' beliefs, ecologies and pedagogic practice within specialised settings overall (Clandinin and Connelly, 1996, p.26). 'Teachers' professional knowledge landscapes' suggest a territory of private and public knowledge, of curriculum requirements and passionate explorations, of emotional knowing and cognitive outcomes. Issues about content, curriculum and pedagogy cannot be separated from emotional issues – they are inseparable from a teacher's practice (Zembylas, 2007).

Teaching transcends the cognitive and technical notions of linguistic education; rather it becomes a complex and personal set of processes embedded in one's ecology (Olsen, 2008), an ecology of care, empathy and compassion amid the ability to be a trailblazer and unafraid to try the obscure. Here there is a specific form of teacher knowledge, a special amalgam of content and pedagogy that is uniquely the province of teachers and their own special form of professional understanding (Shulman, 1987).

Curriculum complexities, language and communication: the uniqueness of the SLD student

When people use the word curriculum, they are generally referring to the content chosen to be taught – the official curriculum, which reflects adopted standards and drives the everyday functioning of schools, sanctions and what the student needs to know (Goodlad & Associates, 1989). Such knowledge is absolute: 'they expect teachers to teach it, they assume all students can and will learn it' (Yero, 2002, p.32), it is driven by the need to articulate coherently through speech and the written word. Yet I argue such notions are bound within simplistic ideals of learning ability and styles and which serve to stop the student from competing in the race at all!

Wood (1999) argues that the curriculum should be child-centred and developmentally appropriate, based on the child's need for play and personal interest not organised into departments of 'petrified' subjects. This is especially true for younger children and those with special needs. Any curriculum which attempts to incorporate precise specifications of what a student needs to be able to do or achieve within 'subjects' only further ostracises those that need help the most.

One needs to look further towards how to deliver within SEN and consider the rather unique and captivating ways students make themselves known and become pliable to learning, acknowledging and accommodating the spoken and written word into multiple sensory fields. Bruner (1996) argued for a spiral curriculum considering environmental and experiential factors where intellect develops in steps dependent on how the mind is used and henceforth how the child engages with educational material and attempts at delivery. One needs to consider that the teacher is rather on the outside looking in, trying hard to understand the student's forms of communication before attempting to deliver a linguistic curriculum objective. This chapter therefore assumes that teachers are central to the child's ecology, that they are a curriculum construct rather than merely a teaching tool, drawing from a belief and tenacity to engage at a student's level and allow expression of thought. Sebba et al. (1993, p.56) advocate that personal and social development will be enhanced by increased access to the whole curriculum by using a balanced range of teaching approaches which facilitate a variety of captive learning styles. One champions the teacher who is unafraid to interpret the curriculum differently for individual students, delivering in ways to empower the student and ready them for adult life. While researching outreach provision for pupils with severe learning difficulty on the autism spectrum, Glashan et al. (2004) found a positive relationship between parental knowledge and involvement in school and the success of the placement for children. Indeed I argue that conceptualising the type of curriculum and how it could be inclusive or tailored to needs could benefit from parental guidance.

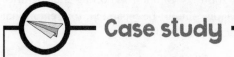 **Case study**

Supporting a child with autism

Adam is six and has autism. He had previously been to mainstream classes where he was disruptive to students, shouting out, throwing things and pulling children's hair. All the staff found him hard to engage with curriculum tasks during class time and he was not receptive to timelines, although he occasionally responded during the one hour he had with his assistant twice a week. He could not stay on task and did not communicate well with other children. He spoiled their games just by staring at them and shouted 'no call the police' when stressed. Generally he gave the opposite answers to questions (saying a pig was a cow, red was blue and chairs were tables. etc.), but became almost mute when approached by children and staff to engage in 'free time' conversations. He could not hold a pen in a tripod grip, instead using a palmar grip on the paper, circling furiously until a hole appeared. He refused to look at books and would not use Makaton symbols when offered or PECS. He was deemed socially isolated and self-isolating by staff, unhappy, unable and aggressive.

Adam moved to a special school where the rooms were large and there were eight students, one teacher and two assistants. The teacher had asked his parents prior to attendance what he liked and disliked, what his triggers were, what frightened him, what comforted him, how he articulated these feelings and how to keep him on task. It transpired that Adam liked cars, transport and travel and being cocooned in a heavy blanket, hated loud noises. He needed people not to give full eye contact as this made him feel threatened and to allow him time to think about questions, supported with a PECS symbol and Makaton to reinforce his linguistic understanding and ability to engage (everything mainstream did not do). He hated smooth pens but loved animal pencil grips (the teacher found this out as he liked to fiddle with her animal toys on her desk, especially cows) and was proud to show children how he could make big circles on the paper like a wheel. With encouragement he began to use a tripod grip to make marks and his expressive written material became more controlled from which one hoped writing could begin. The teacher had spoken to her husband and read up on cars and used this medium to encourage Adam to focus on tasks (counting cars, telling her the colours aloud, searching for the 'C' for cars, looking for the 'A' for Audi. She loved her own heavy quilt as it made her feel relaxed, and with this in mind she brought a quilt into school and bundled him into it. As a result he became much more able to focus on tasks along with a PECS symbol for quilt which he held up if he felt stressed. As a child the teacher had hated big groups and preferred to play alone at times to escape into her own world. She also found that in small focused groups Adam became the boy to go to in role play to be the bus driver or the one in charge of the train which boosted his esteem to be sociable etc. He would offer another child his car if they were upset and while he could not verbalise the letters in books he loved to 'look at the pictures' and with support make up silly stories about characters.

Adam changed, and slowly he began to show emotive language and expression of thought that he had found hard to communicate in the mainstream. The teacher evolved with him, she took the time to think about her world and what she found engaging, soothing and over-stimulating and tried this out in Adam's world to see if she could engage him. It was trial and error and some days unsuccessful but her belief in finding the child trapped within was life-changing for Adam, the teachers and his family as Adam no longer felt as stressed.

In asking whether pupils with special educational needs require distinct kinds of pedagogic strategies, we are not asking whether pupils with special educational needs require distinct curriculum objectives. We are asking whether they need distinct kinds of teaching to learn the same content as others without special educational needs (Lewis, 2005, p.7).

Understanding children's experiences from their inner worlds

Dewey, in *Experience and Education* (1938, p.48), believed understanding students' experiences was central to learning. Educational experience has to be continuous and interactive and lead to other experiences, in essence propelling the person to learn more. Interaction is when the experience meets the internal needs or goals of a person. I argue that within this case study both teacher and student undertook transformation when meeting in the classroom, a reciprocal relationship built upon trust and empathy. If a person has not undergone any reflection they have obtained nothing for mental growth that is lasting. Experiential learning is designed to give one the freedom to explore and find the learning path that is most suitable for him or her (Armstrong, 1977). Similarly, Rogers (2007) believed that that relevancy to the student is essential for learning where personal experiences are the core construct of any course they follow, be it in life or education.

A person cannot teach another person directly; a person can only facilitate another's learning. Each student will process what he or she learns differently depending on what he or she brings to the classroom. A person learns significantly only those things that are perceived as being involved in the maintenance of or enhancement of the structure of self (Rogers, 2007, p.55). Rogers also talked about unconditional positive regard where the instructor's acceptance of being a mentor who guides rather than an expert who tells is instrumental to student-centred, non-threatening and unforced learning. Indeed, one could argue that Rogers' words resonate throughout teachers' lives where SEN is a vast chasm that teachers dip into and find themselves quickly immersed, sometimes sinking and sometimes swimming but only through the process of experience and ecological structures, a self-taught survival skill. If true then perhaps teacher ecologies sit at the core of the nature of curriculum identity. While supportive of such pedagogical practice and contemplation of ecological impact, academic literature continues to suggest that how comfortable a teacher feels around students with profound and multiple learning difficulty influences their attitudes towards teaching them (Hodkinson, 2005; Jones, 2005; Ball, 2005). Moreover, it impacts upon how students are treated (Good, 1981), which is set among assumptions around capability (Terzi, 2005), all of which influence a child's ecology.

Vygotsky (1978) asserted that cognitive development was rooted in the context of social relationships, viewing disability as a product of the individual's interaction with society and focused upon that person's abilities rather than impairment (Grigorenko and Sternberg, 1998). The 'zone of proximal development' was used as a basis for creating diagnostic and teaching tools whereby with some adult or educational aid they learnt from the consequences of actions and emphasised social rehabilitation of the disabled student, focusing on developing individualised approaches. Vygotsky (1987, cited in Glassman, 2001) saw education as consisting of an integration of culture and social goals whereby engaging in an activity would lead the child towards mastery, arguing that free enquiry was eclipsed by culturally significant and appropriate enquiry. Overall, affective factors play a central role in intellectual growth (Dean, 1994) and through negotiation and shared experience comes a mutually held understanding. That said there are tensions surrounding the lack of teacher training (Norwich and Lewis, 2001; Ofsted, 2008; Maddern, 2010; SALT Review, 2009). However, one can only work within the parameters of their own way of being, their empathy, their compassion and their fierce ability to deliver through diversity. Once again I argue that forever in the background is the dominating force of the teacher's ecology, their professional ever-changing landscape within eroding and reforming shorelines.

Noddings (1984) argues for the joy of caring for the student and the need to see things through the students' eyes in order to teach them. Goddard (2005) suggests that building up creativity within a child will enhance interactive aspects of learning. One needs a way to develop an interactive non-prescribed curriculum. Olsen (2008) rightly contends that teaching transcends the cognitive and technical notions of education rather it becoming a complex and personal set of processes embedded within one's ecology.

Arguably, due to ineffective training, the nature of teaching and of teachers' work is often so ill defined that educational beliefs are particularly vulnerable to becoming what Nespor (1987) called an 'entangled domain'. When previous schemas or experiences do not work and the teacher is uncertain of what information is needed or what behaviour is appropriate, teachers are unable to fathom out what to do in such situations and must rely on their belief structures, with all their problems and inconsistencies. Unsurprisingly then, a teacher's identity changes through practice and she/he must constantly interpret experiences and what this means in terms of pedagogic practice or who they are as a person (Wenger, 1998). Kagan (1992) suggested that a teacher's unique beliefs are situated in both context and content which over time shape their identity, which is crucial to the way they make judgements within the classroom (Day et al., 2006; Lasky, 2005). Overall, the way a teacher perceives them or makes specialist teaching meaningful to them influences curriculum choices and judgements regarding what they deem as appropriate for their students.

This great need to cover things no matter what and thus meet 'objectives' seemed to corrode students' educational experience rather than enhance them, steering them towards goals that were unachievable and mismatched with ability, supporting concerns around rigid blanket styles achieving nothing (Carpenter, 1992).

Sebba et al. (1993, p.56) advocate that personal and social development will be enhanced by increased access to the whole curriculum by using a balanced range of teaching approaches that facilitate a variety of captive learning styles. One champions the teacher who is not afraid to study how to interpret the curriculum differently for individual students, delivering in ways to empower the student and ready them for a sociable life. Language is more than words. It is a social tool, a concept that allows children to make friends and to explore the world, and if one removes all day-to-day things from students' lives due to disability they cannot communicate effectively. Overall, to be able to engage with peers is a positive thing and certainly a number of studies, most commonly focusing on pupils who have severe learning difficulties, have reported the development of positive and caring relationships by peers towards classmates who have special educational needs (Evans et al., 1992; Staub et al., 1994). The following excerpts are from Stewart's 2016 research into the experiences and approaches of teachers in SLD settings and illustrate the balances, difficulties and compromises that such teachers are constantly required to make:

> If I used the National Curriculum as my yardstick, none of my students would look as if they could do anything, but they can just use a different form of communication that to the untrained eye and ear sounds too different and so is disregarded. This sort of reflects society's view, they do not appear to achieve targets nationally but that does not mean they are incapable of anything, they can engage but the National Curriculum does not fit, it relies on the written word, exams and problem solving, I throw that book out of the window.
>
> (David, class teacher)

> I kind of start with what they like, can do and what they need educationally, I think a variety should be offered, so they have an awareness of it and can then talk to others about it. I do Macbeth, it's good for experience; they can engage and become included with others on a better level, that's important. In this way I do deliver some of the literacy objectives from the curriculum. That said, young students need to relate to each other and so I have done my homework listening to some rather terrible boy bands and watching Horrid Henry, the Simpsons and Monster High DVDs that my daughter tells me are great. In this way we can have a shared vocabulary in the class, it makes the children feel that their communication with others is normal – that's a good feeling for them.
>
> (Jenni, class teacher)

There is a need for a sense of individuality and personalisation that is based within the premise of being included within national levels, rights and enablement, all of which were entrenched within personal beliefs regarding the creation of an appropriate background which they deemed 'best fit'.

> For those who cannot read or write, they definitely need a social curriculum; their hand malformation would make it very hard to use a tripod grip and so we use other sensory methods. Yes I cover curriculum topics but in a very different way from mainstream, I suppose I cover literature but it's not adverbs, nouns you know more like talking through books and me pulling their fingers through sensory tactile stuff to feel the letters, letting them look in the mirror and practise forming the words, seeing if they can puff out a 'p' as verbal language is not accessible.
>
> (Amanda, class teacher)

Here inclusion is seen as a different entity, a way of enabling as well as a right to have an education. Unlike mainstream provision it changes daily and practices move with the ebb and flow of students' 'ways of being' from day to day rather than an all-out determination to give students what governments feel they are entitled to no matter what the cost. Notions of 'will be offered' and 'will do XXX' become 'will be tried out to see if it fits their need and emotional well-being.'

In view of the particular significance of teachers' experiences, beliefs and values in relation to their pedagogic practice and especially in the context of SEN, it is clear to see how the curriculum and teachers' beliefs and values regarding students' needs are inextricably and potently linked in schools with SLD and PMLD cohorts. Thus their intertwined outcomes determine, in a complex and profound way, the learning experience of these pupils. Often communication and literacy become the ability to be independent, to read visual signs so children can take part in travelling around or merely for them to make choices.

> A practical independent approach is needed geared towards independence . . . things such as washing and dressing oneself are very important. They need environmental numeracy and literacy like getting on a bus, reading a timetable, help with social signs and filling in forms.
>
> (Helen, class teacher)

Dewey (1938) argues for mis-education as being knowledge delivered without any reflection upon content which, if unused, fades away. There is a need for social skills, and experiential learning is designed to provide the freedom to explore and find the learning path that is most suitable for him or her (Armstrong, 1977). Following too much concrete numeracy and literacy work is too much for them. Socially they need to be out in the community learning about life as it is. Just use real-life tools, read signs, talk about events – it's necessary beyond school years (Stewart, 2016).

 **Case study**

Using reflection to improve practice

Anne has been teaching within SEN for years and never stops trying to think of innovative ways to ensure that her students can communicate on their level but also that she can enable them to transcend their language comfort zone. One night at home she is feeling a little lethargic and is trying hard to finish an assignment for her postgraduate qualification that she is struggling with. Both the academic content needed and the ability to engage those reading it is proving a hard task. Frustrated she throws her books to the floor, then laughs, and contemplates that now she knows how her students feel. Her daughter comes into the room wearing a ski mask she has made from leggings and huddled in a sleeping bag. 'Let's get in mummy!' she exclaims, 'and help me build Lego.' Anne climbs into another sleeping bag and finds it rather relaxing. After Lego building she remains in the sleeping bag and switches on the computer, she feels so relaxed, safe almost, that she finds she can zone into her work.

The next day at school two students are becoming frustrated with tasks, Anne notices a Lycra tube in the corner of the room resembling a large pair of tights. She places them over two students' heads shouting 'let's do today's good work task in a fun tunnel.' The two children touch the fabric and press their hands to their faces. Anne helps them to a bean bag and they begin the task again. For seven minutes the children remain calm, almost mannequin-like, and do their work. The next day all the children rush to the tubes eager to do their task; some verbalise their request, others pull the tubes over their heads. Anne makes six more tubes at home and it becomes a regular activity during which students calmly read books, draw sensory marks in the sand or make marks using the palmar grip or tripod.

So how do teachers' beliefs and experiences impact on their understanding of diversity in SLD contexts?

Certainly teachers' ecologies impact upon how they understand diversity (Slee, 2003) as they are set amid teachers' beliefs and multiple sensory, educational and physical approaches akin to Bruner (1996). While teachers appear to take comfort in achieving humility and ignoring the curriculum (Senyshyn, 2011), this adds to the problem within special settings where outcomes appear hard to assess and track for government targets supporting arguments around the impossibility to get through an exam when delivering such a diverse curriculum (Stenhouse, 1975, p.142).

This great need to cover things no matter what and thus meet 'objectives' seems to corrode students' educational experience rather than enhance it, steering them towards goals that are unachievable and mismatched with ability, supporting concerns around rigid blanket styles achieving nothing (Carpenter, 1992). In the research of Stewart (2016), teachers' voices are clear on these expectations:

> Some objectives are crazy, I mean pronouns and similes I am just trying to get people to write; yes I diversify but the whole government ideal is ludicrous.
>
> (Stewart, 2016)

> If I used the National Curriculum as my yardstick, none of my students would look as If they could do anything . . . This sort of reflects society's view, they do not appear to achieve targets nationally but that does not mean they are incapable of anything, a National Curriculum does not fit, I throw that book out of the window . . .
>
> (Stewart, 2016)

 ## Concluding thoughts

Vygotsky (1987, cited in Glassman, 2001), akin to teachers, sees literacy education as consisting of an integration of culture and social goals whereby engaging in an activity would lead the child towards mastery, arguing that free enquiry was eclipsed by culturally significant and appropriate enquiry. Therefore it is unsurprising that professional identities are multifaceted, their construction being a 'continuing struggle' between conflicting identities (Lampert, 1985; Samuel and Stephens, 2000). Olsen (2008) rightly contends that teaching transcends the cognitive and technical notions of education; rather it becomes a complex and personal set of processes embedded in one's ecology. To unfold the enablement of literacy and sensory learning one needs to glimpse the formation of the whole persona, not just 'the teacher', where holistically identity is constructed and reconstructed as people view themselves in relation to other people and notions of professional purpose and attempt to achieve the unachievable (Senyshen, 2011).

References

Almog, O. and Shechtman, Z. (2007) Teachers' democratic and efficacy beliefs and styles of coping with behavioural problems of pupils with special needs. *European Journal of Special Needs Education*, 22(2): 115–29.

Armstrong, J.S. (1977) Designing and using experiential exercises. *Experiential Learning in Marketing Education*, 8–17.

Ball, S.J. (2005) *Education Policy and Social Class: The Selected Works of Stephen J. Ball*. London: Routledge.

Britzman, D. (2003) *Practice Makes Practice: A Critical Study of Learning to Teach*. Albany, NY: State University of New York Press.

Bruner, J. (1996) *The Culture of Education*. Cambridge, MA: Harvard University Press.

Buell, M., Hallam, R., Gamel-McCormick, M. and Scheer, S. (1999) A survey of general and special education teachers' perceptions and in-service needs concerning inclusion. *International Journal of Disability Development and Education*, 46: 143–56.

Carpenter, B. (1992) The whole curriculum: meeting the needs of the whole child. In K. Bovair, B. Carpenter and G. Upton (eds), *Special Curriculum Needs*. London: David Fulton, pp.1–10.

Clandinin, D.J. and Connelly, F.M. (1996) Teachers' professional knowledge landscapes: teacher stories of schools. *Educational Researcher*, 25(3): 24–30.

Cross, D.I. and Hong, J.Y. (2012) An ecological examination of teachers' emotions in the school context. *Teaching and Teacher Education*, 28(7): 957–67.

Day, C., Kington, A., Stobart, G. and Sammons, P. (2006) The personal and professional selves of teachers: stable and unstable identities. *British Educational Research Journal*, 32(4): 601–16.

Dean, A.L. (1994) Institutional affective forces in the internalization process: contributions of Hans Loewald. *Human Development*, 37: 42–57.

Dewey, J. (1938) *Experience and Education*. New York: Macmillan.

Ekins, A. and Grimes, P. (2009) *Inclusion: Developing an Effective and Whole-School Approach*. Maidenhead: Open University Press.

Evans, Salisbury, Palombaro, Berryman and Hollowood (1992)

Glashan, L., Mackay, G. and Grieve, A. (2004) Teachers' experience of support in the mainstream education of pupils with autism. *Improving Schools*, 7(1): 49–60.

Glassman, M. (2001) Dewey and Vygotsky: society, experience, and inquiry in educational practice. *Educational Researcher*, 30(4): 3–14.

Goddard, A. (2005) Special educational needs: critical reflections regarding the role of behavioural objectives in planning the curriculum. *Education, 3–13: International Journal of Primary, Elementary and Early Years Education*, 33(1): 32–9.

Good, T. (1981) Teacher expectations and student perceptions: a decade of research. *Educational Leadership*, 38: 415–22.

Goodlad, J.I. & Associates (1979) *Curriculum Inquiry: The Study of Curriculum Practice*. New York: McGraw-Hill.

Grigorenko, E.L. and Sternberg, R.J. (1998) Dynamic testing. *Psychological Bulletin*, 124(1): 75–95.

Hodkinson, A. (2005) Conceptions and misconceptions of inclusive education, a critical examination of final year teacher trainees, knowledge and understanding of inclusion. *Research in Education*, 73: 15–29.

Hodkinson, A. (2009) Pre-service teacher training and special educational needs in England 1970–2008: is government learning the lessons of the past or is it experiencing a groundhog day? *European Journal of Special Needs Education*, 24(3): 277–89.

Jones, P. (2004) They are not like us and neither should they be: issues of teacher identity for teachers of pupils with profound and multiple learning difficulties. *Disability and Society*, 19(2): 59–169.

Jones, P. (2005) Teachers' views of their pupils with profound and multiple learning difficulties. *European Journal of Special Needs Education*, 20(4): 375–85.

Kagan, D.M. (1992) Implications of research on teacher belief. *Educational Psychologist*, 27(1): 65–90.

Lampert, M. (1985) How do teachers manage to teach? Perspectives on problems in practice. *Harvard Educational Review*, 55(2): 178–95.

Lasky, S. (2005) A sociocultural approach to understanding teacher identity, agency and professional vulnerability in a context of secondary school reform. *Teaching and Teacher Education*, 21(8): 899–916.

Lewis, A. (1995) Policy shifts concerning special needs provision in mainstream primary schools. *British Journal of Educational Studies*, 43(3): 318–32.

Maddern, K. (2010) SEN teacher skills under threat, government adviser warns. *TES*, 12 March, p.3.

Nespor, J. (1987) The role of beliefs in the practice of teaching. *Journal of Curriculum Studies*, 19(4): 317–28.

Nisbett, R. and Ross, L. (1980) *Human Inference: Strategies and Shortcomings of Social Judgment*. Englewood Cliffs, NJ: Prentice-Hall.

Noddings, N. (1984) *Caring*. Berkeley, CA: University of California Press.

Norwich, B. and Lewis, A. (2001) Mapping a pedagogy for special educational needs. *British Educational Research Journal*, 2(3): 313–29.

Ofsted (Office for Standards in Education) (2008) *How Well New Teachers Are Prepared to Teach Pupils with Learning Difficulties and/or Disabilities*. London: HMSO.

Olsen, B. (2008) Introducing teacher identity and this volume. *Teacher Education Quarterly*, 35(3): 3–6.

Pajares, M.F. (1992) Teachers' beliefs and educational research: cleaning up a messy construct. *Review of Educational Research*, 62(3): 327–332.

Porter, L. (2002) *Educating Young Children with Special Needs*. London: Sage.

Richards, G. (2010) Managing current developments in SEN and inclusion: developing confidence in new teachers. *Management in Education*, 24(3): 107–10.

Rogers, C. (2007) Experiencing an 'inclusive education' first hand: parents and their children with 'special educational needs'. *British Journal of Sociology of Education*, 28(1): 55–68.

Rokeach, M. (1968) *Beliefs, Attitudes and Values: A Theory of Organization and Change*. San Francisco: Jossey-Bass.

SALT Review (DCFS) (2009) *Independent Review of Teacher Supply for Pupils with Severe, Profound and Multiple Learning Difficulties (SLD and PMLD)*. Nottingham: HMSO.

Samuel, M. and Stephens, D. (2000) Critical dialogues with self: developing teacher identities and roles – a case study of South African student teachers. *International Journal of Educational Research*, 33(5): 475–91.

Sebba, J., Byers. R. and Rose, R. (1993) *Redefining the Whole Curriculum for Pupils with Learning Difficulties*. London: David Fulton.

Senyshyn, Y. (2011) Respecting students, acquiring humility and ignoring the curriculum. *Journal of Educational Thought*, 45(2): 145–63.

Shulman, L.S. (1987) Knowledge and teaching: foundations of the new reform. *Harvard Educational Review*, 57(1): 1–23.

Slee, R. (ed.) (2003) *Is There a Desk with My Name on It? The Politics of Integration*. London: Routledge.

Staub, D., Schwartz, I.S., Gallucci, C. and Peck, C.A. (1994) Four portraits of friendship at an inclusive school. *Journal of the Association for Persons with Severe Handicaps*, 19: 314–25.

Stenhouse, L. (1975) *An Introduction to Curriculum Research and Development*. London: Heinemann.

Stewart, C. (2016) An Examination of SLD and PMLD Teachers' Ecologies. Unpublished EdD thesis, Durham University.

Stowitschek, J., Cheney, D. and Schwartz, I. (2000) Instigating fundamental change through experiential in-service development. *Teacher Education and Special Education*, 25(2): 142–56.

Terzi, L. (2005) Beyond the dilemma of difference: the capability approach to disability and special educational needs. *Journal of Philosophy of Education*, 39(3): 443–59.

Vygotsky, L. (1978) Interaction between learning and development. In *Mind and Society*. Cambridge, MA: Harvard University Press, 79–91.

Wenger, E. (1998) *Communities of Practice: Learning, Meaning and Identity*. Cambridge: Cambridge University Press.

Wood, E. (1999) The impact of the National Curriculum on play in reception classes. *Educational Research*, 41(1):11–22.

Yero, J. (2002) *Teaching in Mind: How Teacher Thinking Shapes Education*. New York: Basic.

Zembylas, M. (2007) Emotional ecology: the intersection of emotional knowledge and pedagogical content knowledge in teaching. *Teacher and Teacher Education*, 23(4): 355–67.

7

Supporting deaf learners

Rosie Ridgway

 This chapter

This chapter addresses deafness and its effect on learners in inclusive classrooms. Deaf learners experience very different degrees of hearing loss and its impact on learning varies. We will begin by exploring some essential information that teachers need to know to better understand deafness. Several case studies will be introduced to explore different individuals' experiences in primary school classrooms, and some strategies to support learners are discussed.

Understanding deafness

There have been critical discussions of labels and terminology and how they can depersonalise and medicalise people by using deficit language such as 'hearing loss' and 'hearing impairment'. The Deaf community identify with the simple label Deaf (with a capital D) to recognise its importance within Deaf and British Sign Language (BSL) culture. In this chapter, people with all degrees of hearing loss will be described as deaf, and the severity of loss will be specified in case studies and discussion, while references to Deaf culture will have a capital D.

Deafness can be understood in different ways, for example by using a socio-cultural language-based approach. This socio-cultural model addresses the role of language not just in communication, but also in culture and in belonging to a social group (British Sign Language and Deaf culture). A second approach is a bio-medical view, which focuses on the ear and hearing, audiology, diagnosis and corrective technologies. These models (socio-cultural and bio-medical) are widely used (Andrews et al., 2011) to understand deafness and its effect on the individual though they are mediated by factors like their family, the presence of Deaf community support (Leigh, 2009) and individual features such as their communication preferences, degree of hearing loss and the technologies available. This chapter uses a bio-psycho-social approach to understanding and supporting deaf learners, which draws upon psychological dimensions that focus specifically on learning in addition to the bio-medical and socio-cultural models. This work offers guidance for teachers and education practitioners so will be focused on shaping inclusive practice.

What is hearing and what is deafness?

The complex structure of the ear transfers sound vibrations through it (conductivity) so that we can hear. Sound waves are invisible vibrations in the air, which enter the ear and cause a thin membrane (eardrum) to vibrate. The vibrations travel through the eardrum into the middle ear and are exaggerated by the tiny bones there before they are passed into the cochlea. The cochlea (inner ear) is a spiral shaped organ that is lined with thousands of tiny hairs that are sensitive to vibrations. The cochlea converts the vibrations to electrical signals (impulses) which stimulate the auditory nerve (the nerve that connects the ear to the brain) and that is how we hear.

Deafness has many causes (aetiologies) and is classified as a sensorineural, conductive, mixed or central hearing loss. Sensorineural losses are caused by damage to cells in the inner ear or cochlea, which stop sound vibrations travelling to the auditory nerve. This sensorineural damage is permanent. Conductive hearing loss is often caused by infection in the middle ear, where fluid builds up and stops vibrations travelling across the ear. This is sometimes called 'glue ear' (otitis media) which does not typically require treatment and resolves itself within three months. Usually middle ear infections result in temporary loss of hearing, which recovers after the infection. A minority of children who experience repeated, severe ear infections will require surgery to insert a small tube into the middle ear (grommet) to allow fluid to drain from the middle ear and improve vibrational conductivity (hearing). Sometimes repeated infections will cause permanent hearing loss because they have damaged the sensitive inner ear. In addition to the initial grommet surgery it is likely that hearing aids will be used to amplify (make louder) sounds for the child to hear. Mixed hearing impairments are a combination of sensorineural and conductive hearing loss; these affect the outer/ middle and inner ear and is permanent. Many children with mixed hearing impairments will have hearing aids but it is likely that they will still have severe to profound hearing loss.

A central hearing impairment is caused by damage to the auditory nerve and its connection to the brain. It is much rarer than the other kinds of deafness and is somewhat harder to detect as audiology tests rely on patient response (that can be intermittent if there is nerve and/or brain damage). Deafness affects either one ear (unilateral) or both (bilateral). In addition to these different kinds of deafness, there are different patterns of onset. Hearing loss can be intermittent, temporary, progressive (gradual) or sudden; for example, some children are born deaf while for others deafness can be the result of a head injury or even a virus. So there is a diverse range of experiences of deafness which we should be aware of and not seek to make generalisations about 'the Deaf'. Further, sounds are assessed in pitch (frequency) and volume (decibels) and a child's hearing loss is expressed as mild, moderate, severe or profound. This is presented on a simple categorical scale (see below), though deafness doesn't always fit neatly into one category and teachers should consider all relevant elements of the descriptor to support a deaf learner appropriately.

Degrees of deafness:

- **Mild deafness**: 21–40 dB – could hear a baby crying or music from a stereo but could not hear whispering.

- **Moderate deafness**: 41–70 dB – could hear a dog barking or telephone ringing but could not hear a baby crying.

- **Severe deafness**: 71–95 dB – could hear a chainsaw or drums being played but could not hear a piano or a dog barking.

- **Profound deafness**: >95 dB – could hear an articulated lorry or aeroplane noise but could not hear a telephone ringing.

(British Society of Audiology (1988) with guidance from NDCS)

Deafness is described in terms of magnitude of hearing loss (mild, moderate, severe or profound) and is measured in decibels. It is useful for teachers to think about deafness in relation to pitch and volume of sounds so we can evaluate the teaching environment and its effects on the deaf learner. Deafness can affect one (unilateral) or both (bilateral) ears, and can have a number of causes and development pathways (aetiologies). Some children are born deaf, and others can experience progressive, acquired, temporary or intermittent hearing loss. It is important for teachers to get to know the deaf child's individual experience of deafness so that they can respond appropriately.

Before teaching a deaf learner, it is vital to have specific information about the degree and type of deafness and what this means in terms of their learning. It is useful to talk to the child's parents and a teacher of the deaf (or communication support worker) about the child's hearing and how this impacts on their social and communication skills and learning. You might be shown an audiogram chart, which is used to present results of hearing assessments – this shows you at what pitch and volume a sound has to be for the deaf child to hear it. It is also important to talk to the child about what they do and do not find helpful in terms of teaching and communication. With younger children this may be a less reliable source of information as they have had less classroom experience, but it creates space for an ongoing dialogue about learning and communication in your classroom that you can use as a regular means of reviewing your inclusive practice. Think about using visual materials to structure these conversations.

Using the descriptors of deafness above, teachers should consider that for most deaf children, deafness is not 'a world of silence' but a world of *some* sounds. When working with deaf children in class we need to take into account the sound environment at all pitches and its impact on the individual. This means reviewing how noisy it is not just in terms of children's talk or teacher's voice, but intrusive sounds like traffic noise, echoes, chairs scraping on the floor and how much vibration there is, for example from IWB projector fans and computers. Using the individual child's hearing profile and communicating with the learners, their parents and the professional staff, and considering the classroom environment, we can make our classrooms and our teaching much more deaf friendly.

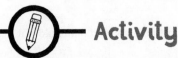

Activity

During your time in school, stop and pay attention the sound environment. List all the sounds you hear (there are more than you think). Try it several times, at different times during the day and in different locations in school. Do you notice that you live and work in a varied soundscape with low-pitch, high-pitch, high-volume and barely audible sounds that surround you? Do you find it easy or hard to ignore these sounds? For deaf children with hearing aids, the soundscape is very different and for some children and adults shouting or loud, sudden noises can be distressing. Think about how you could make your classroom more deaf and hearing friendly, based on your auditory environment audit.

Case study

Acknowledging hearing loss in class

Georgia was seven years old; she had had repeated ear infections throughout her early life before and during school through reception and Year 1. She missed a lot of school during this time because of the problems with her ears, ill health and appointments to review her hearing. Georgia's teacher Miss Cohen has invited her parents into school to discuss Georgia's worrying behaviour and lack of academic progress. Georgia was performing below expectations in English, Maths and Science. Miss Cohen was a recently qualified teacher and was concerned that Georgia was a 'dreamer' who lacked focus, she didn't join in with class discussions and often ignored or seemed puzzled by instructions and stated that she didn't understand. Miss Cohen felt that if Georgia could concentrate more, she would be able to perform better in school. Georgia's parents were frustrated that Miss Cohen was not acknowledging the effect of Georgia's hearing loss on her success in school.

Activity

How could you support Georgia?

- Do you think Georgia's concentration and behaviour was related to attention difficulties or hearing loss? How could we tell?
- What strategies could you put in place to support Georgia during temporary loss of hearing?

Glue ear is a common cause of temporary deafness in childhood. While many children experience hearing loss caused by this, schools and teachers need to consider seriously the implications of temporary deafness on language and literacy development. In Georgia's case, we see that multiple infections had reduced her hearing and she was struggling to succeed without support.

Deaf friendly teaching

Was Georgia's classroom a hearing friendly environment? Miss Cohen and the school SENCo used a listening environment check (see, for example, the Ear Foundation Survey (Ear Foundation, 2006)) to review how much background noise there was in the classroom. They also looked at the layout of the room and Georgia's seating position to make sure she had a clear view of the teacher and other children by arranging seating in a horse shoe (U shape) and encouraging all pupils to communicate when they couldn't see or hear clearly or understand.

Miss Cohen also began training the whole class to be more 'sound aware' – to reduce chair scraping on the floor and monitoring general sound levels. She began using the 'Gimme 5' technique with the whole class so all learners (including Georgia) were practising good listening behaviours. All pupils were encouraged to speak one at a time, even when playing games, so Georgia could understand what was happening. Miss Cohen also began using more visual methods and repetitions in her explanations, and repeating back to the class what each child had said in case Georgia had missed it.

Deaf literacy focus: phonics and cued speech

Georgia needed to have phonics re-taught as a part of the schools catch-up phonics programme because she had missed some critical input. A technique which made a difference for Georgia when recapping phonics was the use by Mrs Fox (the SENCo) of cued speech using visual phonics. This technique involves using a hand shape to distinguish different sounds and is particularly useful when sounds are hard to tell apart by lip reading. Examples of sounds which are difficult to distinguish are : p / b / m and sounds which are difficult to lip read are: t / d / k / n /g. Remember that in phonics we are saying the sound the phoneme makes, not the letter name, so 'k' sounds like the 'c' in cat not 'kay', m sounds like the 'm' in man not 'em'.

It might be a good idea to think about and practise some of these issues so far discussed. With a partner or in a mirror say each sound (p / b / m and t / d / k / n / g) aloud and look at the mouth shapes being used. Repeat this but without voicing the sounds so you are mouthing the sound (but it is silent). If you repeat this again, but changing the order in which you say the sound, your partner can try and guess which sound you are mouthing. When someone is lip reading it is important that you speak normally. Shouting or exaggerating your mouth movements actually makes lip reading far more difficult. (You can practise this in front of a partner too!)

Cued speech can be a useful approach for deaf children with moderate to profound deafness because it gives an additional visual support to distinguish between lip-read sounds which are otherwise difficult to tell apart, for example but and pat. Visual phonics by hand offers a sign for each phoneme which gives a visual to accompany each sound, meaning that recognising and producing sounds and eventual word building have an anchor point (Swanwick, 2016).

Typically, visual phonics by hand is most effective when the learner has a good awareness of BSL finger spelling, but for Georgia (given that she was being reintroduced to the basic phonemes and learning to hear separate sounds) it provided a helpful visual anchor for her learning. In the small group who used visual phonics with Mrs Fox, all pupils began to use this method in their classrooms (and for two pupils who had indistinct speech, it helped them to learn to distinguish and produce sounds more effectively). In lessons other teachers found it helpful to refer learners to use visual phonics alongside their usual teaching.

Kyle and Harris (2006) conducted a research study which compared a range of different predictions of reading achievement in deaf and hearing seven- and eight-year-olds. They found that for deaf children, phonological awareness was a much weaker predictor of reading ability than for hearing children. Instead speech reading and productive (expressive) vocabulary were much more useful. Further research is needed to explore these differences. It seems reasonable that in primary classrooms where there is an expectation that literacy is taught with an explicit focus on phonics, lip reading and cued speech should be used alongside these to offer support to deaf learners by chaining phonic awareness to lip-read meanings.

Working together: parents and schools in partnership

Georgia's parents continued to have regular meetings with Mrs Fox and Miss Cohen to support Georgia's progress. They were pleased by the school making an effort to be more deaf aware while

Georgia was happier in school and was making progress. It was important for Georgia to have positive support from both parents and professionals. There are a number of ways that teachers can engage and work together with parents that are supportive and helpful, but this needs to be sensitive to their preferences. The most important feature of good parent–teacher relationships is communication, the willingness to listen and reach shared understanding. This means that teachers should listen to parents' questions, concerns and observations. Miss Cohen continued to keep Georgia's parents up to date with her progress and development and to communicate about strategies used in school and curriculum developments. Together with other professionals in school Miss Cohen ensured that parents knew what plans were in place to support Georgia and who was responsible for these. There are lots of ways to facilitate this kind of partnership, whether by using a home/school diary or a weekly communication, but they need to be regular and reliable and allow both parties a voice.

A report by the Ear Foundation (2006) found that the terms mild and moderate deafness underplayed the real impact of hearing loss on children's family and education. Parents and professionals stated that children with mild/moderate hearing loss had to use much greater levels of effort and concentration in school and that deafness has a significant social and emotional impact on the child. It is easy to overestimate the level of hearing and comprehension a child with moderate hearing loss has. As a result we teachers sometimes 'expect' a child to be able to ignore background noise, concentrate for long periods and tell us when they don't understand when, in actuality, these are major challenges for most children – and even more so for children with hearing loss.

Problems with diagnosing hearing loss in the classroom

For some children, their hearing deteriorates while they are at school and hearing loss can go undiagnosed. Some warning signs of undetected hearing difficulties to look out for:

- The child seems unfocused.

- The child doesn't join in with group activities.

- The child misses prompts or cues to respond.

- The child misunderstands instructions or doesn't follow instructions.

- The child regularly asks for repetition of instruction or conversation.

- The child regularly complains about noise levels or people speaking quietly.

- Before doing tasks, the child follows rather than leads.

- The child often seems tired and disengaged.

- The child relies on peers or others to help.

- The child talks too loudly or softly.

Who are children with hearing difficulties?

The Children and Families act 2014 requires local authorities to identify the number of children with Special Educational Needs and Disabilities (SENDs) who require support living in their area. It is concerning that the data on deaf children is inconsistent. When we examine the data from the local authorities and compare them with Department for Education data we see a contrast in the data on Deaf and Hearing Impaired children. The Consortium for Research in Deaf Education (CRIDE) conducts an annual survey of education provision for Deaf children to better inform research, practitioners and parents. In 2016 CRIDE report 41,261 deaf children. However, Department for Education figures from the school census report 25,376 children (DfE, 2016). These dissimilarities reflect differences in the definition and identification of deaf children (for example, whether reporting includes just those receiving provision or all children eligible) and possibly other collection differences. Each source can give us some valuable information about Deaf children in the UK today. This chapter references data from the Department for Education because we have a specific interest in the education of Deaf children. In this data the categories and tiers of support used in the UK education system (SEN support and Education, Health and Care (EHC) plans) are referred to. (For an explanation, see this author's discussion in Chapter 5.)

According to Department for Education data (DfE, 2016) there were 20,499 deaf learners in schools (classified as having Hearing Impairment (HI)). This accounts for 1.8% of learners with identified special educational needs; 5,937 of these receive support through an EHC plan or SEN statement and 14,562 at the level of SEN support. The proportion of deaf pupils is relatively even by gender (SEN support girls: 7,270, boys: 7,292; EHC girls: 2,646, boys: 3,291). Deaf learners are more commonly White British (13,078 EHC and SEN support, 64% of those categorised HI) and Pakistani (1,637 SEN at EHC and SEN support, 7.9% of those categorised) than other ethnicities. Where HI is categorised as the primary type of need 26% of those learners have a secondary type of need (3,238 at SEN support, 2,013 at EHC). For learners with other primary types of need, 4,868 also have HI as a secondary type of need (multisensory impairments were not included in this analysis). Where hearing impairment is classified as the primary type of need, speech language and communication needs (SLCN) are the most commonly identified secondary type of need (at SEN support level this includes 1,089 learners 7.5 %; at EHC plan 884 learners 14.9 %) and moderate learning difficulty (MLD) is also a commonly identified secondary type of need (at SEN support 734 learners 5%, at EHC plan 288 learners 4.9%). According to Vernon and Andrews (1990) approximately 38% of children with hearing impairments may also have co-occurring disabilities of another kind (physical, intellectual, social-emotional) that affect their performance in school. It is important to note that hearing impairment is not linked to intelligence, so a deaf child is no more likely to have an intellectual impairment than a non-deaf child; teachers setting appropriate academic expectations is important.

Most deaf children are educated in mainstream inclusive classrooms (DfE, 2016). While many welcome this there are concerns that having teaching dominated by oral approaches will disadvantage children with less access to spoken language. If we examine attainment data, we see that deaf children's attainment is not what we would expect when considering other factors such as age or stage of education (Mayberry 2007, Mayberry et al., 2011).

In sum, then, there are issues with the way data on deafness is collected and reported. Most deaf learners are educated in mainstream inclusive settings. Gender and ethnicity are not strongly associated with Deafness, unlike other Special Educational Needs and Disabilities (SENDs).

Case study

Labelling and including children who are deaf

Connor, aged ten, had profound bilateral hearing loss and had a cochlear implant at the age of 2. He is from a hearing family and before Connor none of them were familiar with signing. Connor's mum and sister have learned some British Sign Language (signing) following his cochlear implant and they communicate using a mixture of lip reading (English) and signing at home (sign-supported English – SSE). Connor's school have worked closely with the sensory support service who have helped to train his class teacher and teaching assistants and offered a teacher of the deaf to the school for one day per week which is divided into Tuesday morning and Thursday afternoon visits. The school head teacher and Special Educational Needs Coordinator (SENco) have encouraged a signing culture in school by offering a signing club for hearing and deaf pupils so that any child in school can learn to communicate with Connor through sign-supported English (with BSL signs) and a community deaf club for deaf children in the local area aged under 12 to meet every two weeks to socialise. Connor was using restricted expressive language when communicating in class and his reading and writing were delayed. He said: 'I smile even when I don't understand; I don't want them to treat me like I'm stupid because I'm deaf. I'm not stupid.'

Supporting deaf children in practice

Connor was already receiving support from Mrs Singh (a teacher of the deaf) and his school and family were working together well. Mrs Lloyd, Connor's class teacher, already used the school tracking system to keep evidence of every child's performance in core subjects. Connor was not performing as well as expected in literacy – his comprehension and writing compositions were not progressing as well as expected. Mrs Lloyd and Mrs Singh decided that a rich language focus was needed to support Connor. This included explicit teaching of vocabulary and verb forms (including endings) to encourage Connor to recognise and use a wider range of vocabulary with more precision and confidence.

This included signed support (when the teacher of the deaf was present), and visual resources alongside written and spoken (lip-read) explanations. These were added to an ongoing 'book' of topic sign vocabulary and activities to take home to practise. Some words which didn't have a simple sign-based correlate (for example, ping and swoosh) would be part of a tricky word discussion, where Connor, his teacher and class would talk about and eventually agree on the definition of the word. These discussions also allowed practice at using such words in writing and checking the understandings of the class. Work on adventure stories in Year 5 offered an opportunity to read and understand as well as compose pupils' own versions of texts. When working on this, both teachers focused on comprehension, vocabulary and helping convey the 'style' of adventure stories. Things that helped Connor improve his comprehension and writing compositions were questioning and discussion of what was happening in the story and what particular expressions meant and how they could be used. Connor said he particularly liked working in a pair on writing tasks so he had someone to talk about his ideas with and they could improve each other's work as they developed their drafts.

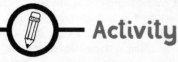 Activity

Supporting Connor to identify word endings

For example:

Has, had, have

Lucy _____ an apple.

Jim _____ an apple, but he ate it.

Sophie and Tony _____ more apples to eat.

Jim says 'Can I _____ your apple?'

Lucy says 'You already _____ one Jim.'

Sophie _____ a spare apple.

What does Sophie say? Write sentences which use **has**, **had** and **have**

What impact can deafness have on learning?

The impact deafness can have on learning depends upon the nature of the individual's deafness (its degree and onset) and the home language environment. Deaf children of deaf parents tend to face fewer difficulties in learning because they experience a first-language environment at home that they can access. They are exposed to communication and socialisation in their own (signed) language, with opportunities to develop awareness of and familiarity with language as carrying meaning, and to develop receptive and expressive language skills. So deaf children of deaf parents have similar learning profiles to other children with English as a second language (ESL) (Swanwick, 2002, 2010). For these pupils, many of the language supportive strategies used in multilingual classrooms can be effective. Early experiences of interaction in infancy are significant in shaping socialisation and communication (for example, turn taking and language development). Carers for deaf infants can develop social turn-taking routines visually and through touch, and long-term studies demonstrate these have positive impact (Meadow-Orleans et al., 2004).

However, children who are deaf who have hearing (and non-signing) parents are at risk of missing out on these experiences (experiential deprivation) and this can cause delays in language and cognition, and potentially social and behavioural difficulties (Lederberg et al., 2013). It's not just that there is a delay in understanding and using language, but in being able to understand other people's social behaviour, so that social interaction and communication can be challenges for deaf children beyond the early years (Anitia et al., 2009).

Deafness can have a big effect on language development, as deaf children can miss out on learning about patterns of speech, tone and language structures. If a child doesn't have access to sign language (for example, if they have hearing parents) then it is common for them to develop 'home signs' which are gestures or signs which hold meaning and work informally with those familiar with them (Goldin-Meadow, 2003). These are fairly limited, however, and early introduction to a signed language is recommended because a broad community uses it and it has richer vocabulary and more social and cultural value for the deaf individual. It is important to acknowledge that British Sign Language (BSL) is a visual and spatial language whereas English is a linear sequential language that has a very different grammatical and vocabulary structure – for learners working across the two teachers need to be sensitive to the challenges which this can pose. For example, in British Sign Language we structure language as subject object verb ('What your name is?') but in English as subject verb object ('What is your name?'). Additionally, in English we use many sound related-words, for example musical concepts which are rather redundant in BSL, so there is a need for bilingual supportive teaching to acknowledge these differences. There is discussion in the research literature about the dominance of 'English only' teaching and the lack of bilingual teaching available in mainstream inclusive classrooms, and how this might disadvantage deaf learners (see Swanwick, 2010, for an overview). Reading and writing require a range of skills, cognitive, perceptive, social and linguistic. Trezek et al. (2010) argue that children who are deaf and without the ability to use phonological awareness are unable to decode new words and this means learning to read is much more difficult for them. Some children who sign learn to read visually (Chamberlain and Mayberry, 2000) rather than phonically, though the mechanism for this isn't well understood. For pupils who are from hearing families where signing isn't available, using only English means they face particular language difficulties as they have missed out on early receptive language experiences (Williams, 2004). Many deaf children leaving the Early Years Foundation Stage (EYFS) aren't reading ready when they enter Key Stage 1 because they don't have a strong foundation language to base reading on (in either English or BSL). Later as children move into Key Stage 2, word problems in science, maths and foundation subjects become increasingly complex and abstract which can pose difficulties for deaf students with poorer language skills (Andrews et al., 2006; Pagliaro and Ansell, 2002).

It used to be that deaf children were identified as having hearing difficulties around age three when they had failed to begin speaking. This 'wait to fail' diagnostic process was catastrophic for children's development because it meant that those children missed out on vital early language exposure. In the last two decades with the routine use of neonatal hearing screening and early interventions through cochlear implants before 24 months of age there has been a shift in the profiles of deaf children. There are now fewer deaf children with a delayed diagnosis and fewer children at risk of missing critical language and socialisation periods of development in their early years that is very positive (Andrews et al., 2011). Yet some children will acquire hearing loss through illness or accident and others may experience worsening hearing that is gradually identified when the child fails to make appropriate progress. There are also pupils in our classrooms whose hearing has been 'corrected' by hearing aids, who still have significant difficulties which require support. Given that a large number of deaf children have cochlear implants and/or moderate loss, it can be easy for hearing teachers and peers to assume a greater level of hearing and understanding than a child actually has. Common issues are that deaf learners may miss some words being spoken, and individual sounds (phonemes) in any word and word endings can be indistinct, lost and challenging to identify for Deaf learners. This partial hearing/partial loss pattern means that misunderstanding is a common issue. For learners, word endings and particular sounds in speech may need specific teaching (see Connor's example in the case study above).

What do hearing aids do?

There is a wide range of devices to assist with hearing loss – digital aids, bone-anchored aids, bone conduction aids, body worn aids, behind-the-ear (post-aural) cochlear implants, etc. Most hearing aids (except bone conduction aids) amplify (make louder) sounds going into the ear – they don't restore hearing levels; they just make sounds louder (all sounds – background noise included). This means that it can be just as difficult to hear people speaking in noisy places. In classrooms and social environments, background noise can easily drown out voices, so the deaf child can find they are missing out on conversations and interactions, for example at dinner times and play times. Digital aids are becoming more sophisticated and can be tailored to suit the individual's hearing loss – we can expect and hope that this technology continues to develop rapidly. Aids are prescribed and fitted for the deaf individual and should be regularly maintained, and a teacher of the deaf or parent should be able to give you good advice about this and routine maintenance if needed in school.

Teaching deaf learners

Different children have very different experiences of deafness, so teachers need to approach this in two ways: inclusive classroom strategies which prioritise communication for understanding, and tailored individual practices to support learners develop specific knowledge, understanding and skills. Communication friendly classrooms prioritise *communication for understanding*. This involves auditing the physical environment of the classroom to make it 'hearing friendly' (as described earlier), reviewing the pedagogical environment so that teaching is designed to include recap, repetition and formative assessment, teaching using multi-mode resources to support learning, and regularly checking understanding as part of routine teaching. This also means we need to review the psychological and social classroom environment, by thinking about our teaching behaviours and what kinds of learning behaviours they encourage: being ready to listen to pupils (a lot), being present with them while they explore and explain their own understanding and considering how meaningful learning objectives are for those pupils. It does not require 'simplification' of the curriculum or lowering of expectations. Using metacognitive strategies to discuss learning and understanding supports the development of complex thinking skills and higher attainment. Thinking about the needs of pupils and supporting them to overcome barriers in order to achieve highly is not 'dumbing down' – it is person-centred high-quality teaching.

Without a solid language foundation, there is no literacy. Without language and literacy children are isolated and significantly disadvantaged. Learners need more than 'functional' language skills to become adept readers and writers – our teaching offers vital support to learners in helping them engage with the world successfully. We can use specific literacy interventions tailored to pupil needs to scaffold their learning.

There is a lack of high-quality, well-controlled, peer-reviewed research in the area of pedagogy for literacy with deaf learners; however, we do know the disadvantages of poor language support on literacy. Rather than discussing various critical and political debates about the advantages of different approaches (where compelling evidence is lacking), let us refer instead to the reflective practice cycle. If we tailor teaching to the individual and context, working together with learners and their families and other professionals to offer the best opportunities for learning that we can, we can support the learners in our classrooms now and have a positive impact on their futures.

Strategies that support deaf learners involve multimodal communication to link concepts together. For example, sign print can be a valuable resource to support children's developing literacy because it links pictures, sign language and written English (orthography) together, making clear the relationships between each (this is called chaining). In sign print teachers can treat sign drawings as text and question children about it, to explore understanding, identification, prediction and comprehension. Unfortunately, sign print has not been widely adopted so it is not uniform and it can be difficult to find enough resources. However, signed stories are abundant and a very valuable resource. Signed stories are stories that the reader signs alongside oral story telling. There are hundreds of free-signed stories available online to support inclusive classrooms, particularly aimed at Early Years and Key Stage 1 students. The advantages of using electronic signed stories are that the stories have 'expert' signers telling the story alongside the text and narration. These signed stories can be played repeatedly, paused, questioned and revisited. In some stories the text also has a 'read along' feature which helps identify which words in the text are being narrated. If this isn't available the teacher or adult can point to the words in the same way as in an ordinary story.

In addition to selecting resources that use multimodal approaches, teachers' own pedagogical style should also be multimodal (Wolbers, 2008). As teachers we tend to rely on our voices as key 'tools' in our teaching toolkit – you may have noticed this if you have had a sore throat and tried to teach your class as usual! Teachers encourage engagement and interaction with text when reading aloud using tone, volume, pace and pitch. When reading with classes including deaf learners, teachers need to find alternative ways to read which rely less on voice alone and offer more visual cues – for example, using a book stand so they have their hands free to point, gesture and sign, or using facial expression and body language to help dramatise the text, and possibly using multisensory approaches to engage pupils. This active engagement with text that links meanings together enhances opportunities for pupils to learn literacy-specific vocabulary, recognise text/sign/word meanings and engage in higher-order literacy and language skills (Gioia, 2001). So that rather than simply trying to 'follow' what is happening in a text, learners are actively constructing their understandings of it (Williams and McLean, 1997). While developing this repertoire of 'performance' reading skills, teachers should be aware that learners will need to shift attention from text to teacher and so may miss information. Teachers should therefore plan repetition as part of this routine.

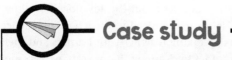 **Case study**

Examining disengagement in deaf children

Mohammed (Mo) was nine, had moderate bilateral hearing loss and had had a cochlear implant. He was good at maths and enjoyed athletics, achieving above age expectations in these subjects. He performed well on computer-based activities with headphones and subtitling. The teaching assistant (Miss Wu) working with Mo had noticed a difference when Mo is working with her and the class teacher Mr Styles. When Mr Styles was leading whole-class teaching, Mo would face toward him, but often closed his eyes or looked over his head (so that he couldn't lip read). This disengaged behaviour was beginning to be evident in Mo's literacy and other subject work, especially where he needed to read and write. His language use was restricted and didn't seem to be improving as expected, despite support from Miss Wu. He relied heavily on tasks being re-explained and closely assisted by Miss Wu. Mr Styles (the teacher), Miss Wu (the teaching assistant), Mo and his dad Mohammed had a meeting to find out what was going on and what they could all do to improve the situation.

Mo said: '[Mr] Styles just keeps going. He doesn't check who gets it. I can look at [the interactive white] board, I can listen [to Mr] Styles [by lip reading] I can't do both [at the same time]. He keeps going ... talk, talk, talk.' Mohammed (Mo's dad) was upset and asked how he could help with school work.

Supporting Mo: understanding children's unique communication needs

Mo was an able student with lots of potential but unfortunately he was becoming disengaged. As Mo moved through Year 4 and into Year 5 there was a risk that as more abstract concepts and methods of teaching were introduced, he might become even more disengaged, particularly if he refused to lip read from the teacher. There were several areas of concern here: one was his academic engagement with a focus particularly on his level of understanding and paying attention, and another related to his participation and why he didn't want to join in.

It was clear that Mo was finding it difficult to keep up with lessons delivered in spoken English without support, so Mr Styles and Miss Wu agreed that handouts and visual reminders would be used in every lesson. This ensured that the key objectives and activities were clear to Mo and that he could refer to this if he 'missed something' and so wouldn't feel left behind. He could also take this home to help him with homework tasks and talk to his dad Mohammed about them. This additional preparation work meant there was a lot more communication between Mr Styles and Miss Wu about exactly what support Mo needed and what was planned for each lesson in advance. Mr Styles altered his planning template so that repetition, time to recap and formative assessment were planned into lessons more explicitly. Using more interactive formative assessment also meant that Mr Styles tracked all pupil progress in more detail. He introduced 'quiz' elements in sessions where new and abstract concepts were being introduced, and allowed pupils to work in small groups and pairs to answer questions which checked understanding.

Miss Wu and Mr Styles agreed that while Mo found relying on teaching assistant support from Miss Wu was helpful, they were keen that he become a more independent learner and that Mr Styles wanted to 'recover' his teaching relationship with Mo. To this end, he spent time working with Mo in class and during social time, such as playtime. Both Mo and Mr Styles felt that they were beginning to understand and like each other more. Miss Wu enjoyed working with Mo in small-group work and with a range of other pupils and felt like she was having more of an impact in the class and that she wasn't 'getting in his way' as much.

Mohammed had meetings with Mr Styles and Miss Wu to discuss Mo's progress each half term, and he spent more time talking about school and doing homework with him. They joined a community football club together and Mo made some more friends. They were all much happier with how Mo was doing in school, and Mo was more engaged and felt like he was making progress. Mr Styles said he learnt a lot about teaching from working with Mo, and was considering further professional development to learn more about inclusive teaching.

 ## Concluding thoughts

This chapter examined deafness using three dimensions: biomedical, psychological and sociolinguistic. The different models meant that we looked at the individual, their environment and how we can adapt our teaching to better support learning. We met Georgia, Connor and Mo, deaf children who prompted us to consider how deaf friendly our classrooms and teaching are, and we also thought about practical support strategies to include and engage deaf learners.

Language is the central consideration for teachers of deaf children, and we need to tailor our teaching to support language acquisition, social communication and literacy development of deaf learners explicitly. If you have access to a teacher of the deaf they can give you advice on making your classroom a more deaf friendly environment (with planning lessons, supporting communication, resources to use to supplement teaching, help with target-setting). They can also give you advice about hearing aids and equipment and special arrangements for tests if needed. If you don't have the support of a teacher of the deaf, don't panic! Your local authority will have a sensory support service which you can contact for advice and support.

This means more than just generic inclusive classroom practice but additional specific intervention focus on the literacy and language skills the pupil needs to develop. It requires use of a reflective practice cycle, careful monitoring and working together with child, parent and other professionals to ensure that this is effective. By targeting specific areas of skill development, we acknowledge our responsibility for the progress of our learners, and demonstrate our high expectations of them – expectations they will be proud to exceed.

References

Andrews, J.F., Gentry, M.A., DeLana, M. and Cocke, D. (2006) Bilingual students – deaf and hearing – learn about science: using visual strategies, technology and culture. *Language Learner*, 3(4): 15–18.

Andrews, J.F., Shaw, L. and Lomas, G. (2011) Deaf and hard of hearing students. In J.M. Kauffman and D.P. Hallahan (eds), *Handbook of Special Education*. London: Routledge, pp.233–46.

Anitia, S., Jones, P., Reed, S. and Kreimeyer, K. (2009) Academic status and progress of deaf and hard of hearing students in general education classrooms. *Journal of Deaf Studies and Deaf Education*, 14(3): 293–311.

British Society of Audiology (1988) Recommended procedures. *British Journal of Audiology*, 22: 265–6.

Chamberlain, C. and Mayberry, R. (2000) Theorizing about the relation between American Sign Language and reading. In C. Chamberlain, J. Moford and R. Mayberry (eds), *Language Acquisition by Eye*. Mahwah, NJ: Erlbaum, pp.221–59.

CRIDE (2016) *CRIDE Survey of Educational Provision for Deaf Children: England Report*. Retrieved from **www.ndcs.org.uk/professional_support/national_data/cride.html**.

Department for Education (2016) *Special Educational Needs in England: January 2016*, SFR 29/2016. Retrieved from **https://www.gov.uk/government/organisations/department-for-education/about/statistics**.

Ear Foundation (2006) Ear Foundation Survey. Online at: **http://www.earfoundation.org.uk/research/previous/european-survey**.

Gioia, B. (2001) The emergent language and literacy experiences of three deaf preschoolers. *International Journal of Disability, Development and Education*, 48(4): 411–28.

Goldin-Meadow, S. (2003) *Hearing Gesture: How Our Hands Help Us Think*. Cambridge, MA: Harvard University Press.

Kyle, F.E. and Harris, M. (2006) Concurrent correlates and predictors of reading and spelling achievement in deaf and hearing school children. *Journal of Deaf Studies and Deaf Education*, 11(3): 273–88.

Lederberg, A.R., Schick, B. and Spencer, P.E. (2013) Language and literacy development of deaf and hard of hearing children: successes and challenges. *Developmental Psychology*, 49(1): 15–30.

Leigh, I. (2009) *A Lens on Deaf Identities*. New York: Oxford University Press.

Mayberry, R. (2007) When timing is everything: age of first language acquisition effects on second language learning. *Applied Psycholinguistics*, 28(3): 537–49.

Mayberry, R.A., DelGiudice, A.A. and Lieberman, A.M. (2011) Reading achievement in relation to phonological coding and awareness in deaf readers: a meta analysis. *Journal of Deaf Studies and Deaf Education*, 16(2): 164–88.

Meadow-Orleans, K.P., Spencer, P.E. and Koester, L.S. (2004) *The World of Deaf Infants: A Longitudinal Study*. New York: Oxford University Press.

Pagliaro, C. and Ansell, E. (2002) Story problems in the deaf education classroom: frequency and mode of presentation. *Journal of Deaf Studies and Deaf Education*, 7(2): 107–19.

Swanwick, R. (2002) Sign bilingual deaf children's approaches to writing: individual strategies for bridging the gap between BSL and written English. *Deafness and Education International*, 4(2): 65–83.

Swanwick, R. (2010) Policy and practice in sign bilingual education: development, challenges and directions. *International Journal of Bilingual Education and Bilingualism*, 13(2): 147–58.

Swanwick, R.A. (2016) Deaf children's bimodal bilingualism and education. *Language Teaching*, 49(1): 1–34.

Trezek, B., Wang, Y. and Paul, P. (2010) *Reading and Deafness: Theory, Research and Practice*. New York: Delmar.

Vernon, M. and Andrews, J.F. (1990) *The Psychology of Deafness: Understanding Deaf and Hard-of-Hearing People*. New York: Longman.

Williams, C. (2004) Emergent literacy of deaf children. *Journal of Deaf Studies and Deaf Education*, 9(4): 352–65.

Williams, C.L. and McLean, M.M. (1997) Young deaf children's response to picture book reading in a preschool setting. *Research in the Teaching of English*, 337–66.

Wolbers, K.A. (2008) Using balanced and interactive writing instruction to improve the higher order and lower order writing skills of deaf students. *Journal of Deaf Studies and Deaf Education*, 13(2): 257–77.

Useful resources

www.communication4all.co.uk

www.ndcs.org.uk/

www.earfoundation.org.uk/

www.signedstories.com/

With thanks for the illustrations by Poppy (aged 10).

8

Expanded noun phrases, adjectives, adverbs and beyond: helping to create a world full of colours and sounds in children's writing

Kirsty Anderson

 This chapter

This chapter will explore the importance of teaching adjectives and adverbs to all children in the classroom in order to maximise the writing capacity of all children, and most importantly to enable teachers to develop young writers who can use language skilfully and creatively to express their thoughts and feelings. The chapter will explore how writing develops in children and the implications for children with language and literacy difficulties. The use of varied language as children extend their writing skills will be highlighted as an essential and ongoing aspect of children's literary development. The chapter will consider how and why difficulties in language development could and should be supported, looking in particular at the use of pictures and drawings to support and stimulate imaginative writing. Finally, the chapter will explore how teachers can make the most of different writing opportunities in the classroom to improve and expand the vocabularies of all children. It is important to note that this chapter does not explore all genres in writing. Narratives and personal recounts form the focus of this discussion.

Children's worlds and the construction of language in their imagination

Stories or narratives offer writers of all ages and stages the opportunity to literally paint pictures of settings, characters and plots with carefully chosen words and phrases. The same vivid descriptions can be included in children's personal recounts; from the adventures they have on school trips to articulating how boring they might have found a school holiday! Moreover, in the current Programme of Study for English (DfE, 2013) children begin their journey in writing with retellings of personal events as indicated in the objectives for Year 1. There is a clear understanding as children develop their writing skills that they need to begin by writing about what they know most closely. The usefulness of a personal experience in aiding the writing process is crystallised in Bereiter and Scardamalia's eight-year study of children's writing, that found memory recall a significant factor in writing success (1987).

When children play they often explore and create imaginary worlds. As they become literate, children enter the exciting imaginary worlds found in the huge range of children's literature available. Some stories prove more popular and captivate audiences for generations: the terrible teeth and terrible claws of Julia Donaldson's Gruffalo for instance, and of course for older readers the exciting world inhabited by Harry Potter, so creatively described by J.K. Rowling. In both of these examples children are greeted with carefully chosen language that enables them to walk in the shoes of the key protagonists. Teachers are tasked with facilitating reading for pleasure so will make careful selections in the stories they share. Throughout the reading of different stories teachers may comment on the effectiveness of different vocabulary. If the vocabulary within a story is focused on developing a command of useful nouns and verbs, children with any language difficulty will struggle to enjoy the story. Of course, stories for children are filled with language that both excites and engages. Sharing stories is a natural opportunity to encourage children to become interested in the language they choose to use in their own writing. Teachers are skilled at promoting language and literacy development in the classroom. The environments are often colourful, with rich reading materials for children to explore with support and independently. Stimulating opportunities for imaginative play should be offered, such as puppets and role-play areas, particularly in the early years.

Effective practitioners plan to include writing opportunities within structured language and literacy activities. These can range from mark-making and scribbles in the very early years to keeping a personal word bank and writing a journal for older children. But throughout these learning opportunities it should always be noted that for some, writing is much more challenging. Writing is a detached activity, reliant on the skills of an individual, which can lead to great frustration for children with language and literacy difficulties. Teachers can support children to have ideas, through replicating a fairy tale for example. They support children to have enough ideas, using various planning scaffolds or prompts to serve as an aide-memoire. Both of these steps can be fruitful, but children with language and literacy difficulties may have a variety of challenges that need to be considered, so even with support some children will struggle to write an engaging story. When working with children then it is crucial to develop understanding and use of a wide range of vocabulary, including adjectives and adverbs. Essentially it is the rich languages of action and emotion that will help children develop best as writers. Writers who write exciting, adventurous or even heartbreaking stories or autobiographies understand the importance of emotional responses in the audience. It may also be the case that having a wider vocabulary leads to a writer utilising a greater diversity of language more naturally. If children are limited to learning simple nouns and verbs, then the stories they write will lack the exciting, emotional language used by their more articulate peers. Children need to have the chance to experiment with exciting language in their writing but even more importantly through enriching expressive vocabulary with adjectives, adverbs, expanded noun phrases and knowledge of descriptive verbs. Children can then learn to express their emotions in all aspects of their lives.

Learning to write

Writing is a particularly difficult process to learn and consequently to teach. The most important aspect to note when teaching any children to write is the difference between writing and speech. Although it is often suggested that children write as they speak, the real challenge is more complicated. Communicating through speech involves at least one other person to engage in a dialogue. Where writing is detached, speech is very much involved. The other person or people provide helpful reminders when talking by asking questions, sharing responses and showing their emotions. Writing, on the other hand, is dependent on writers developing an independent internal dialogue without an immediate audience. Speech involves interaction with an immediate audience – which doubtless is challenging for some children – and with interaction come reference words such as 'that', 'this', 'there' which direct the listener, gestures and intonation or – put simply – emotions. When children learn to write they need to be taught to incorporate these emotions into their language choices and to consider the emotional responses the audience may have. While talking children can be interrupted, asked questions and even start again; writing on the other hand demands much more precision. Repetition and questioning can help children's speech to be understood. Children need to learn grammatical rules as well as developing a rich, effective and engaging vocabulary to use. Spelling, punctuation and grammar are essential rules useful in helping children to ensure their writing makes sense.

When developing as writers children progress at different rates through different phases, with emphasis on the following stages:

- scribbling, forming letter-like symbols, writing strings of letters;

- writing initial sounds to represent words but without spaces;

- using consonants to represent words and some punctuation of sentences which are understood as basic units of meaning;

- initial, middle and final sounds included and writing is more readable;

- transitional phase: writing is clear with much spelling recognised;

- standard spelling.

The developmental phases are connected and will improve gradually. Stages of vocabulary development in spoken language can affect when a child is ready to learn spelling patterns and rules. The National Curriculum (DfE, 2013) includes example words for the phonics and spelling patterns taught and learned in Years 1 and 2, and word lists for Years 3 and 4 and for Years 5 and 6. Although proficiency in spelling does not necessarily determine proficiency in story writing and expression, it is an important part of classroom teaching and learning. Developing knowledge and skills of spelling patterns and rules can help the fluency of children's writing. It is important to encourage this fluency, and to support children building their confidence so that even without knowledge of the correct spelling they are willing to 'have a go'.

Obviously children do not form a homogenous group in any classroom. As such it is important to recognise that the challenges faced by children are likely to differ from child to child, though there are some commonalities that can be presented:

- disabilities such as muscular dystrophy or cerebral palsy may result in difficulties with the physical act of writing and/or speech;

- speech and visual or hearing impairments may reduce the range of language a child has had the opportunity to explore;

- children with English as an Additional Language (EAL) are aiming to close the gap between themselves and their peers who are effectively a moving target;

- assessment of progress and attainment is measured in English, presenting further challenges for EAL pupils;

- children with emotional or behavioural difficulties may have a limited expressive vocabulary, for instance if there has been a traumatic experience or a lack of emotional support provided in the early stages of development;

- writing is the dominant form of assessment for any subject in schools, meaning that children with any of the above (or other) difficulties may not see conventional success. This may further exacerbate difficulties if self-esteem plummets as a result.

Clearly then it is essential that teachers take every possible opportunity to improve both spoken and written vocabularies in children. When sharing stories teachers must pause (at suitable points) to discuss the language read. After starting with the likes and dislikes of different words teachers can help children to construct their own range through ensuring that children can define the word and explain why it most effectively describes an event, location or character. For instance, if a character is *strolling* this conjures a very different image from one who is *rushing* and even more so from one who is *tiptoeing*. The best teachers will use questions, actions and illustrations to ensure all pupils not only understand what these descriptive verbs are portraying, but also how the character that is strolling, rushing or tiptoeing *feels*. Children can of course be encouraged to indicate their understanding of emotions through questioning, though it is not the only option. Children might use emojis to indicate what emotion they think a word expresses. Children are likely to be familiar with emojis, making them more accessible. It is even possible for emojis to tell a story or recount an event for some children. Teachers may also use software such as Clicker that includes images and smiley faces to accompany the selected vocabulary.

Writing stories

There are a number of complexities to consider when children learn to write stories. Children need to consider which words to use, how these words are spelled and the selection of an appropriate order for them. If vocabulary is limited then this can inhibit fluency, range and importantly the impact the story has on the audience. Even children with limited vocabularies are capable of imagining complex narratives, however, as an observation of play will demonstrate. It is important then that teachers are willing to make a link between children's imaginative play and their developing writing skills. Teachers could scribe children's adventure stories as told through their play and therefore help children to see the link between written stories and the feelings or emotions – the impact – that these can have on the reader, particularly if they are one of the players who is experiencing this play.

To support children learning to write teachers need to act as model, scribe, editor, reader and publisher. To encourage children to write vivid, exciting and engaging stories the modelling stage is vital. When children work independently and begin to develop ideas the content of the stories should be the focus. The meaning, purpose and desired impact should be established initially, with the mechanics of grammatical rules approached secondly. Focusing on the content first can help children to achieve success, improving their self-esteem. Teachers can support children to improve the content by clarifying that sentences are what Kress (1994) explains as complete thoughts. When the thought is finished, punctuation signifies the move to a new sentence topic.

It should be noted, however, that there is a wide range of stories that children can learn to write. Children need to be taught the unique features of different genres, which include the specific language features of the genre, such as the action and dialogue included in adventure stories.

 **Case study**

Writing for an audience with a purpose

A trainee teacher in a Year 5 class, Liv had the freedom to focus on composition with the pupils during her English lessons. The school had separate spelling and grammar (SPaG) lessons which focused on the transcription aspects of writing, so Liv was tasked with teaching the class to plan and draft their narrative writing, through identifying the audience and purpose and selecting the appropriate grammar and vocabulary, and understanding how these change and enhance meaning. The mixed-ability class included Aminul, who was fluent in Bangladeshi and English, but sometimes struggled to articulate some words and phrases which were difficult to translate from his home language. Liv paired pupils of similar ability to work as an audience for each other's adventure writing on the theme of being cast away on a deserted island. The pupils collaborated on the purpose of their stories: to entertain. Liv planned for the pupils to collaborate so that children could bounce ideas from each other. Liv spent several sessions modelling effective partner work so that the pairs were not simply sharing ideas, but were able to carefully consider the effectiveness of the chosen vocabulary. Aminul and his partner Bilawal planned complex adventure stories, with rich descriptions adding to the reader's understanding. They explored phrases to describe characters and settings, adding detail which would offer the reader useful clues about the events in the story. The two boys followed Liv's guidance carefully, questioning the impact of the language they selected. Rather than simply using nouns and verbs to set the scene, they made use of noun phrases and adverbs to enhance the intended meaning. The desert island had 'high and jagged cliffs' and the protagonist 'explored cautiously', suggesting danger and fear for the reader. The collaborative work, combined with a thoughtfully modelled understanding of the impact of selecting vocabulary carefully, meant that the writing successfully matched the purpose and entertained the audience.

In order for strategies like that deployed by Liv to be successful it is essential that these become commonplace in the classroom. Paired work can be a resounding success but takes time to become embedded. It is useful to start with shorter opportunities such as games. Language games like 'word tennis' can further expand vocabularies. In any similar word games children can be encouraged to keep a personal dictionary of the words they learn. Children could use symbols (like the emojis mentioned earlier) or even colours to indicate emotions associated with the word or phrase they have learned.

Case study

Colourful social stories

Jacob attended a mainstream primary school that included an Additionally Resourced Centre (ARC) for children with specific physical and medical needs. He had the life-limiting degenerative disease Duchenne's muscular dystrophy. Significantly, this illness impacted on Jacob's ability to move, and left him feeling frustrated and angry at his inability to play some games with his more mobile peers. Moreover, Jacob was aware that his illness was life-limiting. His class teacher, Allison, was keen that Jacob should enjoy his experience in school, fully achieving his potential. Allison wanted Jacob to take part in all aspects of classroom life, but his physical difficulties led to emotional difficulties as this ten-year-old boy needed to process his developing understanding of the debilitating illness he had. Jacob's illness left him physically tired, and meant he missed school for treatment sometimes. Consequently, there was a gap between Jacob's language and literacy skills and those of his peers. At the same time, Allison was conscious that his classmates needed to build their emotional capacity to empathise with Jacob's experiences. The children in this class needed a range of vocabulary beyond noun and verbs. Indeed the class, including Jacob, needed an understanding of the vocabulary to enable them to articulate their feelings. Inspired by Anna Llenas's (2016) book *The Colour Monster*, Allison began to plan to support her class not only to have the appropriate vocabulary, but also to be able to apply it in context. Allison felt that the rules for Standard English were important, but knew that her class needed to explore the rules in context rather than simply be reminded to use 'more interesting vocabulary' or 'remember to use an adverbial phrase to open your sentence'. Instead, Allison would include these in her shared writing, and articulate the impact of this language. To help the class understand and articulate feelings, they would regularly write social stories together. Allison started with the idea that feelings could be described as colours. Like the monster in Llenas's book (2016) Allison encouraged her class to think about what colour they might be when doing various activities. By asking 'what colour do you think Jacob is when he finds it hard to do PE?' the class began to empathise with his difficulties. Similarly, Jacob was able to literally illustrate his emotions simply by selecting a colour. On days when he was especially tired or had missed some of the shared learning, Jacob used the colours as a signal for Allison and the class, who were then able to support him effectively.

Colour can be incredibly powerful in helping children learn to identify the emotion they feel. Through exploring colour as an extension of a feeling children can then begin to recognise that colours are not simply adjectives but may be used as more descriptive nouns and even verbs.

Painting with words: stimulating ideas and punctuating pictures

Children may have limited vocabularies for a variety of different reasons. Vocabulary can be improved and stimulated in context. For many children this will be a natural part of growing up, as they like, or dislike, the varied opportunities offered to them. However, it is fair to say that there is not a 'one-size-fits-all' approach to this. Although the spelling lists provided by the National Curriculum (DfE, 2013) are useful, these do not include all words. Words useful to help children write adventurous and exciting stories need to be developed by the teacher. Emotive vocabulary makes sense in context, and so teachers should consider this when thinking creatively about how they can foster vocabulary for their pupils. Art works can and should be used to do this, as visual and verbal literacies complement each other well. Importantly, art works can be accessed by all children, as pointed out by Pearson and Thompson in their chapter in Bearne's book *Differentiation and Diversity* (1996). Just as language develops naturally through different experiences, vocabulary can also be extended and improved through the exploration of pictures and art works. It is easier for children to talk about and then write about something they can see. They can make sense of their past, present and future through exploring pictures, all the while enhancing their linguistic repertoire.

In the Early Years and often in Key Stage 1, children are encouraged to illustrate their stories as part of their regular and routine learning. This use of drawings can be a useful memory aid for older children too, especially those with language and literacy difficulties. In an Australian study with EAL children, Adoniou (2014) found that children wrote significantly more when they had an accompanying illustration of their experience. Although Adoniou's (2014) study was linked to non-fiction rather than fiction writing, the popularity of story maps as planning tools in the classroom indicates that drawings do enable children to write better stories as they have something to act as a reminder or stimulus of ideas.

Children's vocabulary can and must be enhanced, and creative approaches such as utilising works of art and children's own drawings are incredibly useful. At the same time, however, there are grammatical rules and conventions that must be learned. Teachers will frequently bemoan the forgotten punctuation in children's stories and descriptive writing. To counter this, teachers might consider punctuation as more than a set of rules. Just as the vocabulary children used forms a palette of colours that describe their emotions, punctuation can be thought of as a specialised tool that adds precise detail to their writing. Children need to understand that punctuation adds the detail that in speech is added through intonation and pauses. Explaining punctuation in this way can be much more effective than simply repeating grammatical rules out of context. Rules will only make sense if the function of the punctuation is clear. Pauline Gibbons (1993) explored the importance of understanding the difference between punctuation in writing and intonation in speech in her work developed to support EAL learners. Gibbons explains the importance of children recognising both the form and the function of language and punctuation, rather than relying on repetition of rules. This is useful for all teachers when focusing on punctuation, as this is often difficult for children to recall and use consistently.

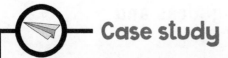

Case study

Colouring emotions to develop literacy confidence

Annie's Year 5 class were confident and keen to share their ideas, thoughts and feelings. The children came from a range of different backgrounds, and many had English as an additional language. Far from necessarily having a language deficit, Annie believed her class had a language difference. After sharing stories Annie's class would talk about their likes and dislikes, and she encouraged this during shared writing opportunities. With more opportunities to develop confidence in their spoken language Annie noticed the children's emotive vocabularies were limited, more so than she expected. Characters were often described as being 'sad' or 'happy' or, if pushed, 'really happy'. She was confident that with some creative teaching she would be able to encourage the use of a wider range of emotive vocabulary. Annie planned to develop children's use of more descriptive and engaging language, starting by unpicking the use of particular techniques in the stories they shared.

Annie selected *Skellig* by David Almond, a story about Michael and Mina's meeting with a strange creature. Rather than noting all of the beautiful language used in the engaging story, Annie chose to explore the use of references to colour with her pupils. When the story made use of colour in its vivid descriptions, Annie collected these phrases on a 'working wall' for her class. As a class they would discuss the phrases, like *I called him Doctor Death because his face was grey and he had black spots on his hands and he didn't know how to smile* ... and reflect on how they might use similar language in their own writing.

To further develop this, Annie worked with her class to develop the links they made between colours and emotions. She gave each pupil a set of coloured cards – a colour fan. At the start of each school day, Annie would ask the children to hold up the card that best described how they felt that day. The class started this journey quite slowly. Even though they were often keen to talk, they were worried about the challenge of developing new language skills. When Tomi held up the light blue card he explained it was because he was feeling sad that day. Annie guided the class to explore different ways of expressing sadness, including use of the phrase 'feeling blue'. From this small start, Annie supported her class to understand phrases like 'green with envy' or 'white as a sheet'. As their understanding grew, the class began to use similar phrases in their writing, and to recognise the clues associated with colour. When Bettina described a car in her story as 'red and powerful', Annie questioned what she meant. Bettina confidently explained that the red car in her story would be fast moving, loud and dangerous! It was clear that through literally exploring the colourful language of emotions, the children in her class had begun to improve and expand their capacity to articulate their feelings.

Through understanding how colour can link to emotions, Annie was able to support her class. Linking language and colour is very helpful for children, particularly as colour is a part of our everyday lives.

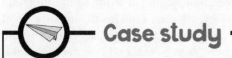

Case study

Enriching and extending children's vocabularies

Anthony was a trainee teacher on placement in a Year 6 class. The school he was developing his teaching skills in included an Additionally Resourced Centre (ARC) for children with emotional and behavioural difficulties. Anthony's English classes included children with mixed abilities and a range of emotional needs. One of the pupils in the class, Freddie, had experienced prolonged periods of absence from school that resulted in both a lack of confidence and lack of interest in his writing tasks. Anthony's class teacher asked him to plan lessons that would teach the class how to plan, draft, evaluate and edit their writing. Anthony used shared and modelled writing techniques to 'think out loud' and explain his own word choices. He encouraged the children to talk to each other about their language choices as they worked, and made particular use of talk partners to explain each other's interesting vocabulary choices in the plenary sessions. Though useful for some children, Freddie's lack of confidence in his knowledge of varied language exacerbated by his frequent absence from school meant that he was reluctant to talk about his ideas. Anthony came up with a creative solution that meant Freddie would be able to demonstrate his developing learning, and more importantly begin to experience success. Anthony started by asking Freddie to highlight his favourite words from his own writing. After a week, he instructed Freddie to define the favourite word in the margin of his book. In doing this he knew Freddie would be improving and enriching his existing vocabulary through careful exploration of the dictionary. Anthony then challenged Freddie in his feedback by offering a range of synonyms Freddie could have used. Finally, Anthony asked Freddie to explain the intended impact of his chosen vocabulary on the audience. Freddie was expanding his vocabulary, developing his self-efficacy and considering the impact of his words on his audience.

While developing his teaching skills with the Year 6 class, Anthony realised the importance of ensuring children are taught to understand the relationship between form and function in language. Rather than simply telling Freddie that his work would be more interesting with a more varied range, or having a checklist of word classes to include, Anthony taught Freddie to understand the effect or function of the selected vocabulary in his writing. Feedback and marking are essential tools for teachers to utilise in the classroom. In an ideal world children and teachers would have the opportunity to discuss the written work, aiding improvements through the chance for children to explain their ideas one to one. Realistically, however, this is not always possible. Teaching children to respond to written feedback and marking on their compositions is an important aspect of the teacher's role. By making use of stimulating and challenging questions like Anthony does, teachers can use feedback and marking to further enrich children's vocabularies, increasing the range of powerful vocabulary which is literally at the pupil's fingertips.

 Concluding thoughts

This chapter has outlined the value of developing and enriching children's vocabularies. Nouns and verbs enable us to communicate, but through the addition of adjectives and adverbs, playing with word order and sentence structure and, importantly, understanding the function of the words selected in their work, children can become powerfully expressive writers. Language has the potential to make us laugh or cry, and everything in between. Children can learn to delight in using language deliberately to provoke a specific response in the reader. This is essential for all writers but for some children with language and literacy difficulties, the ability to express oneself in writing can provide a tool through which to communicate difficulties. For others it may widen the range of language at their disposal, helping to close the gap with their peers. Most of all, it gives children the skills to add vivid colours to the language they use. Stories are not enhanced simply with a range of naming and doing words. There is a limit to the number of ways to vary sentences based on subject-verb-object. Adding variety, however, makes the range of sentences limitless. For children who are challenged in any way, limitless power is a marvellous thing.

References

Adoniou, M. (2014) Drawing conclusions: what purpose do children's drawings serve? *Australian Art Education*, 36(1): 25–33.

Almond, D. (1998) *Skellig*. London: Hodder & Stoughton.

Bereiter, C. and Scardamalia, M. (1987) *The Psychology of Written Composition*. New York: Macmillan.

Department for Education (2013) *English Programmes of Study for Key Stages 1–2*. London: DfE.

Gibbons, P. (1993) *Learning to Learn in a Second Language*. Newtown, Australia: Heinemann.

Kress, G. (1994) *Learning to Write*. London: Routledge.

Llenas, A. (2016) *The Colour Monster*. London: Templar Books.

Pearson, K. and Thompson, G. (1996) Visual literacy: access for all. In E. Bearne (ed.), *Differentiation and Diversity*. Abingdon: Routledge, ch. 3.

9

L2 language acquisition in the classroom: perspectives, problems and children's lives

Elaine Lopez

 This chapter

The aim of this chapter is to help all people working with or supporting primary aged children to understand what language can realistically be learnt in a classroom, some of the problems that may arise through the course of this development as well as what is actually not a problem but rather a natural part of L2 language acquisition. Finally the chapter looks at the impact this may have on children's lives outside the classroom.

Languages and the National Curriculum

Foreign languages are now a compulsory subject at Key Stage 2 (age 7–11) in local-authority main-tained primary schools in England, as they form part of the National Curriculum. This also applies to pupils who speak English as an Additional Language (EAL) even though they may already speak two or more languages. The outcome of language learning at this stage is expected to be on 'practical com-munication' and teaching is not restricted to modern foreign languages: an ancient language may also be chosen. The National Curriculum document provides a list of expected outcomes which, for those with no background in bilingualism or second language (L2) acquisition, may be difficult to interpret in real terms. In addition, there are many issues surrounding support for and attainment of EAL pupils as they adapt to and integrate into English-medium education, which also relate to L2 acquisition.

I will do this by focusing on several areas of interest. When considering what language can be realisti-cally learnt, I will address the expectation that children make better language learners. I will explain the need to have realistic expectations of just how much language a child can be expected to learn in a school classroom, be they foreign language learners or EAL pupils. I will move on to explain some of the characteristics of L2 development including errors you may observe and whether these can be overcome, and how much exposure is required in order for a child to make real and measur-able progress. Some of the things you may observe are *not* a problem, such as *transfer*, where one of a child's existing languages may impact on/interfere with their use of another language, or when a child appears to be making very slow progress. In the final section, I will briefly touch on what happens outside the classroom in order to present a 'whole-life' perspective of L2 acquisition. Throughout the chapter, I will address what are sometimes two diverse perspectives. The first is children in a foreign language (FL) classroom, some of whom may have other needs around language and literacy devel-opment. The second perspective is EAL learners who need to improve their English proficiency in a timely manner in order to fully participate in, and benefit from, mainstream schooling.

Realistic expectations of language acquisition

L2 acquisition is incredibly complex because language itself is incredibly complex. It takes time and effort to learn a second language and the task may at times seem insurmountable, especially when compared to L1 acquisition that appears to take place effortlessly for the large number of chil-dren who display typical development. This part of the chapter will consider what expectations we should hold for children learning an L2, be that in the FL classroom or as EAL learners, as well as some of the reasons behind these expectations.

The widespread belief that children make better language learners is often attested to Lenneberg's (1967) observation that the brains of children are different to those of adults and therefore, after puberty, there is a rapid decline in the ability to respond to the physiological demands of language learning. He proposed the Critical Period Hypothesis (CPH), which suggested that children have a neurological advantage and that up to the age of puberty innate biological structures in the brain enable acquisition of the L1. When expanding this to L2 acquisition, Lenneberg stated that 'auto-matic acquisition from mere exposure to a given language seems to disappear [after puberty], and foreign languages have to be taught and learned through a conscious and labored effort. Foreign accents cannot be overcome easily after puberty' (Lenneberg, 1967, p.176).

The reality is more likely a 'sensitive period' during which language learning may be easier for younger children under the right conditions, and many researchers point out that evidence for the CPH is weak (Singleton, 1995; Marinova-Todd et al., 2000; among others). It also appears that there are several sensitive periods for different areas of acquisition such as pronunciation, grammar and morphology. In fact, older children and adults learn some aspects of language faster than young children due to their more advanced cognitive development and metalinguistic awareness. Singleton (1995) identifies what he calls a 'paradox' in the results of research in this area. For classroom-based learners (such as those in an FL classroom in an English primary school) there appears to be no benefit to an early start whereas for learners in a naturalistic setting (such as EAL learners) in most cases starting younger does indeed equate to a better outcome. A recent overview of research in this area by Muñoz and Singleton (2011) found that there are a multitude of factors which influence the ultimate attainment of L2 learners, be they children or adults, and not all of these can be explained by so-called 'maturation effects'. When it comes to realistic expectations of language learning for all children, they question whether Native Speaker-like proficiency is a relevant target, and point out that even very young L2 learners differ from their monolingual peers, most likely as the result of already speaking another language.

Foreign languages in the primary classroom

It is likely that the recent decision to introduce languages to the primary school curriculum was motivated by this belief that younger children make better language learners than adults. However, foreign language instruction is not compulsory at Key Stage (KS) 1 so the youngest primary-aged children are not required to learn a foreign language. The national curriculum document provides a list of attainment targets for language learning at KS2 (ages 7–11) and, as a researcher who has worked on second language acquisition for several years, some of these appear to be unrealistic giving the constraints on learning discussed in this section. One example is the target that children will be able to 'engage in conversations' and another is the target to 'develop accurate pronunciation and intonation' (Department for Education, 2013, p.2). I will return to these attainment targets later. An additional concern relates to the current provision of languages at primary level, as highlighted in the Language Trends survey. This is an annual assessment of language teaching and learning in primary and secondary schools in England, funded and managed by the British Council. According to the most recent survey (Tinsley and Board, 2016, p.8):

The principal challenges reported by primary schools are:

- Finding enough curriculum time to accommodate languages
- Improving the confidence of classroom teachers who teach languages
- Accessing professional training on a regular basis
- Recruiting suitably qualified teaching staff.

In the 2015/16 survey, only half of primary schools in England reported having access to specialist expertise on the teaching of languages, a statistic which suggests that the other half have not been able to access such expertise. This is a concern, since it is widely accepted that teachers need to have a certain level of proficiency in the target language in order to provide children with the high-quality exposure to language that is needed for them to develop an acceptable competence. Singleton (1995, p.162) points out that, at every stage of learning, input should be 'appropriately focused, appropriately abundant and appropriately enhanced'. Furthermore, in an overview of research into age effects in language learning, Marinova-Todd et al. (2000) conclude that:

> Investment in elementary foreign language instruction may well be worth it, but only if the teachers are themselves native or nativelike speakers and well trained in the needs of younger learners; if the early learning opportunities are built upon with consistent, well-planned, ongoing instruction in the higher grades; and if the learners are given some opportunities for authentic communicative experiences in the target language. (2000: 28-9)

As mentioned above, pronunciation and intonation are key measures of the National Curriculum, and in terms of age effects, this is one aspect of language that does appear to be more easily acquired by younger children. There are many instances of adults who have been resident in the UK for many years, speak English perfectly fluently, and yet retain their L1 accent because they arrived as older children or adults. The same phenomenon is observed with regional accents. Despite this tendency, there are issues both with expecting children to have 'accurate pronunciation and intonation' when they are only exposed to the target language for minimal amounts of time, and when that target language may come from a teacher who themselves is not an expert in the L2 (Tinsley and Board, 2016). There are also issues with EAL pupils in the FL classroom, who may already be acquiring the correct pronunciation of their L2 (English) then being measured on their pronunciation of a third language such as Spanish or French, as transfer of pronunciation is almost inevitable.

None of this is intended to suggest that languages should not be taught to primary-aged children. It is merely the intention to enable the reader to develop a realistic expectation of what level of language development is possible with short periods of exposure to the FL. This is particularly pertinent in light of some of the issues highlighted in this section. However, to finish on a positive note, academic research suggests that young language learners . . .

- have good phonological capabilities;

- have a strong instinct for interaction.

More generally they may . . .

- be less self-conscious;

- have a capacity to find fun in what they do;

- be given opportunities to develop understandings of other languages and cultures;

- develop positive attitudes towards multilingualism at an early age.

All of this suggests that introducing languages in primary schools is a good idea, as long as there is an awareness of the limitations and issues highlighted above.

Realistic expectations: English as an Additional Language

Of pupils in England 16.2% aged 5–16 were recorded as EAL in 2013 (Strand et al., 2015), and this percentage had almost doubled in just 15 years. In the primary sector, nearly one in five primary school children in England (19.4%) is classed as 'not having English as a first language' (Tinsley and Board, 2016, p.13). However, the distribution of EAL pupils is skewed as over half of schools have less than 5% EAL students, but approximately one in 12 schools have a majority of pupils with EAL (Strand et al., 2015). It is at primary level where the differences between the attainment of EAL pupils versus those with First Language English are most marked, as by aged 16 this difference is largely eliminated. Strand et al. note that the problems at primary level are unsurprising, since EAL children may begin school with markedly lower exposure to English than their L1 English-speaking peers. However, there are a number of additional risk factors, the most marked being EAL children who are identified SEN and those who arrive in the English education system during KS2.

One of the key issues for EAL children will be learning to read and write in English, and additional support in this area may be necessary. According to Bialystock (2001, p.152), there has been surprisingly little research into the literacy development of bilingual children, and she points out a number of differences between individual children that may impact on literacy. Much of this comes back to the child's two languages, and includes issues such as whether they are balanced (i.e. they have a similar level of proficiency in both English and their L1) or, more likely, unbalanced bilinguals, as well as their early exposure to text and whether both languages have the same or different scripts. For bilingual children, it is more common to learn to read in one language first and the second language later on (Baker, 2014), and this is certainly considered preferable when one of a child's languages is stronger. Furthermore, learning to read in an L2 is helped if a child is already literate in their L1, even when there are differences between the scripts (as for Arabic or Chinese speakers with L2 English). When there is a difference between scripts there will be less *transfer* of language (see below) but, as Baker points out, children can still transfer their knowledge that words carry meaning, or their ability to guess words and meaning based on the storyline, any pictures or their knowledge of the world. However, not all EAL children will begin school literate in their L1. Customs around learning to read differ between countries and cultures. It can be affected by the availability of age-appropriate books in a language although, as Baker (2014) explains, in some places children are simply not expected to begin to read until they start school.

In terms of L1 development, the home languages of EAL pupils formed a key part of the Language Trends survey (Tinsley and Board, 2016), since they are recognised by many schools as 'an important resource' (p.13). As exemplified in the survey, positive support comes in the form of allowing some use of home languages within the classroom, or providing encouragement and opportunities for pupils to reflect on their own multilingualism. Despite this recognition, active support for continued L1 development is less common within schools, and the majority of schools with high levels of EAL pupils have no involvement in teaching home languages. Therefore, a lack of development in the L1 will likely impact on the development of EAL learners' English, and this should be considered in terms of expectations towards these pupils. In terms of expectations towards practitioners, teachers and schools are encouraged to celebrate linguistic diversity while many simultaneously lack the linguistic support or training that is needed to make this a reality. Safford and Drury (2013) report on surveys with new teachers who state feeling underprepared for dealing with bilingual pupils, and who are (justifiably) concerned about assessment of these pupils. They suggest that a monolingual curriculum and assessment structure problematises the many bilingual learners in English schools, as do policies which make it difficult for teachers to distinguish needs related to language learning from specific physical and cognitive needs.

Language development takes time, but it is also important to recognise that different genres and registers of English may be acquired at different rates. This could, potentially, lead to situations where EAL pupils have learnt the informal, social language necessary to communicate fluently with their peers but still struggle with assessment and using the more formal discourse required in class. Baker (2014, p.153) makes a distinction between 'conversational language and classroom language', and explains that a different type of competence is required in order for students to be successful in the classroom. This is partly due to the complex language used when explaining key concepts, which is something that teachers should consider in terms of their own expectations of EAL pupils. In addition, Lightbown (2000) explains that there can be a long period of time between the developmental stage where an L2 can be understood in social contexts and the stage where complex ideas conveyed in the second language can be understood.

To summarise, the expectations for FL and EAL learners are very different, principally due to the amount of exposure they have to the target language and their need (and therefore their motivation) to be able to use the new language. However, in both cases it is necessary for adults to have realistic expectations of how language and literacy develop in an L2, the impact of the school environment on this development, and the potential problems that may arise. The next section will consider this final point in more detail.

A perspective on L2 acquisition

In order to explain the expectations highlighted above, this section will detail some of the natural processes of L2 acquisition. It will touch on how or why these might occur, how they may manifest themselves in the language of the children you care for or work with, and why they do not require a solution (or cannot be solved). Many of the diverse and complex reasons for language and literacy delays introduced in other chapters of this book are magnified and intensified when these children are expected to engage in foreign language (FL) learning. As explained previously, L2 acquisition can be problematic, but these problems may be lessened if they are understood by those involved in the care and education of children. Furthermore, understanding the complexity of L2 acquisition will help you to see that some of the behaviours or learning patterns of children are not actually a problem, in the hope that this will lead to a more relaxed and enjoyable learning environment for all involved. This section will touch on just some of the insights which have emerged from research into L2 acquisition and which are of relevance to readers of this book.

Input

The amount of input, or exposure, that an L2 learner has to the target language is instrumental in determining how much language they will acquire. Input may be meaning-based, where the focus is on understanding the message, or form-based where the focus is on learning something about the language itself (such as its grammatical structure). Examples of form-based input are likely to be abundant in an FL classroom, but extra provision may be required in order to provide input about English to EAL learners. The quality of input is also important so that, while authentic examples of language are important, the input must be *comprehensible* (i.e. close enough to the learner's current level of understanding) in order to be of any benefit. One influential hypothesis by Krashen (1981) states that comprehensible input is that at 'i + 1', where 'i' is the learner's current level. This means that examples of the target language should be just slightly above the learner's current level in order to maximise the benefit. The implication is that both FL and EAL learners require exposure to abundant, high-quality examples of the target language that is just slightly above their current proficiency level if they are to improve. Therefore, placing an EAL learner in a classroom which is far beyond their current proficiency level and expecting them to naturalistically acquire a language is unrealistic. This also relates to the difference between conversational English and classroom English highlighted in the previous section. If the classroom English is too complex to be comprehensible then EAL pupils will not be able to make sense of it, nor acquire more language simply by being exposed to it. Safford and Drury (2013) point out that issues have arisen in English schools since the 1990s, when a policy shift led to bilingual learners being included in mainstream classrooms, due to what they call 'a strongly centralized, monolingual national curriculum and assessment system' (p.73). The method used for categorising newly arrived pupils according to 'native English speaker developmental norms' mean that bilingual children may be incorrectly labelled as underachievers since their L1 language knowledge and capabilities will not be measured.

A related area is output, which is the language produced by a learner. Many scholars believe that it is through using language or interacting with others that a learner is able to develop. Two speakers can *negotiate meaning* by checking comprehension, asking for clarification or modifying what they are saying in order to allow for successful communication, and so providing opportunities for all language learners (EAL or FL) to engage in such interactions is important.

Language transfer

As highlighted above, transfer is an important consideration when developing literacy in an L2. Language transfer affects all language learners at all levels of proficiency and cannot be avoided. It can occur at the level of grammar, vocabulary and/or pronunciation. It may be positive when transferring the structure or words of a language will facilitate the use of the new language. An example would be for Spanish-speaking learners of English and the use of the definite and indefinite articles (*a/an* and *the*). Both languages have a similar article structure; therefore, Spanish speakers will have an element of positive transfer. They are less likely to omit the articles and also less likely to use them wrongly as opposed to, say, Polish-speaking learners of English who have no articles in their L1. That is not to say that Spanish speakers will not have any problems with the English article system, just that transferring their L1 article system means that they will experience fewer problems than learners who have no article system to transfer.

However, transfer can also be negative, in that it hinders development of the L2 in the classroom and beyond. At the level of vocabulary, a popular example is the Spanish word *embarasada* that means *pregnant* and not *embarrassed*. This leads to the scenario of English speakers accidently claiming to be pregnant when they actually wish to express a sense of embarrassment. Transfer of lexical items such as this can be overcome relatively simply with some explicit correction, although they may reoccur when an L2 learner is tired, distracted or under some other sort of pressure. Transfer of grammatical items can be considerably harder to overcome, and there is very little that teachers can do about this.

Fossilisation

This is something you are unlikely to see among children learning a foreign language since they will be of relatively low proficiency. However, if you deal with EAL learners then you are likely to experience/observe the phenomenon of fossilisation as learners reach a higher level of proficiency in English. Fossilisation refers to an error which appears to be 'stuck' (or fossilised) and which no amount of exposure to the language, explicit instruction on this form or error correction seems able to overcome. For many years, the prominent explanation for fossilisation errors has been that second languages are represented differently in the mind than first or native languages. This relates in part to the Critical Period Hypothesis (see above) and the belief that adults or older children can never become native-like.

Recently, L2 acquisition research has become much more interested in, and able to measure, how language is accessed and used in real time. This growing body of research demonstrates that many of the previously held assumptions about L2 acquisition may in fact be oversimplifications. What we find is that, in some cases, a second language is represented correctly in the brain and errors that appear to have fossilised are actually related to what we call 'processing difficulties'. What this means in real terms is that when children of a high proficiency are using their second/additional language in real time they are unable to retrieve the information as quickly as they would their L1, possibly due to extra demands on their working memory, and therefore more errors occur. It is important to be understanding and sympathetic of this phenomenon, as there is often very little that an L2 learner can do to overcome it.

U-shaped development

Another phenomenon which you may encounter in classroom-based L2 learners is U-shaped development. More commonly talked about for young children acquiring their L1, this is when a learner may use a grammatical form correctly for a period, and then begin to use it incorrectly. As Lightbown (2000, p.444) explains, 'their apparently high level of accuracy, based on the use of memorised chunks, suddenly drops and then rises again as they come to create novel sentences.' The period of incorrect use may continue for some time, and can be a source of frustration for teachers since it appears that the learner has taken a step backwards. In fact, this incorrect usage is a sign that learners are beginning to analyse parts of a word or sentence. The classic example from L1 development is acquisition of the regular past tense in English. Initially, young children may use *went* since they have heard the word and are repeating it as an 'unanalysed chunk' of language. Once they begin to realise that the past tense is generally formed by adding -ed to the end of a word, the correct word *went* is replaced by the incorrect word *goed*. This is a sign that the child's language development is progressing and they are beginning to analyse and understand the language. This exact same example can appear in L2 development among EAL learners, depending on the stage. Other common examples include overuse of the do auxiliary as in *I don't can do it* and some unusual patterns of question formation.

There are many other phenomena that occur in L2 acquisition and are of relevance, but a detailed discussion of these is not possible within the space of this chapter. Any introductory-level textbook on L2 acquisition will be able to provide more details. In terms of primary-aged FL and EAL learners, these four areas were highlighted since they can be easily observed or, in the case of input, changed to make L2 acquisition easier for children. In terms of the previous section on realistic expectations, some level of understanding of acquisition processes, however basic, can help to ease pressure on language learners and may even turn the acquisition process into a source of fascination.

L2 acquisition and children's lives

Language development does not only occur in the classroom and so this final section will consider what support may benefit both FL and EAL learners outside of school.

FL learners only have minimal exposure to the target language in class time, and therefore anything that can be done to maximise the amount of input outside school will benefit their L2 development. This could take the form of after-school clubs, access to books in the L2, or even watching videos accessed for free over the Internet. For primary-aged children, watching their favourite cartoon in French, Spanish or German (or whatever other language they are learning) is generally an enjoyable and entertaining experience. It is not realistic to expect primary-aged children to become fluent speakers of the language in the time available, but encouraging a positive attitude to language learning outside of the classroom can help to maintain an overall positive attitude to multilingualism, which is important in the current climate of globalisation. Ideally, I would see this as the main aim of primary language learning, as there is very little evidence that the small amounts of exposure available in an FL setting will have long-term effects on children's L2 development. Problems may occur if children become anxious about their own development, especially when compared to their peers, and so additional support and reassurance may be required. A particularly problematic period is the transition from primary to secondary school when motivation for language learning is known to drop considerably, but with more research taking place in this area it is hoped that recommendations can be made to schools which will ease the transition and make this motivational drop less likely to occur.

For EAL children, this chapter has mainly discussed the development of their English, since the focus has been on acquisition *in* the classroom. However, much of children's lives occur outside the classroom, and for EAL learners it is necessary to also think about their native language(s). The current status of support for the home language in English primary schools was highlighted above. As we saw when discussing literacy development, it is important, if not critical, that the first language is maintained and, where possible, continues to grow and develop alongside the language of schooling. In addition, Conteh and Brock (2011, p.358) explain that bilingual learners need 'safe spaces' in order to be empowered and that this in turn will help them to develop into 'confident, successful learners and citizens'. Bilingualism has many benefits for cognition and, to name just a few examples, bilinguals are known to be better able to focus their attention and have better executive function, and recent research has even shown that as they age they are less likely to suffer from dementia or its onset may be delayed. In addition, there is the importance of maintaining contact with a child's culture and developing the first language in order for the child to communicate with their extended family or their parents who may not be proficient in English.

Many educators believe that there are benefits in making links between the teaching of the national language, the mother tongue (where this is different) and new languages being taught (Tinsley and Board, 2016, pp.13–14). Very occasionally, the complexities surrounding the linguistic development of bilingual/multilingual children are not recognised in classroom contexts, or when recognised they are seen as a disadvantage. In some extreme cases, the use of languages other than English outside school is actively discouraged, mostly because of a lack of understanding of what these complexities mean and how they can be overcome. According to Safford and Drury (2013), in the 'monolingual mindset', language learning and multilingualism are not always appreciated, and it may be left to the multilingual person, in this case the EAL child, to negotiate any gaps in culture or language. There is much that schools can do to assist children with this, and it is encouraging to see the examples of positive support for home languages which were highlighted in the most recent Language Trends survey (Tinsley and Board, 2016).

 ## Concluding thoughts

This chapter aimed to provide some insight which would help those working with/supporting primary-aged children to develop realistic expectations around what language can be learnt in a classroom. The chapter began with an introduction to some of the issues that may arise through the course of this development, such as a lack of exposure to the target language in an FL classroom, or exposing EAL learners to language which is too far beyond their current level of proficiency and therefore incomprehensible. Other issues raised in this book include lack of resources and suitably trained teachers, although looking through the past few years of the Language Trends survey there are signs that this is changing for the better. The second section provided the briefest of introductions to processes of L2 acquisition to help readers understand what is actually *not* a problem but rather a natural part of L2 language acquisition. The final section looked at L1 and L2 development outside the classroom, and the different considerations needed for FL and EAL learners.

The benefits of being bilingual far outweigh any of the problems or issues raised in this chapter, and so the intention is not to present L2 acquisition as a concern or problem that must be dealt with. Rather, by helping all those working with children, be they EAL learners or FL learners with language and literacy difficulties, to understand more about L2 acquisition and its complexity the aim is to make L2 acquisition less of a mystery or something to be feared so that the linguistic diversity of our primary classrooms can be encouraged and celebrated.

References

Baker, C. (2014) *A Parents' and Teachers' Guide to Bilingualism*, 4th edn. Bristol: Multilingual Matters.

Bialystock, E. (2001) *Bilingualism in Development: Language, Literacy, and Cognition*. Cambridge: Cambridge University Press.

Conteh, J. and Brock, A. (2011) 'Safe spaces'? Sites of bilingualism for young learners in home, school and community. *International Journal of Bilingual Education and Bilingualism*, 14(3): 347–60.

Department for Education (2013) *Languages Programmes of Study: Key Stage 2. National Curriculum in England.* Available at: **https://www.gov.uk/government/uploads/system/uploads/attachment_data/file/239042/PRIMARY_national_curriculum_-_Languages.pdf** (accessed 20 June 2017).

Krashen, S. (1981) *SLA and Second Language Learning*. Oxford: Pergamon.

Lenneberg, E.H. (1967) *Biological Foundations of Language*. New York: Wiley.

Lightbown, P. (2000) Anniversary article. Classroom SLA research and second language teaching. *Applied Linguistics*, 21(4): 431–62.

Marinova-Todd, S.H., Marshall, D.B. and Snow, C. (2000) Three misconceptions about age and L2 learning. *TESOL Quarterly*, 34(1): 9–34.

Muñoz, C. and Singleton, D. (2011) A critical review of age-related research on L2 ultimate attainment. *Language Teaching*, 44(1): 1–35.

Safford, K. and Drury, R. (2013) The 'problem' of bilingual children in educational settings: policy and research in England. *Language and Education*, 27(1): 70–81.

Singleton, D. (1995) Second language in primary school: the age dimension. *The Irish Yearbook of Applied Linguistics*, 15: 155–66.

Strand, S., Malmberg, L. and Hall, J. (2015) *English as an Additional Language (EAL) and Educational Achievement in England: An Analysis of the National Pupil Database*. Available at: **https://v1.education endowmentfoundation.org.uk/uploads/pdf/EAL_and_educational_achievement2.pdf** (accessed 12 June 2017).

Tinsley, T. and Board, K. (2016) *Language Trends 2015/16: The State of Language Learning in Primary and Secondary Schools in England*. Available at: **https://www.britishcouncil.org/sites/default/files/language_trends_survey_2016_0.pdf** (accessed 20 June 2017).

Further reading

One chapter cannot cover everything about this complex issue and therefore the following book and online resource are recommended as accessible introductions and guides to those who wish to further explore the topic.

Baker, C. (2014) *A Parents' and Teachers' Guide to Bilingualism*, 4th edn. Bristol: Multilingual Matters.

Bilingualism Matters provides training, advice and information on child bilingualism to anyone interested in or involved with raising, educating and caring for bilingual and multilingual children – see:

www.bilingualism-matters.ppls.ed.ac.uk

10
Using multicultural narratives to explore loss and grief

Kulwinder Maude

 This chapter

This chapter will explore literacy development of refugee and asylum-seeker children from a range of ethnic groups who may have experienced loss and grief due to various reasons and how we can support them both in their own and their new cultural settings. Types of losses experienced by primary-aged children will be discussed and how they might appear to cope with them. There will be a discussion about how, through the use of multicultural literature, teachers in primary schools can help such children deal with the pain of loss and grief along with rebuilding their lives in the new culture. Finally a framework for working with a chosen few multicultural texts will be shared. Milton (2004) defines a loss as when anything that is valued or anyone we are attached to is removed from our lives. Grief is the process by which we adjust to living with a significant loss – it is the pain of 'letting go'. In the context of refugee and asylum-seeker children, this loss can be compounded due to the extreme confusion or urgency with which they might find their circumstances changed or changing.

Who are refugee children?

> *Refugee children are ordinary children in extraordinary circumstances.*
>
> (Hope, 2008)

UNHCR's founding mandate defines refugees as people who are outside their country and cannot return owing to a well-founded fear of persecution because of their race, religion, nationality, political opinion or membership of a particular social group. When people flee their own country and seek sanctuary in another state, they often have to apply for 'asylum' – the right to be recognised as bona fide refugees and receive legal protection and material assistance. Studies (Völkl-Kernstock et al., 2014) have revealed that often the most vulnerable war victims, children, are at increased risk of developing mental health problems if not supported appropriately, in addition to lack of formal school education which many children in the Western world may take as a given.

Loss and grief in childhood experienced in migration (forced or otherwise)

Refugee and asylum-seeker children often experience the loss of people, places, pets and possessions throughout their lives as the dependants of migrant parents or carers (although some children have become unaccompanied minors as well; Völkl-Kernstock et al., 2014). Gilbert (2008) has coined the term Third Culture Kids (TCKs) for children who accompany their parents to live all or part of their childhood outside the country for which they hold a passport (Pollock and Van Reken, 1999; Useem, 1993). This term might equally apply to asylum-seeking and refugee children who are currently in primary schools in the UK. As many of them have had to leave their countries of birth without prior warning or consent, often there is a sense of loss and grief involved with this sudden loss of normalcy. This is very commonly reported as a lingering concern among adult TCKs, that is adults who were TCKs as children (Barringer, 2000; Cockburn, 2002; Pollock and Van Reken, 1999; Schaetti, 2002). Many of the attributes that particularly characterise TCKs — prolonged adolescence, feelings of rootlessness, alienation and inability to make commitments (Barringer, 2000) – can be tied to unresolved grief issues (Schaetti, 2002). This is where schools have an important part to play in creating *safe and normal* spaces where children can process their grief and rebuild their lives with renewed enthusiasm and hope for the future. Primary school teachers are in an ideal situation to support children who may be experiencing loss and grief due to circumstances beyond their control and to prepare all children for future (eventual) experiences of loss.

Before going any further, it is important to address the unique characteristics of children's grief that may complicate the ability of adults to recognise and respond to the needs of such children. In general, grief centres on the process of making sense of a loss, regardless of the age and developmental stage of the individual (Silverman, 2000). Each child makes sense of a loss in the context of his or her developmental stage and related capabilities (Oltjenbruns, 2007; Silverman, 2000), and the child may 'regrieve' the loss as he or she moves through new developmental stages and has a new appreciation for what exactly was lost, especially if the situation in their own homeland (in the case of refugee children) is changing on a day-to-day basis for a prolonged period (Oltjenbruns, 2001).

Children's grief often does not look like adult grief (Oltjenbruns, 2007; Sekar and Katz, 1986), and adults (teachers and carers) may not recognise that the child is grieving. In the classroom, on a day-to-day basis, children may appear to lack feelings about the loss, but it may be that they feel overwhelmed by their grief and shut down emotionally in response (Wolfert, 1983). Adults may minimise the seriousness of the loss, or they may ignore or disparage the child's response (Crenshaw, 2002), thus marginalising the grief experience of the child. On the other hand, parents/carers and teachers may recognise the child's grief, and may try to protect the child from the pain of loss by encouraging them to focus on the positive or by keeping them away from the experiences that serve as reminders of the loss. The result may be that the children feel isolated in what may seem to be overwhelming and unnerving emotions (Oltjenbruns, 2001). Such feelings, if unresolved, can affect the future development of refugee children. Those that have an immediate complicating effect are the fact that losses often are hidden and, being hidden, are not acknowledged; they experience a lack of permission to grieve and a lack of time to process the loss; and finally, a lack of comfort may be offered to the children as they attempt to deal with their losses. Although individual situations and stories may vary for refugee children, they may feel a sense of responsibility toward their parents/carers and may hide their feelings from adults (Pollock and Van Reken, 1999). They may deny and/or suppress emotions related to loss, potentially leading to later complications (Oltjenbruns, 2007). Many of the losses experienced, particularly those that are hidden, are ambiguous. *Ambiguous losses* are those that lack clarity and can lead to sharply different assessments of exactly who or what has been lost (Boss, 2004, in Gilbert, 2008). Often the children are too young to make sense of what exactly happened before they left home (city or country of birth). With uncertainty or lack of awareness about how to respond, teachers in the classroom may respond in a way that does not meet the needs of the griever (Gilbert, 1996). This, combined with a lack of knowledge about the nature of children's grief, increases the likelihood that children will not receive the support they need, thus complicating their grief.

The grief experienced by refugee children clearly has characteristics of disenfranchised grief (Doka, 2002; Schaetti, 2002). Their socially ambiguous losses may not be openly mourned or socially supported. Essentially, this is grief that is restricted by 'grieving rules' ascribed by the new culture and society in which they may find themselves piecing their lives together on a day-to-day basis.

Often refugee children change schools as they move from one local authority to another. It may be further compounded by the grief that results from the loss of trust in the availability of adults to be sensitive to their emotions. Losses that are not successfully resolved in childhood have an increased likelihood of recurring in adulthood. Thus, how losses and the resulting grief are dealt with continue to influence the lives of refugee children into adulthood (Gilbert, 2008).

Before we discuss different types of loss and grief any further, let us consider what it might look like in a typical primary classroom.

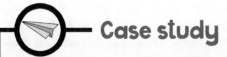

Case study

Fleeing from the trauma of civil war

Noor is seven years old and managed to escape from Syria where the civil war has been raging for some time. He came to the UK with his mother and a younger brother, Salim, aged five, along with some other extended family members. Noor's elder brother was killed in the bombing in Aleppo, which Noor had witnessed. Naturally, he is traumatised by this event. His father stayed behind to find a safe passage for Noor's grandparents. Due to the unrest it is very difficult for his father to stay in touch with regular information about his well-being. This causes a lot of anxiety for Noor's mother which Noor shares as well. None of the family members who came to England speak any English; their native language is Arabic. Noor and his younger brother attend local schools, but Noor attends the junior school and Salim attends the infant school. Since the schools are on separate campuses, Noor and Salim don't get to see each other.

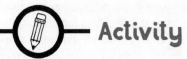

Activity

Make a list of some of the main areas where Noor would need support. Here are some suggestions:

- During 'Circle Time', which is used in many primary schools to facilitate PSHE (personal, social, health and economic education) related issues, use the 'Seeking Safety' activity booklet available for free download on https://www.amnesty.org.uk/files/activities_-_seeking_safety.pdf. Use this to highlight discussion around Noor's situation inviting him to contribute if he feels comfortable. It is important that you share your intentions for the activity with the child beforehand.

- Get in touch with any Arabic-speaking staff members if possible or involve other parents or the wider community to arrange for interpretation so that the parents and refugee children know what is expected of them. Aim to collect as much information about the family as possible.

- Refugee children may be in need of psychological support before they are fully ready to concentrate on their schoolwork. Speak to the SENCo to arrange support.

- Arrange a buddy within the class with an Arabic-speaking child, if possible, to help with school routines and make friends initially.

- Offer time and support right from the start to develop a trusting relationship with the child. Gradually, if the child wishes to share, listen and acknowledge the traumatic experiences that the child has been through.

- Use children's literature to establish a shared understanding, raise awareness and stimulate discussion within the classroom. The role of multicultural literature in raising awareness will be discussed in detail later in the chapter as well.

Types of loss and grief

Disenfranchised grief

As we age, we may experience a range of losses as we make the transition to another developmental period. These losses can be profound as we move to later life, but can even be significant as we give up childhood activities and toys to embrace the responsibilities of adolescence and emerging adulthood. This takes on a new dimension in the case of refugee children, who may have to suddenly grow up or take additional responsibilities due to changes in circumstances. *Self-disenfranchisement* (Gilbert, 2008) can also be seen, particularly when it is related to a parent's/carer's financial situation or mental health in the new environment. Evidence exists to suggest that the process of grieving is more easily resolved if those grieving have the opportunity to discuss events and their feelings (Gilbert, 1996). Contrary to this, refugee children may feel comfortable growing up, not focusing on loss and keeping their feelings to themselves. In such circumstances, as well as being good listeners and good communicators, teachers need to be able to use the language of loss, grief and death easily and naturally. With multicultural classrooms, the children will be members of families with a range of different religious beliefs and cultural practices regarding loss and grief. Milton (2004) suggests that rather than be fearful of this, teachers can use this to their advantage by enlisting parental help and exploring these cultural and religious differences together thus developing more understanding of each other.

Loss of persons

Refugee children may have experienced the deaths of family members, including both in the immediate and extended family. The death of a parent is an already devastating loss, and it may compound their sense of loss, because it often results in an end to a familiar lifestyle or a move to a country that may seem alien compared to the country in which they had been living. Some children may have experienced or witnessed the deaths of friends, caregivers and other adults in their lives. Although they may not have known the individuals involved, it may be that refugee and asylum-seeking children have had the experience of surviving a coup and seeing dead bodies and, in some cases, witnessing executions. In most cases, their grief becomes disenfranchised. There may be other losses as a result of high mobility of the peer network. In the UK, The Immigration and Asylum Act 1999 introduced a policy of dispersal that compels asylum seekers to move to different parts of the country if they wish to receive support with accommodation. This means that asylum seekers' lives can be characterised by periodical displacement within the UK as a result of migration policies rather than choice (Bourgonje, 2010). Although it may be easier to make use of the Internet to stay in contact with friends, they may miss the easy, relaxed camaraderie of close physical proximity. Over time, children may learn to adapt to the loss of friends as a normal part of their life. But initially they would need support and a listening ear in order to adapt to the new cultural and educational settings.

Loss of places

Moving away from their home country or place of birth is a commonly cited loss by refugee and asylum-seeking children. Often these children have the challenge of adjusting to adverse events in the past while forging important emotional, social and intellectual developmental trajectories in a new setting (Reed et al., 2012). The smells, tastes, cultural rituals and site-specific opportunities in addition to the physical aspects of the country – geography and climate – are often cited as missing (Gilbert, 2008) in their lives, especially, if there are no warnings of an impending move. The loss becomes compounded in most extreme situations, for example emergency evacuation because the situation has become too dangerous and potentially life-threatening. In addition to this, they can be burdened with challenges that include altered family dynamics, such as assuming the role of carer for younger siblings or psychologically and physically injured parents. Children who resettle across international borders often combine these tasks while managing a new language, education system and culture, typically in difficult economic and legal circumstances (Eisenbruch, 1988). Leaving one school and moving to another can be a significant loss as well. In addition to struggling with a different curriculum, the change in school means the loss of the support network in the form of friends and even the one-to-one support provided by additional adults etc. linked with that place.

Lost opportunities can often be tied to specific places, either where they (refugee children) were or where they wished they were. Older children may feel the loss of exposure to culture in the form of TV shows, museums and performance venues that may be available in their home country. This has an impact on the extent to which refugee children can be a part of the popular culture in the host country. A high degree of displacement during the younger years can manifest itself as a sense of detachment from places. In extreme situations, children may feel no intimate connection with any particular place.

Case study

Sharing experiences of children's homes

Amanullah (a refugee child from Afghanistan) enjoyed the guided reading session that involved collecting information about sandstorms and river systems in the deserts as a part of reading comprehension in Year 6. He had spent his initial years in the mountains of Afghanistan before his family was granted asylum in the UK. His eyes lit up as he shared his memories of taking shelter in the shops to avoid the sandstorms in the late afternoons and later taking a dip in the nearby river. He remembered the names of all his friends who used to jump in the river with him. He was sad that he might never see them again due to the conflict in Afghanistan. However, sharing his memories and experiences with his classmates in England surely added to the development of camaraderie and social networks that children build in their schooling years.

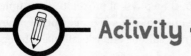

Activity

Read the case study above and think about the following:

- How could school help Amanullah familiarise with popular culture in the host country?
- How could teachers capitalise on the wider experiences of the refugee children through cross-curricular teaching and learning? Think about individual subjects that might facilitate the exchange.

Loss of pets

Grief over the loss of pets can be a source of unrest for children who may have been attached to them before leaving them behind. For those for whom pets were meaningful parts of their lives, the loss of these animals can be quite painful. This can be particularly true when the animal serves the role of friend or companion to the child. As a teacher, it is important to be mindful of such feelings and provide opportunities within the classroom to bring these feelings to the surface, maybe through discussions (picture books) or debates about why and how to look after pets.

Loss of possessions

Refugee children remain at increased risk of developing mental health difficulties due to the traumatic experiences and multiple losses which the majority of these children have suffered (Hodes, 1998; Rousseau, 1995, in Ehntholt et al., 2005). Among the various losses which will be incurred, although possessions may hold less meaning for adults at times of extreme conflict, personal possessions are generally precious to young children, especially if there is a danger of having to choose what they can take when leaving home, forever in most cases. Refugee children may be attached to a range of objects: articles of clothing, toys, books, blankets, jewellery, dishware, decorative hangings and artwork and photographs to name a few. Hence it is important to be mindful that from the point of view of refugee children, the institution (school, fellow classmates, other professionals) has everything – a fixed place in society, a voice, status, money, etc. – which has been lost to them (Summerfield, 2000).

Existential losses

Existential losses involve the loss of security in knowing that what they have thought of as real is actually reflective of reality (Janoff-Bulman, 1992), that is that the world they knew up to this point as reliable and predictable will continue to be so. For refugee and asylum-seeking children, this may include the belief, built over time, that relationships are fluid, that nothing stays the same and that the ability to adapt to change is highly valued in the adult world. Following a loss, meaning must be attributed in such a way as to allow the individual to regain a sense of order, control and purpose in life (Gilbert, 1996). Teachers in school can help in the process of empowerment by arranging for interventions (short and long term) that would help children regain control and power over their circumstances. Initial assessments and support structures need to take account of factors such as values and beliefs in the countries of origin, the personal cultural values of the children, the varying environments and experiences during different stages of migration, as well as the legal status of family members. Such information can be gathered during initial interviews with refugee families in the first few weeks of children joining school.

Loss of a safe and trustworthy world

A common belief is that children need to feel secure in their lives and their relationships in order to function and develop well (Erikson, 1963). One aspect of a secure attachment to one's assumptive world is a sense that the world is safe and trustworthy. Refugee children share the painful loss of home and separation from culture with other immigrant children. However, what is potently different in the case of refugee and asylum-seeking children is the assault on the human psyche and the loss of lives and entire social communities, resulting in the loss of trust and safety (Falicov, 2002).

Case study

Understanding children's feelings of loss of security

I left all my friends, everyone behind! left alone here.

(Abdi, a ten-year-old refugee child talking about his friends in school in Syria)

Abdi's friends, who had been close, had become estranged or simply stopped corresponding and essentially disappeared from his life once he had moved to England. Although he described efforts to maintain contact especially with his elder brothers in the extended family, he also described himself as having become aloof and cautious about forming relationships in the school and the community in England. He spent most of his time helping the teachers and hardly went out to play during playtime. The most common loss that relates to safety and trust is the one related to trust in a social setting – the loss of a sense of belonging. Although this feeling of loss is more common when children make the transition from primary to secondary school, it could happen when children try to make friends in new surroundings. In addition to that, his feelings were essentially raw as his family had witnessed a political coup of which he had a mixed understanding, followed by riots as a part of the disruption in his home country. He said some of his family members had seen dead bodies in the streets and witnessed murder. He became quite emotional in describing his fears as his parents and other extended family members attempted to do what they could to keep the families safe. He used terms like 'bloody', 'terrifying' and 'horrible' in an attempt to describe what he had gone through.

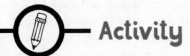

Activity

Reading this case study, discuss the following questions:

- How could you help Abdi rediscover a sense of normality and belonging?
- How could you encourage Abdi to talk about his experiences with a view to encouraging other children to talk about their losses as well?

Loss: 'Who I thought I was'

If refugee children go through primary school without adequate support in developing self-esteem and social networks, there is a danger that they can experience a delayed adolescence in which they deal with the issue of identity long after one would normally expect it to be resolved (Schaetti, 2002;

Useem and Cottrell, 1996). Gilbert (2008) highlights that such children can be highly adaptable in taking on the appearance and accent of indigenous children, but missing the fine details of life of what they may see as an alien world. Here teachers and additional adults can help by building meaningful relationships with refugee children aimed at mentoring them into the dominant culture both inside and outside school.

Fantino and Colak (2001) highlight uprooting, disruption and insecurity as the by-products of migration affecting the psychological and social development of refugee children. This makes the process of identity formation a more difficult balancing act between two or more sets of cultural notions and values. We often hear 'children adapt quickly'. Perhaps we should ask: 'To what? In relation to whom? At what price?'

 Case study

Understanding possible selves and aspirations

Abdi started primary school with a temporary asylum certificate that presented him as younger than he actually was. He had finally been granted asylum in England after living with his aunt in Ethiopia in order to save him from the civil war in Somalia. In ideal circumstances, he should have been in a secondary school, but due to some confusion with his paperwork he was offered a place in Year 6 instead. Abdi was extremely keen to learn English and wanted to become either a pilot or a footballer. He developed a close relationship with the teaching assistant who used to work with him learning English. He often asked for additional homework and would often stay in class helping her out with classroom chores and practising his spoken English when other children were not around. Abdi would often speak about his formative years in Somalia and later Ethiopia where he looked after his aunt's land and shops along with his uncle. Often nostalgic, he compared his experiences in both worlds and longed to become a footballer so that he could help his country and community, just like other celebrity footballers such as Ronaldo. The teaching assistant, realising his potential and innate desire to learn, started arranging for extra homework for maths and English so that Abdi would be better prepared for the secondary school.

 Activity

Reading this case study, think about the following as a teacher:

- How could you encourage Abdi to feel a part of the classroom community and make friends?
- How could you value his experiences and include him in the curriculum?
- Bolloten and Spafford (1998, p.109) state that 'Raising awareness of what it means to be a refugee ... is a vital step in understanding the needs of refugee children.' Discuss how that could be achieved.

Loss of a place they can call home

This loss is related to the loss of security in their personal identity. Young refugee children are often not able to verbalise their struggle through childhood to define home. So, rather than thinking of the loss of home, they relate better to the concept of experiencing grief at the recognition that home (as they knew it) is somehow absent from their lives (Gilbert, 2008). As a society we place much emphasis on the individual, making the refugee family and their history almost invisible. Refugee children become children without a history. As a result, when helpers and practitioners analyse the behaviour of a refugee child out of context, there is a tendency to *pathologise* that behaviour (Fantino and Colak, 2001). Many ordinary cultural practices of refugee families are often misunderstood in our classrooms, hospitals, social services and social life.

 **Case study**

Language and the settling in process

When Noor first came to the UK, for the first few weeks at school, he did not want to speak about his home in Aleppo. Gradually he started talking a little about how his mother is worried about his father and the rest of the family. One could clearly see the nostalgia in his eyes as he spoke about his childhood days spent there without the fear of bombs dropping overhead. It was never a straightforward sentence, rather a glimpse of a rainbow as he drew a picture of a house in a reading session.

> I can jump to the terrace of my friend's house from our rooftop, Miss! You can't do that here.

He missed his elder brother who was killed in the bombing. Initially, Noor did not want to talk, draw or remember the war, his brother or his former home. He only wanted to draw butterflies and happy faces. Questions about the future and memories of the past were selectively put out of mind. He had nightmares that kept him terrified for days and changed the expression on his face. While his mother dealt with her own illness and losses, Noor was placed in a position that seemed to overwhelm him. Between his practical duties of taking care of his younger brother, learning a new language, adapting to a new culture and worrying about the future, he had neither the time nor energy to grieve. Activities and social connections outside the family were limited because of the family's recent arrival and language barriers. Since the teacher started showing genuine interest in Noor by encouraging him to talk to her about his home, Noor started expressing a sense of relief and optimism that was evident in his behaviour and progress at school.

 **Activity**

Reading this case study, think about the following:

1. How could schools/teachers influence the welcome that refugee children receive in the host community/country?

2. What are some of the key factors that influence the adaptation of refugee children as compared to immigrant children? Think about mental and physical trauma, mourning of losses incurred, homesickness etc.

Role of multicultural literature in supporting refugee children in school

Multicultural literature focuses on people of colour from diverse cultural, linguistic and religious groups (Canales et al., 2002, in Boles, 2006). Hefflin and Barksdale-Ladd (2001) discuss the importance of children relating to characters and situations found in books reflective of their own culture. This longing for a sense of belonging is more potent in refugee children. Here multicultural literature can provide children with a sense of affirmation about themselves and their culture (Colby and Lyon, 2004). In the Western system of education, children are often encouraged to make personal connections with what they are reading so it is important for refugee children to be able to see themselves and situations that they can relate to. Carefully selected multicultural literature can be used to create a classroom where all children are valued (Colby and Lyon, 2004). Since reading is so personal, teachers need to examine the literature available to students. Colby and Lyon (2004) further emphasise that children need to receive affirmation of themselves and their culture through literature (Bieger, 1995/6), and be able to connect text to self in order to promote greater meaning (Dietrich and Ralph, 1995; Keene and Zimmerman, 1997; Rosenblatt, 1978).

For younger refugee children, teachers can use multicultural literature to encourage the development of vocabulary, stimulate the imagination, facilitate empathy, increase knowledge of one's own heritage and foster positive self-concepts and identity (Taylor, 1997, in Boles 2006).

Ford et al. (1999) identified six main goals of multicultural literature:

1. Increase in sense of self-worth and a sense that they have a chance for a successful future.

2. Achieve educational equity which has three basic conditions:

    (a) an equal opportunity to learn;

    (b) positive educational outcomes for both individuals and groups; and

(c) equal physical and financial conditions for students to grow to their fullest potential cognitively, academically and affectively.

3. Support cultural pluralism by helping children develop understanding and respect for people who are different from them.

4. Create a sense of empowerment in children so that they become independent learners and feel empowered to take an active role in improving the lives of others.

5. Work in groups in harmony by providing knowledge and skills to prepare children to work with members of their own and other cultural groups.

6. Teaching from a multicultural perspective, challenge assumptions and stereotypes starting with the classroom. For example, teachers need to select literature that does not promote stereotypical perspectives.

(Adapted from Ford et al., 1999)

Choosing multicultural literature

When choosing books for refugee children, it is important to make sure that the themes selected are relatable to the experiences of such children (Meier, 2003). Canales et al. (2002) highlight that the selected texts should represent authentic experiences portrayed in a true-to-life and balanced manner; be consistent with the values, beliefs, customs, traditions, needs and conflicts of the specific culture; be free of stereotypes in language, illustrations, behaviour and character traits; and finally the language used must show sensitivity to the culture.

Drama is a classic area where emotions such as empathy can be given maximum exposure, and the works of Day (2002) and Watts (2004) demonstrate the strengths as well as the limitations of confronting refugee issues through the medium of drama. Hope (2008) highlights that other subject areas, such as art and music, can be used as backdrops for generating conversations which can empower refugee children. The links with history and geography are also clear, but also whole-school initiatives, such as Refugee Week, can exploit the tremendous educative potential of books, giving them the context for discussion to have maximum impact. However, there is a danger of the focus being lost after the Refugee Week.

Strategies for teaching multicultural literature

Engagement with multicultural literature should be focused on making reading fun as well as generating thoughtful insights. Meier (2003) suggests a good starting point can be teaching book reading behaviours explicitly by asking questions, the answers to which are found directly in the text. Teachers can go further by making books come alive for refugee children through the use of props, for example dolls and puppets to act stories out in the class. This helps children form powerful attachments to the literature (Meier, 2003).

Children in primary schools should be introduced to multicultural texts consciously instead of simply exposing them to literature. It can be argued that English lessons are the obvious vehicle for the introduction of children's literature about the refugee experience and Habib (2008) discusses the importance of choosing class texts of contemporary relevance not only in English but other cross-curricular subjects as well. Kruse (2001) proposes that introducing a text implies that you are establishing an acquaintance with that text, along with a possibility that further dialogue will ensue, suggesting pleasant and sustained engagements with diversity. However, stories about refugee experiences may not always be pleasant. Hence, it requires a commitment on the part of the teachers to normalise the discourse, however unpleasant. Encouraging children to make connections with the refugee literature and apply the lessons learnt to their everyday lives would help to routinise the use of multicultural texts in the classroom. Finally, it is significant that teachers do not simply tell a story or experience but take the time to discuss what children have read, as with any good piece of literature.

Examples of how teachers can use refugee literature in class through sample texts

In this section, we shall look at four examples of multicultural children's literature that can be used to highlight the narratives of young refugee lives. Along with the individual texts, a framework for working with refugee literature is also shared.

Case study

Here I Am by Patti Kim

This is a picture book (suitable for all ages) illustrating the trials and trepidations experienced by a young boy who arrives in a strange land where he doesn't understand the language or the customs. The weather is cold and wet and he misses his home. Gradually he begins to make new friends and finds that not everything in the new country is disagreeable. He eventually settles into his new life and feels comfortable in his new home.

Activity

- Make a list of what you would pack if you had just a little time. What would you miss? What would it be like to be forced to leave home suddenly?

- Create a Welcome Pack focusing on what could help make a refugee child feel more comfortable and less scared in his/her new home.

- With older children, make a collage explaining what 'refugee' means – someone who is forced to flee their home because they fear they will lose their lives or freedom if they stay.

- Together using drama, imagine arriving in a new country without knowing the language or customs. Help the children 'walk in the shoes' of a refugee child by asking:

  – What would it be like to have to leave home quickly and suddenly?

  – What would you pack if you had just a little time? (Many refugees leave their homes with little warning and cannot even bring basic necessities.)

- What would you miss?
- How would you feel?
- What could help make a refugee feel more comfortable and less scared in their new home?

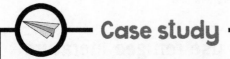

Case study

Azzi in Between by Sarah Garland

This is a thoroughly absorbing tale of a little girl called Azzi who comes to a new country with her parents as a refugee. The excitement of coming to England is overshadowed by the sadness incurred as a result of having to leave Grandma behind in the war zone. Through her incredible resourcefulness and sheer tenacity, we see Azzi not only survive but thrive in her new world.

This book is suitable for both Key Stage 1 and 2.

Activity

- Explore feelings from different perspectives. For example, compare 'feelings' in the story before and after the arrival of Grandma using the *colour, expression and body posture* in the illustrations as cues. Write a diary extract from the perspective of Azzi or Grandma.

- In order to develop visual literacy, sequence the jumbled pictures from a section of the story. You can differentiate by asking children to match the illustrations to the text first. Different groups work on different parts of the story. Once finished, the children present their sequences and give reasons for their decisions and predictions for the next part of the story.

- Perform a role-play – prepare short dialogues to rehearse between pairs where one is Azzi and the other is the teacher in the new school. You can prepare dialogues during a guided reading sessions beforehand.

- Children can create a comic that shows the journey from their birth country to a country of their choice. Their finished work should show an understanding of shot types, colour and composition used in comics and film. In *Azzi in Between*, Sabeen's and Grandma's stories in particular can be used as inspiration.

Other literature case studies

Case studies

Oranges in No Man's Land and A Little Piece of Ground by Elizabeth Laird

These two novels are suitable for Key Stage 2 as they introduce children to the desperately coura-geous lives of children growing up in war zones. These texts serve as a powerful means of giving children living in the Western world opportunities to walk in the shoes of similar young children (likely to become refugees) who frantically try to live a normal life among the horrors of war in the cities of Beirut (Lebanon) and Ramallah (Palestine) respectively.

Oranges in No Man's Land

Ayesha is left alone to look after her two younger brothers when grandma falls ill. It's up to the brav-ery of little Ayesha to cross the checkpoint and venture into enemy territory in order to see Dr Leila.

A Little Piece of Ground

Like most 12-year-old boys, Karim dreams of being a champion footballer. Unfortunately, his life in Ramallah is severely hampered by the presence of Israeli troops and tanks. Despite the dangers, between curfews, Karim and his friends clear a patch of wasteland to use as a football pitch and sneak off to play whenever they can, but when the soldiers return, Karim finds himself trapped and in real danger.

Activities

Some activities linked with both these texts:

* Frame of comparison can be used during guided reading to explore the texts in detail.
* *Oranges in No Man's Land* was written in 2006. As a class, focus on how the situation has changed in modern-day Lebanon. Use pictures, maps and photographs to create a news report.
* When Ayesha crosses the Green Line to the other side of Beirut, Dr Leila allows her to dine in her house. But not everyone is happy about her being there. Imagine if Ayesha came to stay with your family. Write a story that portrays Ayesha seeking refuge in your house for a day. Would she be welcome? Would she get along with all of your family? Additionally, children could focus on writing recounts from the character's perspective.

- When Ayesha crosses the Green Line, she ensures that she remains quiet: she knows that if her accent is heard, they'll know where she's from. Do you know anywhere else in the world (or at school) where people have been judged by their accent? Discuss how it feels.

A Little Piece of Ground, another text by the same author, can be used for further discussion and raising awareness perhaps during book club sessions. Further information can be found at the following links:

- 3cenglishstudies.weebly.com/uploads/1/3/7/3/13739250/a_little_piece_of_ground_activities.pdf
- https://education4liberation.files.wordpress.com/2012/10/lpg-pack.pdf

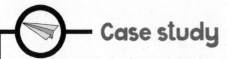 ── **Case study** ──

Alpha: Abidjan to Gare Du Nord *by Bessora Barroux (translated into English by Sarah Ardizzone)*

Alpha is a story of a young refugee who takes on the arduous journey of escaping from the horrors of everyday life in Abidjan (Ivory Coast) to seek a safer future in Europe. This is a powerful retelling of the horrors encountered by one refugee and how the human spirit triumphs through times of extreme desperation. This book is recommended for Upper Key Stage 2 where children should be able to empathise with human suffering caused as a result of the breakdown of civic society due to multiple reasons.

 ── **Activity** ──

- Use the following frame for comparison in order to explore the book in depth.
- In consultation with the children, choose a language of focus and work together to prepare a book of phrases. Don't emphasise what children would like to be able to say. Instead ask them to imagine what someone newly arrived in the area would like to hear. Imagine that the refugee is the same age as the children and has had a hard and possibly dangerous journey here.
- Focus on including emotional, practical and fun elements in the book. Children can work in groups to come up with phrases related to basic needs, entertainment and leisure, goods and services, or social opportunities. They could include questions – but also statements – of welcome, support, friendliness and concern, expressing interest, giving information and offering invitation.
- In preparing for secondary school, children in Year 6 can discuss a range of situations – from someone almost destitute to someone whose main problem is social isolation. Try to end up with a mini phrase book of useful and relevant material.

A framework for comparison of books for particular content

Table 10.1   Questions about the different features of (picture) books dealing with refugee stories

1. Cover

- What do you notice on the cover of the picture book?
- What are the most important features on the cover?
- What is the title of the book? What does this title mean to you?
- Has the book won any awards? Are they displayed on the cover?
- What colours dominate the cover design?
- What is in the foreground? What is in the background? What is the significance of the placement?
- Are there any visual images in the background to consider?
- What refugee clues (if any) are provided on the cover?

2. Representation of asylum seekers and refugees

- Are asylum seekers and/or refugees represented on the cover? How are they portrayed?
- Is the main character looking at you? How does this affect you?
- If the character is looking at you, what might he/she be demanding from you?
- Is the character looking away or at someone or something else? How does this affect you?
- Is this asylum seeker or refugee character a historical figure or fictional? How do you know?

3. Setting

- What setting is portrayed on the cover and other illustrations?
- Describe the setting in geographical terms, e.g. find its location on a map.
- When do you think this story is taking place?
- What visual and textual clues are provided on the cover, jacket and within the author's note?
- How is the setting important in the context of this picture book about refugees?
- How is colour, texture and motif used to represent the setting of the story?

4. Illustration style

- Are the illustrations realistic, folk art, surreal or impressionistic?
- How might the style of illustration add to the mood or theme of the book?
- How does the style contribute to the understanding of a refugee's experience?

5. End pages

- What do you notice about the end pages?
- Do the end pages contain a visual narrative?
- Do the end pages contribute to the visual continuity of the picture book?
- Do the end pages represent the story of refugees in any way?

(Continued)

Table 10.1 (Continued)

6. Book jacket (where book jackets are included)
• What information is contained in the front and back book jacket?
• How does the jacket information (if any) help to establish historical background information for the story?
• How does this information help you to understand the story?
• What clues are given about the historical facts (if any) and fictional aspects being presented?
7. Title page
• What information is included on the title page?
• Was a visual image included on the title page?
• Is the image within the story? If so, what is the significance?
• If the image is not within the story, what symbolic meaning does it hold?

Adapted from Dolan (2014).

A word of caution for teachers

While engaging with characters emerging from the war zones of the world, it is important to remember not to fall into the trap of reinforcing the stereotypical constructions that cast the war-torn regions as a place of ultimate violence, poverty, religious oppression and patriarchal tyranny. There is an urgent need to disrupt these generalisations, diversify thematic foci (not just war and political tyranny), and present young readers with heterogeneous characters and settings from all over the world.

 Concluding thoughts

We need to understand refugee children's traumas, journey, losses and assets with an alliance-building attitude or strategy of 'not knowing', creating an openness of inquiry that allows a co-construction of problems and building of therapeutic alliances. Through exploring various issues affecting refugee children's understanding of loss and grief, we offer hope and strategies to support such children in the classroom via multicultural narratives. Finally, it is important to remember to assure children that they are safe, and focus on positive ways to make a difference rather than on despair.

References

Barringer, C.F. (2000) *Counseling Third Culture Kids*. Paper presented at the Annual Conference of the American Counseling Association, San Antonio, TX. [Online]. Available: **www.eric.ed.gov ERIC #: ED451459**.

Bieger, E.M. (1995/1996) Promoting multicultural education through a literature-based approach. *Reading Teacher*, 49(4): 308–12.

Boles, M. (2006) The Effects of Multicultural Literature in the Classroom. Unpublished Senior Honors Thesis, University of Michigan, at **http://commons.emich.edu/honors/62**.

Bolloten, B. and Spafford, T. (1998) Supporting refugee children in East London primary schools. In J. Rutter and C. Jones (eds), *Refugee Education: Mapping the Field*. Staffordshire: Trentham.

Boss, P. (2004) Ambiguous loss. In F. Wash and M. McGoldrick (eds), *Living Beyond Loss: Death in the Family*, 2nd edn. New York: Norton, pp.237–46.

Bourgonje, P. (2010) *Education for Refugee and Asylum Seeking Children in OECD Countries: Case Studies from Australia, Spain, Sweden and the United Kingdom*. Brussels: Education International.

Canales, J., Lucido, F. and Salas, R.G. (2002) Multicultural Literature: Broadening Young Children's Experiences. In *Early Childhood Literacy: Programs and Strategies to Develop Cultural, Linguistic, Scientific and Healthcare Literacy for Very Young Children and Their Families, 2001 Yearbook*. Corpus Christi, TX: Texas A & M University.

Cockburn, L. (2002) Children and young people living in changing worlds: the process of assessing and understanding the 'Third Culture Kid'. *School Psychology International*, 23: 475–85.

Colby, S. and Lyon, A. (2004) Heightening awareness about the importance of using multicultural literature. *Multicultural Education*, Spring, pp.24–8.

Crenshaw, D.A. (2002) The disenfranchised grief of children. In K.J. Doka (ed.), *Disenfranchised Grief: New Directions, Challenges, and Strategies for Practice*. Champaign, IL: Research Press, pp.293–306.

Day, L. (2002) 'Putting yourself in other people's shoes': the use of forum theatre to explore refugee and homeless issues in schools. *Journal of Moral Education*, 31: 21–34.

Dietrich, D. and Ralph, K.S. (1995) Crossing borders: multicultural literature in the classroom. *Journal of Educational Issues of Language Minority Students*, 15, Winter.

Doka, K.J. (2002) Introduction. In K.J. Doka (ed.), *Disenfranchised Grief: New Directions, Challenges, and Strategies for Practice*. Champaign, IL: Research Press, pp.5–22.

Dolan, A. (2014) Intercultural education, picture books and refugees: approaches for language teachers, *CLELE Journal*, 2(1).

Ehntholt, K., Smith, P. and Yule, W. (2005) School-based cognitive-behavioural therapy group intervention for refugee children who have experienced war-related trauma. *Clinical Child Psychology and Psychiatry*, 10(2): 235–50.

Eisenbruch, M. (1988) The mental health of refugee children and their cultural development. *International Migration Review*, 22(2): 282–300.

Erikson, E.H. (1963) *Childhood and Society*, 2nd edn. New York: W.W. Norton.

Falicov, C. (2002) 'Foreword', in *Therapeutic Care for Refugees: No Place Like Home*. London: Karnac, p.15.

Fantino, A. and Colak, A. (2001) Refugee children in Canada: searching for identity. *Child Welfare*, 53(5): 587–96.

Ford, D.Y., Harris, J.J. and Howard, T.C. (1999) Using multicultural literature in gifted education class-rooms. *Gifted Child Today*, 14–21.

Gilbert, K.R. (1996) 'We've had the same loss, why don't we have the same grief?' Loss and differential grief in families. *Death Studies*, 20: 269–83.

Gilbert, K. (2008) Loss and grief between and among cultures: the experience of third culture kids. *Illness, Crisis and Loss*, 16(2): 93–109.

Habib, S. (2008) Refugee boy: the social and emotional impact of the shared experience of a contemporary class novel. *Changing English*, 15: 41–52.

Hefflin, B.R. and Barksdale-Ladd, M.A. (2001) African American children's literature that helps students find themselves: selection guidelines for grades K-3. *Reading Teacher*, 54(8): 810–81.

Hodes, M. (1998) Refugee children. *British Medical Journal*, 316: 793–4.

Hope, J. (2008) 'One day we had to run': the development of the refugee identity in children's literature and its function in education. *Children's Literature in Education*, 39: 295–304.

Janoff-Bulman, R. (1992) *Shattered Assumptions: Towards a New Psychology of Trauma*. New York: Free Press.

Keene, E.O. and Zimmerman, S. (1997) *Mosaic of Thought*. Portsmouth, NH: Heinemann.

Kruse, M. (2001) Escaping ethnic encapsulation: the role of multicultural children's literature. *Delta Gamma Bulletin*, 26–32.

Meier, T. (2003) 'Why can't she remember that?' The importance of storybook reading in multilingual, multicultural classrooms. *Reading Teacher*, 242–52.

Milton, J. (2004) Helping primary school children manage loss and grief: ways the classroom teacher can help. *Education and Health*, 22(4): 58–60.

Oltjenbruns, K.A. (2001) Developmental context of childhood: grief and regrief phenomenon. In M.S. Stroebe, R.O. Hanson, W. Strobe and H. Schut (eds), *Handbook of Bereavement Research: Consequences, Coping, and Caring*. Washington, DC: American Psychological Association, pp.169–97.

Oltjenbruns, K.A. (2007) Life span issues and loss, grief, and mourning part 1: The importance of a developmental context: childhood and adolescence as an example. In D. Balk, C. Wogrin, G. Thornton and D. Megher (eds), *Handbook of Thanatology: The Essential Body of Knowledge for the Study of Death, Dying, and Bereavement*. Northbrook, IL: Association for Death Education and Counseling, Thanatology Association, pp.143–50.

Pollock, D.C. and Van Reken, R. (1999) *Third Culture Kids: The Experience of Growing Up Among Worlds*. Yarmouth, ME: Intercultural Press.

Reed, R., Fazel, M., Jones, L., Panter-Brick, C. and Stein, A. (2012) Mental health of displaced and refugee children resettled in low-income and middle-income countries: risk and protective factors. *Lancet*, 379: 250–65.

Rosenblatt, L.M. (1978) *The Reader, the Text, the Poem: The Transactional Theory of the Literary Work*. Carbondale, IL: Southern Illinois University Press.

Rousseau, C. (1995) The mental health of refugee children. *Transcultural Psychiatric Review*, 32: 299–331.

Schaetti, B.F. (2002) Attachment theory: a view into the global nomad experience. In M.G. Ender (ed.), *Military Brats and Other Global Nomads: Growing Up in Organization Families*. Westport, CT: Praeger, pp.103–19.

Sekar, C. and Katz, S. (1986) On the concept of mourning in childhood. *Psychiatric Study of the Child*, 41: 287–314.

Silverman, P.R. (2000) *Never Too Young to Know: Death in Children's Lives*. New York: Oxford University Press.

Summerfield, D. (2000) Childhood, war, refugeedom and 'trauma': three core questions for mental health professionals. *Transcultural Psychiatry*, 37(3): 417–33.

Taylor, G.S. (1997) Multicultural literature preferences of low-ability African American and Hispanic American fifth graders. *Reading Improvement*, 37–48.

Useem, R. (1993) Third culture kids: focus of major study. *Newslinks*, XII(3). [Online].

Useem, R.H. and Cottrell, A.B. (1996) Adult third culture kids. In C.D. Smith (ed.), *Strangers at Home*. Bayside, NY: Aletheia, pp.22–35.

Völkl-Kernstock, S., Karnik, N., Mitterer-Asadi, M., Granditsch, E., Steiner, H., Friedrich, M. and Huemer, J. (2014) Responses to conflict, family loss and flight: posttraumatic stress disorder among unaccompanied refugee minors from Africa. *Neuropsychiatry*, 28: 6–11.

Watts, M. (2004) Telling tales of torture: repositioning young adults' views of asylum seekers. *Cambridge Journal of Education*, 34: 315–29.

Wolfert, A. (1983) *Helping Children Cope with Grief*. Bristol, PA: Accelerated Development.

Examples of refugee literature

A Little Piece of Ground by Elizabeth Laird. Published 1 October 2006 by Haymarket Books

ISBN 1931859388 (ISBN13: 9781931859387)

Alpha: Abidjan to Gare Du Nord by Bessora Barroux (translated into English by Sarah Ardizzone). Published 2014 by Gallimard BD ASIN B00SBARVVC

Azzi in Between by Sarah Garland. Published 2012 by Frances Lincoln Children's Books

ISBN 1847802613 (ISBN13: 9781847802613)

Here I Am by Patti Kim. Published 2015 by Picture Window Books

ISBN 1479519316 (ISBN13: 9781479519316)

Oranges in No Man's Land by Elizabeth Laird. Published 2006 by Macmillan Children's Books

ISBN 0330450271 (ISBN13: 9780330450270)

11

Digital stories: helping children to develop and prevail with digital media

Caroline Walker-Gleaves and Alan Gleaves

 This chapter

This chapter will look at the use and critical importance of stories and storytelling in the construction of language and literacy within the primary classroom. It will examine the ways in which teachers can use stories to help children develop their feelings and thoughts, and also how stories might be used to help children overcome difficulties, where problems with language and literacy stand in the way of children articulating their stories. It will focus on the use of digital literacies to help teachers develop digital storytelling practices and techniques so that children can use different forms of media and representation to develop their language and literacy skills in ways that are congruent with youth culture.

What and who are stories for?

There are oral traditions within many cultures all over the world, including African, First Nation and Jewish cultures, and in these there is a critical importance attached to tales and narratives that is intertwined with the value of life itself, and what it means to experience difficulty and hardship, and to overcome these. These structures are *stories* – and stories in this sense are able, for individuals and communities and cultures, to promote learning, celebrating, remembering, becoming and overcoming all kinds of experiences and events (Hiemstra, 2001). Not only that, stories, when they are told to and shared between individuals who have significance in people's lives, are enriching and healing, and may well contribute to children's emotional and spiritual development. According to Robin (2008a), when children who are experiencing some kind of difficulty are helped to write, tell and share stories, they become different, and undergo a kind of transformation, where they begin to feel different about their lives and their identities, and how they might then begin to have some control over them, however small at first.

Stories in the classroom

Stories and storytelling can be very difficult for children with particular language and literacy difficulties, and the Primary National Curriculum adds a further layer of complexity for many children, the story and storytelling element being based around the recognition of themes and structures of already known stories, rather than the use of these structures to explore the children's own experiences and events (Department for Education, 2013). For example, in the sections on Reading Comprehension in the Years 3 and 4 Programmes of Study (2013, p.35), the statutory requirement says that children should be:

> ... *increasing their familiarity with a wide range of books, including fairy stories, myths and legends, and retelling some of these orally.*

and in the non-statutory guidance, children should be (p.36):

> ... *taught to recognise themes in what they read, such as the triumph of good over evil or the use of magical devices in fairy stories and folk tales.*

My teacher tells me off if I can't remember the proper ending.

(Liam, aged 8)

We have to write stories about things that the teacher says but I like to write about me.

(Shula, aged 9)

These two comments illustrate something very important that happens with stories as soon as many children learn how to put ideas, imagery and language together – they are told to write in specific formats, about ideas and events that are public and well known and, most of all, they become aware very quickly that there are 'right' and 'wrong' kinds of endings, but whatever else, it is stressed frequently, how important it is to remember these very specific pieces of information and ideas. These very particular frameworks and methods, however, present considerable difficulties for many different kinds of children, especially children with learning difficulties in which memory and structure play a part, for example as in dyslexia or dyscalculia (Petterson, 2004).

This situation presents a problem that is already apparent for teachers considering the use of stories and storytelling in their classes. We know from research in anthropology, psychology, sociology and early education and child development that stories are natural processes in the way that humans construct and understand meaning within experiences and events (Konner, 2010). But critically, both Konner (2010) and Frank (2010) point to why stories are much more than simply being able to tell *about* things, or to recognise structures within *other people's* stories: stories are about a recognition of individuals – from deeply personal feelings to big cultural themes (Liu et al., 2003). Stories amount to the way in which private history becomes a properly validated and authorised experience, and even for very young children, the ways in which different kinds of stories are able to give freedom to worries, to thoughts, to imaginations, is nothing less than what Frank (2010, p.2) means when he says: *Stories may not actually breathe, but they can animate.* In other words, stories bring things – ideas, feelings, people – to life. And here, digital technology can make a huge difference to teachers' practices and pupil learning – because its basis of richness of expression and nuance can allow thoughts, feelings and emotions to arise that confound more textual forms of expression (Marsh et al., 2015).

But this process of bringing to life is often very difficult for both children and teachers, because of two things: first, how do teachers teach children how to learn that all kinds of stories are valuable and worth telling and sharing, and second, how do teachers learn how to use the raw material of stories and assemble it into ways that both reflect what children are saying, and also give them the best chance of presenting their stories in the first place. For some children, thinking of an idea is an easy process, but for other children, frequently those with language and literacy difficulties, it is the start of a nightmare of anxiety and exclusion from the classroom and from other children. There are many questions that teachers must ask concerning stories and language then: Why do we remember some stories and not others? What affects our ability to tell and retain stories? Is this the same for all children? How do children develop their own voice within their story? And what kinds of stories work best in words, pictures or music? All of these are time-consuming processes, but behind them sit the concept of digital storytelling and behind that, the basis for using digital technology at all, the idea of digital literacy.

Understanding digital literacy

According to Hague and Peyton (2010) digital literacy is a critically important element of the educational experience for all young people in an increasingly digital culture. They make this claim on the basis of it becoming, over the last decade, such an embedded part of children's lives that it amounts to an 'entitlement' in inclusion and educational terms. If we turn the question around, it becomes more obvious why all teachers and professionals associated with learning and children's language and literacy development should imagine embedding and using digital culture when it is so critical and key to children's lives. So perhaps the question for educators, parents and other professionals alike, should be to continually ask: 'Why would I avoid using all the technological means to help my pupils or children learn and enjoy what they are learning?'

Digital literacy gives children and young people the ability to take advantage of the diverse new and emerging opportunities associated with digital technologies but at the same time being aware of the very real problems and difficulties that technology can bring, especially if a child or young person has difficulties with language and understanding meaning for example. Most importantly, however, if formal schooling is to prepare children to make sense of the world and to thrive socially, intellectually and economically, then teachers, parents, carers and other professionals must also be able to use and adapt the social and cultural practices of digital literacy that enable people to make the most of their multiple interactions with digital technology and media.

But as Marsh et al. (2005) point out, it is important to understand how teachers and pupils can engage with the concept of digital literacy, especially when language and digital literacy is quite so complex and multifaceted – it involves critically engaging with technology and developing a social awareness of how factors like advertising, people's agendas and very diverse individual viewpoints can affect the way that children use and understand technology. Digital literacy therefore means being able to:

- understand how to communicate effectively and with a sense of who the audience is and what difference that makes to the tone and content of what someone is writing or saying;

- communicate better in terms of being decisive and specific about which medium (e.g. music, film, text, a mixture) will best convey their stories and also will be the most appropriate way in which it can represent their emotions and thoughts, especially if children have language and literacy difficulties.

Understanding the potential and power of digital media

The practices of language and literacy that stand behind the processes of creating and constructing ideas, artifacts and stories with digital technologies need to be situated in children's social, cultural and language contexts, especially when it should be remembered that children and young people exist and interact in situations where there are countless relationships, often loose but very influential, with others. This is most evident in the way that language trends and norms become transferred with ease, and yet that are often misunderstood, especially for children with language and literacy difficulties. The research of Ofcom (2015) shows, for example, what can happen in social media contexts when vulnerable children appropriate terms and phrases that they do not understand, and this leads them to be open to exploitation by others. Such behaviour shows clearly that each 'act of digital literacy' (Shifrin et al., 2015) children engage in has 'sociohistorical' antecedents; it is an act of literacy because it is related to and supports these broader understandings, activities and interactions around the creation of meaning (Formby, 2014). Critically, it also supports the growth of children's awareness of their own stories – personal narratives – and the differences between sharing a narrative and eliciting understanding and empathy in other children, and telling a narrative where children may feel compelled to relate something of their context or past but which other children may not understand. Such a combination of personal narrative and digital literacy is very powerful and has the capacity to help teachers understand the links between the wider e-safety, social and language elements of digital literacy as a means of developing children's storytelling.

Digital literacy as applied to children with language and literacy difficulties works in several linked ways: it will often act as a positive means to develop another area, by a process of multiplying the opportunities for children to be heard and understood while at the same time teaching them that using digital media may have other, unintended consequences. So it is important that children therefore learn the importance of:

- being able to produce and understand meaningful and sensitive communication;
- understanding that the media they use should be carefully tailored to the audience and that, sometimes, particular media are not suitable;
- being able to understand that the content of what is produced or written in a different medium may not be suitable, since it may last a long time or be used to exploit in future;
- understanding that the best way to relate a piece of content is that the medium and the content itself are not in conflict and that the use of digital media, just because you can use it, doesn't mean always that it should be used;
- in relation to writing their own stories, children should understand that there are reasons for using particular digital media to convey content, and that they may be far more successful if they choose their media carefully, so that it accurately represents both their cognitive and emotional states.

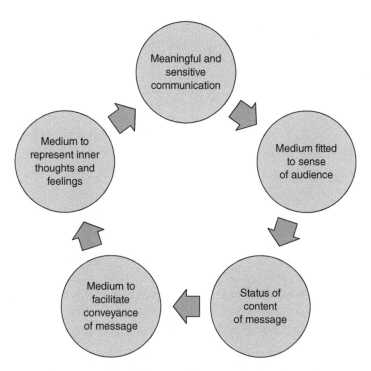

Figure 11.1   The domains of digital literacy considerations for children with language and literacy difficulties.

Caroline Walker-Gleaves and Alan Gleaves

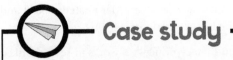

Case study

Creating personal narratives

One of the most important ways to combine digital literacy and storytelling is to create a personal narrative. But before encouraging children to write or tell their own personal narratives, it is very important for children to hear and think about other people's personal stories, to establish what form and shape a story might look like and, critically, what elements of a story could be introduced to others – first, in establishing what to reveal and what not to reveal, and second, in establishing more than simply facts as important story elements. Earlier on, this chapter presented the notion that much of the current National Curriculum rests on remembering different story structures and very specific details and endings of stories. Using personal digital narratives gives children an opportunity first-hand to realise that stories are also about feelings and thoughts and that used digitally, through different media, these can be compared and contrasted to reveal different viewpoints.

A very good example of such a personal narrative may be found in the following example:

http://digitalstorytelling.coe.uh.edu/view_story.cfm?vid=244&otherid=featured&d_title=Featured%20Digital%20Stories

This story is one of dislocation and alienation, as it relates to a mother who brings her children to the USA from South Korea in order to give them a better life and to give them what the mother sees as better opportunities to learn, to succeed and to be happy. But the story is one of difficulty and loneliness as the mother and daughter have opposite feelings about what is happening to them: these centre on friendship, leaving their heritage behind, making new lives, learning a new language and, most of all, wondering who they are any more and whether they will ever feel they belong.

Such a story provides a clear way for children to be able to relate their own personal narratives using digital means, to use the affordances of digital literacy and digital technology, and to amend, edit and understand their own stories, as well as to begin to understand the impact on other children who may not have had similar experiences but who can use these experiences to reflect on stories of their own.

There are other wider socio-cultural reasons why this type of story may be a very useful one for teachers, too, such as facilitating discussions about current issues, such as children who are refugees and who may well be unaccompanied, what children experience during migration, war and strife across the world, and also the difficulties that many of the children will be facing in terms of re-settlement due to other reasons, such as being in care, fleeing domestic violence and so on. Children who can use this type of story to develop their own narrative can provide a very positive way to deal with some very difficult and emotional family issues. However, as emphasised earlier, this is where the judgement and care of the teacher is paramount, in considering both the inherent nature of the digital literacies as well as the make-up of the story elements that will help the children's emotions as well as their abilities with language.

In short, technology can play a very important role in scaffolding young children's language and literacy development, through storytelling vehicles such as apps and e-books, where children can record their own versions of stories, and cut and paste these for alternative endings for example.

However, research into the use of technology in children's language development suggests strongly that interacting with technology in a storytelling and narrative manner is not a replacement for adult interaction, for example with a teacher. Technology can play an important role in the encouragement and inducement of storytelling and language development especially for children who have impoverished language backgrounds (Formby, 2014).

Why is digital storytelling important in primary education?

In 2007, neuroscientist Michael Merzenrich, a professor at the University of California at San Francisco's Keck Centre for Integrative Neurosciences, asserted that adding computers to conventional teaching strategies is an unsophisticated approach and that it is not surprising that it adds very little to students' experiences in the classroom. He stated:

> In a world run by computers, where almost every kid in that class will have some sort of a computer in their pocket and on their desk in their future life and job, wouldn't it make sense to measure the impacts of serious computer-based training on our school children's reactions to, and their facile uses of computers?
>
> (Merzenich (2007), p.1)

In this section, we discuss the significance of digital storytelling in a primary classroom, and use research to explore how digital storytelling can bridge gaps in relation to children's language and literacy development, teachers' technology practices and the principles of digital literacy that we discussed earlier. This combination of qualities and opportunities supports a concrete framework by which teachers can begin to adapt digital storytelling as a powerful medium for language and literacy, especially for children experiencing difficulties.

The basis for using digital technology is evident if you walk into any class of children from the very early years up to compulsory age schooling and ask them if they know 'the singing AA baby' or the beauty blogger 'Zoella' or the meme 'Charlie bit my finger' . . . They will, and they will know all the words to the songs, the actions, the mixes of the songs, the beauty episodes and so on. All these 'memes', digital clips and viral videos represent critical parts of the culture of young people who have come to be known as 'digital natives' (Prensky, 2001). Indeed, many researchers have pointed out that the transmission of ideas moves faster at this point in history than it has ever moved before, and also that such ideas and stories have moved from the fringes of youth culture to the mainstream (Shifrin, 2015). This means that the use of digital media is now not a question of if it is used in class, but when and how it is used, to both capitalise on the lived experience and familiarity of it in informal terms, but also to give a level playing field of achievement and progression to all those children it is able to 'reach' educationally by virtue of its multimedia richness and its capacity to represent diversity and, in turn, present diverse ways of learning, creating and developing children's individuality and, critically, their language.

Much research suggests that young people growing up immersed in technology use has led to the development of the 'digital native' (Prensky, 2001), who is immersed in, and fluent in, youth culture and digital forms for presenting and creating content (Hull, 2003). The digital native may be contrasted with the 'digital immigrant' in relation to four distinct domains:

- learning location – where learning may take place;

- learning architecture – the structure of how concepts and understanding might occur;

- learning 'grammar' – the usual manner in which learning and teaching might occur;

- relationships – the characteristics of how children might relate to significant others in learning contexts.

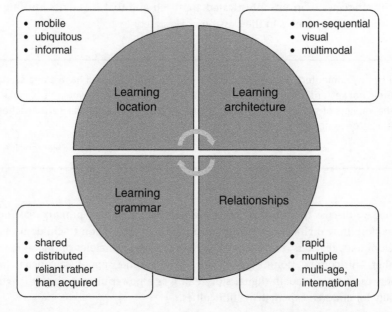

Figure 11.2   The domains of the digitally literate education

Digital culture and the use of language

While there is much research to suggest equally that digital nativity is merely a guide to how technology has begun to influence children's and young people's behaviour, there is also emerging evidence to suggest that, currently, classrooms are undergoing paradigm shifts where new teachers especially amount to being digital natives teaching digital natives. As such, they arguably accept uncritically some of the very strong beliefs about digital technology as an enabler of children's learning without first having considered its shortcomings and limitations, or as Lei (2009) puts it: 'Digital natives need to develop a systematic understanding of the technology, subject matter, pedagogy, and how these aspects work together' (p.93).

In fact, it is the intersection of digital nativity with digital immigration in which the richest use of language, technology and stories have the biggest impact upon children and adults alike. Using the earlier mentioned examples as illustrations – the AA singing baby advert is arguably engaging not simply because the baby is smiley and funny (which she is) or the father oblivious to what is happening in the seat behind him (which he is), but also because the advert has a combination of comical and narrative elements which are irresistible and can only be achieved by digital means. These include the imperfect animation of the singing and song lyrics, the involvement of the AA man who is increasingly engaged with the action as well as the music, and finally the question of whether the baby is going to be discovered by the father before the car is fixed. In other words, although the clip focuses on advertising a product, it is ultimately the story and the characterisation that is ultimately the most engaging part of the video.

So, digital storytelling is the art of combining narrative with digital media such as images, sound and video to create a short story (Robin, 2008b). Whether a simple clip of a few seconds or a longer narrative of minutes, digital stories interweave different media to support the art of telling a tale. In the *Digital Storytelling Cookbook*, Lambert (2007) identifies seven elements that are critical components of effective digital stories:

1. *Point of view*: outlines the point of the story and the perspective from which the story is told.

2. *A dramatic question*: sets the tension of the story by identifying issues to be resolved.

3. *Emotional content*: engages the audience through common emotions and themes (love, pain, humour).

4. *The gift of your voice*: helps the audience make meaning of images.

5. *The power of the soundtrack*: sets the mood of the story.

6. *Economy*: balances the auditory and visual tracks of meaning.

7. *Pacing*: sustains the attention of the audience by establishing and modifying the rhythm of the story.

A quick survey of these, however, suggests that digital storytelling is not as straightforward as it first seems in relation to its application to the particular focus of this chapter, that is providing an opportunity for children with difficulties in language and literacy to use it as a medium in which to overcome the emotional or socio-cultural nature of their difficulty. Indeed, although the medium of digital storytelling offers tremendous opportunities for teachers to engage pupils – for example through the integration of visual images with written text or the use of music to suggest meaning and relate difficult emotional issues – digital stories need a great deal of thought and preparation to fully enable teachers to use them to make differences to children's language and literacy. Fortunately, there is research that gives teachers opportunities to reflect on how this might be achieved.

For example, when using digital storytelling with middle- and high-school students, Bull and Kajder (2004) found that digital stories helped struggling readers visualise ideas by offering a platform for visually communicating meaning, especially in cases where children's vocabulary might be limited or even in specific contexts where certain elements of language might be sparse or missing, for example descriptive language such as adjectives and adverbs. Other research has found that when children have created their own personal digital stories, multiple media (music, song, pictures, language) are able to act as leverage for cognitive, interpersonal, emotional, language and technical skills (Petterson, 2004). But these specific examples need further exploration if teachers, parents, carers and other professionals are to understand how to develop the ideas further for teaching and learning in children with language and literacy difficulties.

Understanding the basis of digital media and language development

There are numerous theorisations that offer insights into the language and literacy development of children when combined with other contexts, such as the use of media, the social and relational nature of the teacher and classroom and, of course, the existing language and literacy capabilities of individuals. Such relevant theorisation includes, for example, the theory of media richness, which draws upon the extent to which different multimedia formats may enhance learning or may actually be redundant if the cognitive load of an individual is compromised (Paivio and Clark, 1991). The theory of relational zones (Goldstein, 1999) draws on the primacy of caring relationships and the constructivist principles of the Zone of Proximal Development to offer an explanation of how and why children are more engaged in close personal and caring relationships which can often occur when teachers work with children to produce digital narratives for example. However, although both offer partial explanations as to pedagogic processes that make digital literacy particularly potent as a means to enhance children's literacy, neither is able to offer a reasoned account of how media combines with language development to offer a convincing explanation of how and why language construction environments may work and be useful in the development of digital storytelling especially in young children.

For this, an alternative theoretical approach rests on Krashen's input hypothesis, which claims that 'we move along the developmental continuum by receiving comprehensible input. Comprehensible input is defined as second language input just beyond the learners' current second language competence in terms of syntactic complexity' (Krashen, 1985: 2). In digital storytelling, the 'just beyondness' is provided by the media input, whether music or visuals. For many children with language difficulties, whether these originate in cognitive terms, cultural terms, or social deprivation terms, the visualizations central to digital storytelling used as examples of how to construct a digital story first by a teacher, then by the pupil themselves, will support the comprehension of language, and the 'second' or 'new' language input will be more easily understood. Such visualization provides simultaneous language and conceptual scaffolding through cultural context or other clues, and it helps with the natural associations of images and words.

However, what is critical to understand in this process is that the developmental continuum works in three overlapping ways: teachers may construct digital stories for children to listen to and watch; teachers may co-construct digital stories *with* children, where the children might choose media to fit alongside particular words, or verbalise thoughts when teachers choose particular media to stand behind a story. But children may also consciously work independently and steadily over time to construct longer and more adventurous personal narratives, where the mixture of language and media may become increasingly nuanced and subtle if a teacher works alongside a child, so that children extend their own developmental competence. According to Paivio and Clark (1991), a model of 'dual coding' explains the gradual improvement of language acquisition: 'combining pictures, mental imagery, and verbal elaboration could be an effective method in promoting understanding and learning from text by students ranging from grade school to university level' (Paivio and Clark, 1991, p.163). This model is not the only one to explain language competence, however; another framework developed by cognitive psychologists is the 'image schema theory', which claims that knowledge is not static, propositional and sentential, but situated, shaped by the arc of lived experience (Gibbs and Colston, 1995). Not only that, but Gibbs and others suggest that image schemas proliferate in individuals' daily lives, and are dynamic in their constructions of imagery and how they transform our thinking. Accordingly, research suggests that the purpose of our cognitive functions is to make real our external experiences through providing representations of reality that may be continually adjusted and tested. In line with these theorisations, advocates of this theoretical orientation assert that digital stories provide the most stimulating, fertile and inclusive ways possible of achieving such representations, since they:

- make it possible to bring the outside in with their variety of sounds and pictures and haphazard nature;

- make it possible for children to work individually and collaboratively, to practise, to edit, to reinvent their stories and to present them perfectly in the way that they wish to;

- enable teachers to offer the most sensitive and measured support and interaction to enable each child's digital story come to life.

Indeed, the many and unique affordances of digital storytelling – such as the combination of music and visualisation that can offer a much greater possibility of eliciting more diverse memories than text alone, as well as the technical nature of digitisation, e.g. being able to edit, replay, listen and adjust what is told and what therefore is ultimately heard – makes pupils both more conscious and confident of their ability to tell a worthy story that will hold the attention of an audience (Merchant, 2015). Furthermore, the iterations of language development in a digital and oral sense suggest, according to recent research, that many pupils whose previous pieces of writing were stilted and did not present richness of emotions, language or otherwise were able to present them in subsequent pieces of work in an entirely new light, with more risk, more creativity and more intimacy (Mullen and Dusbabek, 2006). As such, children's work becomes less an object in meeting memory refinements or structural details, but more an assessment-in-progress model of really understanding the relationship between children's personal experiences and their language *and* emotional development (Ohler, 2008). Quite simply, the use of digital storytelling gives students more control over how they present themselves to the world. And this becomes a gateway to a much more nuanced experience of teachers helping their pupils to learn language and literacy, and of pupils constructing more multi-dimensional accounts of themselves and their feelings and of revealing the complex and multifaceted ways in which all of these interact in their everyday lives.

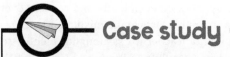

Case study

A process of teacher reflection in practice

Kim is a newly qualified teacher (NQT) and has a young boy in her class, Luke. He is seven years of age and loves music. He lives with his mother, brother and two half sisters, and all his siblings have different fathers. Two of the fathers always seem to come to the house each month at the same time and repeatedly there have been fights culminating in serious assaults on Luke's mother which have been reported in the press. Luke has been witness to all of this and has drawn pictures that have been disturbing to the teacher in his art sessions at school. Luke is often the last to leave the class on a daily basis and has told the teacher that he doesn't want to go home. Kim, the teacher, has become increasingly concerned for the welfare of Luke, as well as being concerned for his educational progress. He seems to be unable to engage with lessons and she is worried that he is beginning to turn inwards and not be able to express himself and so deal with his emotions in a way that will allow him to make sense of what is happening to him.

Kim went to an NQT session at her local university and was listening to some research about how digital storytelling might help a young pupil like Luke. In particular, the research suggested that digital storytelling might be able to offer Luke and children like him opportunities to explore their emotional needs and so stop being a barrier to learning in general.

The research suggested that surprisingly little is known about how emotions and emotional states affect children's language development, but there are social psychological theories linking affect and cognition and these are based, in turn, on the influence of identity, relationships and inter-personal context, confidence, resilience and agency. Standing behind these are theories of how emotions influence the storage and retrieval of information from long-term memory, and how affect influences the processing of information: in other words, the ways in which emotional states affect what is usefully remembered are then brought to bear on the significance of this information in making sense of future emotional reactions and contexts. Linnenbrink (2006), for example, proposed an associative network theory suggesting that emotional state is associated with information stored in long-term memory and, as such, that particular emotions can limit the memory of particular kinds of information – so if negative emotions in the first place limit the storage of information, such as language for example, then when such language is remembered later on it may itself give rise to further negative emotions, so limiting more learning and acting as a negative learning cycle.

While much of this is still in the exploratory phase, research has since exposed much more complex relationships between language, emotions and children's behaviour, but critically research is emerging to suggest that teachers may play a critical role in advancing positive learning environments in which digital stories can act as bridges between children's inner emotional landscapes and their ability to develop much greater language ability. The research that enables such developments relates to what are called 'Identity Construction Environments' (ICEs) (Bers and Cassell, 1998). These were originally objectives of digital storytelling that were meant to engage children in learning processes that combined personal development with civic education, rather than separating them out as most educational programmes do. For example, in one, a Storytelling Agent Generation Environment (SAGE), children talk about their lives with a virtual 'sage' who listens and then responds with a relevant tale. Such a program is an example of an ITS (Intelligent Tutor System) whereby each subsequent telling of a life story generates a greater bank of stories from which the sage may construct a relevant and appropriate tale.

Why is this research relevant to Kim's experiences with Luke? Well, immediately, Kim could see direct similarities between the ICE analogue of personal development and civic education, and personal development and very specific vocabulary development, a critical area of need for Luke. Kim contacted a nearby university Education department and asked if she could speak to someone about perhaps doing some research in this area and using already established ICEs as models, and develop similar programs as apps that she could use with pupils like Luke who might respond to the use of such digital stories in combination with teacher-centred learning in the classroom.

 ## Concluding thoughts

This chapter has raised many issues concerning the links between digital technology, storytelling, digital literacy and the problems that some children may face in relation to language and literacy development. While examples of digital storytelling that have been presented in the research are motivating to a diverse range of pupils, they are particularly potent to children experiencing difficulty with linguistic expression, whether that is through being a struggling reader, a hesitant writer or a child with very specific and particular learning difficulties or impediments. The nature of digital literacy and digital storytelling is not as straightforward as some literature suggests, and many teachers find it hard to make sense of the proliferation of technical skills required and the technological preparation for developing specific elements of learning. But it is worth thinking about the rationale for using digital stories in the first place since this will open the possibility of being a more creative and responsive practitioner in relation to solving the 'problem' that will present itself in every class, no matter what age or stage a child is at. As such, in conclusion, we return to the research that suggests that digital storytelling has proven to 'engage struggling readers and writers who have not yet experienced the power of personal expression' (Bull and Kajder, 2004, p.47).

References

Bers, M.U. and Cassell, J. (1998) Interactive storytelling systems for children: using technology to explore language and identity.' *Journal of Interactive Learning Research*, 9(2): 183–215.

Bull, G. and Kajder, S. (2004) Digital storytelling in the language arts classroom. *Learning and Leading with Technology*, 32(4): 46–9.

Department for Education (2013) *Primary National Curriculum in England*. Accessed at: **https://www. gov.uk/government/publications/national-curriculum-in-england-primary-curriculum**.

Formby, S. (2014) *Children's Early Literacy Practices at Home and in Early Years Settings: Second Annual Survey of Parents and Practitioners*. Nottingham: National Literacy Trust/Pearson.

Frank, A. (2010) *Letting Stories Breathe: A Socio-narratology*. Chicago: University of Chicago Press.

Gibbs, R.W. and Colston, H. (1995) The cognitive psychological reality of image schemas and their transformations. *Cognitive Linguistics*, 6: 347–78.

Goldstein, L. (1999) Relational zones: the role of caring relationships in the co-construction of mind. *American Educational Research Journal*, 3(3): 647–73.

Hague, C. and Peyton, S. (2010) *Digital Literacy Across the Curriculum*. Bristol: Futurelab.

Hiemstra, R. (2001) Uses and benefits of journal writing. In L.M. English and M.A. Gillen (eds), *Promoting Journal Writing in Adult Education: New Directions for Adult and Continuing Education*. San Francisco: Jossey-Bass.

Hull, G.A. (2003) Youth culture and digital media: new literacies for new times. *Research in the Teaching of English*, 38(2): 229–33.

Konner, M. (2010) *The Evolution of Childhood: Relationships, Emotion, Mind*. Cambridge, MA: Harvard University Press.

Krashen, S. (1985) *The Input Hypothesis: Issues and Implications*. London: Longman.

Lambert, J. (2007) *Digital Storytelling Cookbook*, Centre for Digital Storytelling. San Francisco: Digital Diner Press.

Lei, J. (2009) Digital Natives as preservice teachers: what technology preparation is needed? *Journal of Computing in Teacher Education*, 25(3): 15–23.

Linnenbrink, E.A. (2006) Emotion research in education: theoretical and methodological perspectives on the integration of affect, motivation, and cognition. *Educational Psychology Review*, 18: 307–14.

Liu, H., Selker, T. and Lieberman, H. (2003) *Visualizing the Affective Structure of a Text Document*. Conference on Human Factors in Computing Systems, CHI 2003, Ft Lauderdale, FL.

Marsh, J., Brooks, G., Hughes, J., Ritchie, L. and Roberts, S. (2005) *Digital Beginnings: Young Children's Use of Popular Culture, Media and New Technologies*. Sheffield: University of Sheffield. Avaiable at: **www.digitalbeginnings.shef.ac.uk/DigitalBeginningsReport.pdf**.

Marsh, J., Plowman, L., Yamada-Rice, D., Bishop, J.C., Lahmar, J., Scott, F., Davenport, A. et al. (2015) *Exploring Play and Creativity in Pre-Schoolers' Use of Apps: Final Project Report*. Available at: **www.techandplay.org**.

Merchant, G. (2015) Apps, adults and young children: researching digital literacy practices in context. In R.H. Jones, A. Chik and C.A. Hafner (eds), *Discourse and Digital Practices: Doing Discourse Analysis in the Digital Age*. Abingdon: Routledge, pp.144–57.

Merzenich, M. (2007) Developing training strategies for remediating learning difficulties in children: using technology in practice. Lecture at UCSF Keck Centre for Integrative NeuroSciences, Dean's Distinguished Lecture Series, December 2007.

Mullen, L.J. and Dusbabek, R.J. (2006) We arrived at fantastic shapes: an investigation into students' use of materials to learn. *Journal of Visual Literacy*, 26(2): 151–78.

Ofcom (2015) *Children and Parents: Media Use and Attitudes Report*. Accessed at: **http://stakeholders.ofcom.org.uk/binaries/research/media-literacy/children-parents-nov-15/childrens_parents_nov2015.pdf**.

Ohler, J. (2008) *Digital Storytelling in the Classroom: New Media Pathways to Literacy, Learning, and Creativity*. Thousand Oaks, CA: Corwin Press.

Paivio, A. and Clark, J.M. (1991) Dual-coding theory and education. *Educational Psychology Review*, 3(3).

Petterson, R. (2004) Gearing communications to the cognitive needs of students: findings from Visual Literacy Research. *Journal of Visual Literacy*, 24(2): 129–54.

Prensky, M. (2001) Digital natives, digital immigrants. *On the Horizon* (MCB University Press), 9(5): 1–6.

Robin, B. (2008a) Digital storytelling: a powerful technology tool for the 21st century classroom. *Theory into Practice*, 47(3): 220–8.

Robin, B. (2008b) The effective uses of digital storytelling as a teaching and learning tool. In *Handbook of Research on Teaching Literacy Through the Communicative and Visual Arts*, Vol. 2. New York: Lawrence Erlbaum Associates.

Shifrin, D. et al. (2015) *Growing Up Digital: Media Research Symposium*. American Academy of Pediatrics. Available at: **https://www.aap.org/en-us/Documents/digital_media_symposium_proceedings.pdf**.

12

The language of mathematics and the particular difficulties of children with foetal alcohol spectrum disorders

Caroline Walker-Gleaves and Janet Degg

 This chapter

This chapter will examine three interlinked areas: the nature of mathematical learning in the primary school, the mathematical literacy that is used and, in turn, is required for children to be able to both learn mathematical knowledge, and also for them to be fluent in using and relating mathematical ideas, and the difficulties of a particular group of children in navigating and negotiating both. An important element of these two subjects will be the exploration of realistic approaches to mathematics as a way of introducing mathematical language to readers of this chapter. However, it will also aim to do something very important in keeping with the purpose of this book, and that is, to view the whole of the conceptual nature of mathematical learning and language through the lens of a very particular group of children who have language difficulty, particularly in the context of mathematics, and that is children who are located on the Foetal Alcohol Spectrum, and who have attendant difficulties and disorders. Children so assessed and diagnosed as having these disorders are termed therefore children with foetal alcohol spectrum disorders (FASD).

Defining and understanding FASD

Of course, there are many areas of learning difficulty and disability that impact upon children's language development, but FASD is an important area to consider, for two reasons. First, the education system at all levels in the UK is currently witnessing an increasing number of children with new and emerging disabilities for whom teachers are often ill equipped, for reasons of funding, time or lack of specialist professional support (Carpenter, 2009). FASD is one such emerging disability and is currently the most common, non-genetic cause of learning disability in the UK (BMA, 2007) affecting around 1 per cent of live births in Europe (Autti-Ramo, 2002), and costing an estimated £2.9 million per individual across their lifespan (Peadon et al., 2008). Second, FASD is a learning disability that is increasing across all areas of the spectrum due to the greater incidence of alcoholism among both men and women, but particularly as a result of the growth in chronic and persistently high levels of drinking in women over the early and late childbearing ages in Western Europe (Kesmodel and Kesmodel, 2002).

Foetal alcohol spectrum disorder (FASD) is associated with a range of disabilities, including physical, behavioural and cognitive deficits (O'Connor et al., 2002). Particularly critical for this chapter is the fact that one specific area of concern in children with FASD is the use and development of speech and language and their impact upon wider learning capability, social difficulties and the associated problems of life skills and emotional regulation (Mattson et al., 2006). As a result, children with FASD face difficulties with learning language ranging from minor but specific difficulties, to complex and debilitating difficulties that require teachers' creativity, care and, above all, imagination and persistence in trying to find ways to engage and improve the educational progress, achievement and life chances of this group of children.

Foetal alcohol spectrum disorders

FASD is a catch-all, an organising term for a set of disorders caused by the consumption of alcohol by a mother while pregnant (Connor and Huggins, 2005). Alcohol is known physiologically as a 'teratogenic compound', and as such it chemically interferes with the normal development of the embryo or foetus in the uterus, through which it passes via the placenta. While it is in the developmental stage *in utero*, the foetus has an undeveloped and incomplete blood filtration system, and as a result is almost completely unprotected from the effects of alcohol which may be circulating in the blood system (BMA, 2007). As a result, a foetus in the uterus of a mother who is ingesting alcohol is at risk from foetal damage. There has been a great deal of controversy in recent years concerning the extent of alcohol consumption that is considered safe for a well-developed and healthy baby, but most research suggests that due its teratogenic properties, alcohol should be considered a potentially serious threat to the growth and development of all embryos and foetuses.

The physical characteristics of infants born to mothers who drank alcohol during pregnancy were first recognised in 1968 by Lemoine et al. in France (Lemoine, 1997). The effects of heavy drinking in pregnancy on the foetus were independently characterised again in 1973 by the American paediatricians, Ulleland, Smith and Jones (Jones and Smith, 1973) who originated the umbrella term Foetal Alcohol Syndrome (FAS) and identified four categories of associated features:

- Pre-and postnatal growth deficiency – the babies were short in length, light in weight with a smaller than normal head circumference, and they did not 'catch-up' with healthy children as they grew older.

- Physical anomalies – the best known of these traits is the physical cluster of facial features common to these children.

- Central nervous system dysfunction – this can be a significant problem for the child and includes learning difficulties, problems with concentration and distractability as well as difficulties with executive function.

- confirmed maternal alcohol consumption.

The term foetal alcohol spectrum disorders (FASD) has been significantly more developed in recent years, operating as an organising and categorising term for a group of disorders caused by the consumption of alcohol by a mother while pregnant (BMA, 2007). The utility of the inclusion of the word 'disorders' is such that it emphasises the complex nature of the condition, and the continuity of difficulties and disability that individual children face. This is very important for teachers to understand within their classes, since it stresses that capacity of children with FASD to be able to learn in a multitude of different ways, and for teachers to develop their inclusive practices in a manner that capitalises on the strengths of children with FASD while also recognising potential difficulties.

However, while FAS is a clinical diagnosis (Hoyme, in Mukherjee et al., 2006), FASD is not and therefore within the educational arena there has been almost no systematic research on the needs of students with FASD or on the best educational strategies (Ryan and Ferguson, 2006) nor any systematic training for teachers to educate young people on the consequences of maternal alcohol consumption. However, although there have been many changes in the awareness of teachers as to the potentially devastating effects of FASD for children, parents and teachers alike, the situation is still extremely concerning. Ryan and Ferguson (2006) point out, for example, that most children with FASD are not diagnosed, not acknowledged in relation to specific difficulties, not considered in relation to how inclusive practices might help them learn and, moreover, struggle on under the diagnosis of a variety of other terms (such as dyslexia, dyspraxia, ADHD, OCD, ODD) for a very long time without teachers and other professionals ever realising that they may have a problem (Sigman, 2008).

This situation is often and further compounded by the fact that many such children having FASD may well be looked after, and so the focus is frequently on their emotional or transient needs rather than recognising their educational needs. And finally, if any of this group of children are fostered or adopted, then their difficulties may not be registered or recognised at all, since it is possible that teachers do not even know the familial status of children if they are under a Care Order. By all accounts, and by all reasoning, it is therefore very important for all teachers to have at their disposal a sound knowledge of the difficulties, the emotional states and the learning needs of this group of children and a range of interventions and strategies at their disposal in order to personalise learning for them. For such children, the already complex problems of educational progress and attainment are compounded by many other differential diagnoses that impact on almost every aspect of their education. This, of course, includes the ability to make and sustain relationships, an aspect which is covered in another chapter of this book and which in itself is a precursor to effective language and literacy development (Taylor and Houghton, 2008).

Table 12.1 presents the most significant impairments associated with FASD.

Table 12.1   Most significant impairments associated with FASD

Area of impairment	Synthesis of observed impairments associated with children with FASD
Cognitive impairment	• Impaired auditory learning • Impaired non-verbal intellectual ability • Memory function impairment including visual, short-term, working memory, explicit memory functioning, conscious memory recall • Impaired strategic manipulation of information to improve recall • Impaired initial encoding of information • Visual-motor integration and visual-perceptual deficits, including reading disorders, impaired visual-spatial perception • Slow information processing • Impairment of higher level receptive and expressive language • Impaired comprehension • Impaired arithmetical reasoning and mathematical skills (e.g. money management and telling time) • Cognitive inflexibility • Poor executive function ('dysexecutive syndrome') • Impaired concept formation • Poor abstract reasoning/metacognition • Impaired ability to plan • Impaired ability to make decisions • Impaired ability to respond to urgency or pressured contexts
Behavioural/ emotional difficulties	• Difficulty in focusing attention and maintaining attention in the presence of distractors • Poor impulse control/response inhibition • Disorganisation • Impaired persistence • Perseverative behaviour • ADHD (usually earlier onset, inattention subtype; often unresponsive to medication) • Developmental, psychiatric, and medical conditions, attachment disorder, post-traumatic stress disorder • Chronic and acute frustration with own limitations • Anxiety disorders
Social difficulties	• Emotional immaturity (e.g. age inappropriate emotional interactions and responses) • Lack of effective reciprocal social behaviour (leading to alienation from others) • Difficulty in understanding the social consequences of behaviour • Lack of social perception including difficulties with detecting and understanding non-verbal communication/subtle social cues • Understanding another's perspective • Self-reflection and insight into own actions

Area of impairment	Synthesis of observed impairments associated with children with FASD
Physical difficulties	• Gross and fine motor function difficulties
	• Sensory processing difficulties
	• Speed of movement
	• Compromised inability to fight or flight

Sources: This table is constructed using relevant literature and frameworks for current FASD diagnosis, including Government of Australia (2002); Hughes (2006); Jacobson (2002); Jirikowic (2007).

 **Case study**

Experiencing children with FASD

Janey was ten when I first encountered her as a primary teacher specialising in science. As such, Janey was not in my form, but I did teach her science several times a week, alongside children from other classes, in rotation. So I got to know her very well, and yet not well enough to forget that she was somehow different, and therefore stopped questioning her ability and progress and just got used to her uniqueness. In fact, I saw her just enough to see that she was very different to other children in many linguistic and cognitive ways, and also just enough to remind me each time I taught her that there were indeed some extremely specific and notable aspects of her difficulties that were significant enough to develop my own strategies and also to see that it was perfectly possible for me to be able to make a concrete difference to Janey's progress. Also, of course, this process served to show me that Janey herself could improve her learning and therefore life chances.

Janey was very compliant in class, very bubbly on some days and yet very sad and withdrawn on others. She did, however, have some quite inappropriate behaviours and often came to school wearing provocative clothing – never dirty but almost always age-inappropriate for young children – and she also had sexualised behaviour and knew and repeated language that was clearly from multi-player games that I knew had an age 18 rating. Janey lived with her mother, who was an alcoholic and well known to the school, while her father, who was much older and infirm, was also an alcoholic. Janey's house was known in the area as a drinking den for people, varying in ages from teenagers up to people in their 60s and 70s who were in poverty and for many of whom transience had become a part of their lives for a variety of reasons. Janey had many difficulties spanning a range of areas, including emotional, behavioural, social and cognitive difficulties. These included specific things such as not being able to tell the time, not being able to tie shoelaces, not being able to make decisions, especially if there were many items to choose from, not being able to coordinate tasks related to timing such as planning how long it might take to do something, and, most of all, coming back to school day after day with hardly any memory of what had gone before.

But there was a problem with Janey and her difficulties. In discussing her needs with other teachers, two things quickly emerged – first, that the teachers – my colleagues – disagreed with the notion that Janey might have FASD on the basis that her difficulties were so wide ranging, so diverse and so resistant to any obvious classification that it wasn't possible for her to actually be diagnosed with anything specifically. In short, my colleagues (though not all of them) felt that Janey did have problems, but that her lack of progress and somewhat strange behaviour was a function of her living arrangements with her parents and the wider dysfunctional circle of people orbiting her life. Another group of colleagues thought that it was likely that Janey did have some learning difficulties, but that these were not full-blown disabilities, and that in any case, probably not very much could be done about them because she was a child who was just 'a bit slow' as a result of her lack of socialisation, early stimulation and her current lack of rich social environment that would improve her learning ability. I myself was thoroughly confused. Turning to the literature was largely impossible because it was almost non-existent, veering between medical literature, highly pathologised studies of individual 'disease' aetiology and forensic analysis, highly situated social accounts of families in difficulty and the social outcomes of such children, and psychological analyses of particular personality types with attendant questionnaires that had little utility for teachers trying to put techniques and knowledge into practice. There was literature on foetal alcohol syndrome, but a lot of it seemed not to apply to Janey – for everything that the 'how to' guides said, I could see or had seen something about her behaviour and ability that just didn't fit. So alongside and somewhat instead of I turned to the literature on inclusion and inclusive education, and began to read studies of children with vague but undiagnosed difficulties, or problems that defied specific educational responses. Instead, I looked at how teachers might develop pedagogical strategies that were inclusive and developmental for all children, as well as promoting mindsets that could make teachers more 'agentic' – that is, have the capacity to act and to make a difference in a pedagogic, rather than pathologic, sense. I started by taking detailed notes and observations about all the things that helped Janey, and all my reactions to, and difficulties with, understanding the differing ways in which she struggled or succeeded with the different aspects of the curriculum, and together we became like a little action research partnership.

FASD, mathematical thinking and language

As has already been outlined, children with foetal alcohol spectrum disorder (FASD) have a number of cognitive difficulties, but studies such as that of Ueckerer and Nadel (1996) demonstrate that mathematical ability seems particularly damaged, and such research suggests that it is the wide-ranging nature of mathematics that causes particular difficulties for children with FASD. This is on the basis that it draws upon many areas of executive functioning that are potentially at risk as a result of the serious effects of excessive alcohol consumption, including spatial awareness, iteration, generalisation, prioritisation, reading, hierarchical knowledge and memory. One study suggests that a particular problem concerns that relationship between mathematical skills and brain white matter structure in children with FASD and supports the hypothesis that the left parietal area for mathematical tasks is somehow compromised in such children (Lebel et al., 2010). This research is potentially ground-breaking in that it not only exposes the wide-ranging nature of FASD in relation to brain activity, but also, and critically, the 'associative' nature of brain activity in relation to mathematical processes: specifically, the findings support the notion that there are activity networks that link higher-level thinking, such as decision-making and iteration, and cognitive processing, such as spatial awareness and linguistic ability. But furthermore, different areas seem to be related to different processes, like addition and subtraction, and more demanding areas of mathematics involve more areas which are interrelated in 'networks'.

The most compelling evidence for the effect of *in utero* alcohol exposure on mathematics difficulties among young children comes from a seminal longitudinal study by Streissguth et al. (1999) of over 500 parent–child dyad participants, with about 250 of the mothers classified as heavy and recurrent drinkers and about 250 as infrequent drinkers or as abstaining from alcohol (based on the maternal report of alcohol use during mid-pregnancy). From pre-school to adolescence, these children were tested on a variety of outcome variables including IQ, academic achievement, neurobehavioural ratings, cognitive and memory measures, and teacher ratings. Of all these outcome variables, the most significant correlated academic area with alcohol exposure was performance on arithmetic and this occurred at ages from pre-school to primary through secondary at ages 4, 7, 11 and 14 years. Put simply, the more alcohol that these children had been exposed to (and this bearing in mind that it was a self-reporting study with the difficulties associated with this, especially in relation to addictive and non-compliant behaviours) then the poorer they performed and continued to perform over a whole cohort-generation of education (a decade), especially in arithmetic, arguably one of the most fundamental and gateway skills for all individuals, alongside language and literacy.

However, despite studies emerging that suggest the wide-ranging and severe chronic impairment that may result from alcohol, it is a different matter when it comes to actually intervening at the level of individual teachers. One of the greatest challenges for educators and teachers of children with FASD is the fact that such children's learning landscape and behaviour is not congruent with general theories of learning development; in fact, it often seems to confound them, with children with FASD presenting complex and incompatible behaviours and traits associated with their age, their experiences and their superficial achievements (Timler et al., 2005). For example, their immediate recall is often highly impressive, and gives the impression both of high levels of engagement and rapid processing and understanding, but this frequently masks repetitive and 'parroting', where children with FASD may be able to repeat what has been said, particularly if learning features a lot of drill and practice, with fast recall and simple responses practised over time. Nevertheless, this in itself raises questions of what may constitute learning for such a child, on the basis that teaching and learning for understanding may simply not be appropriate or realistic, so if repeating tasks to perfection may lead to concrete learning and development, then such mechanisms should not be overlooked. This particular facet of FASD has direct importance for the progress of children in mathematical terms.

Intervening in FASD – does it work?

There is very little intervention research among children with FASD, even less impact research on mathematics and FASD, and correspondingly even less that deals with very specific aspects of FASD and the emerging research on how FASD may respond to particular pedagogical activities in line with what we currently know about executive functioning and associative mathematical network activity. In other words, adopting particular language and repetition approaches may be cognitive shortcuts to the development of arithmetic skill which in turn have a cyclic effect on higher-level skill (Coles et al., 2009). The research of Coles et al. (2007) featured a mathematics intervention study programme for children aged three to ten years with FASD that included intensive, interactive and individual maths tutoring with each child. It also focused on cognitive functions such as working memory, language and descriptive work and visual-spatial skills that are involved in mathematics. Children were assessed before and after the six-week intervention, and after the intervention children in the maths intervention group showed more improvements in mathematical performance than children not in the maths intervention. This was the very first study to demonstrate improvements in mathematical thinking, processing and understanding among children with FASD, and raised important questions for teachers and other professionals alike, including:

- What is the longer-term sustainability of such an intervention for teachers and schools in terms of finance and staffing?

- Is the research base concrete and definitive enough so that teachers can be trained to intervene and adopt it?

- Does the intervention have long-lasting effects on children with FASD?

- How long should the programme be?

- Does the programme work irrespective of the age of the child with FASD?

- Can the positive benefits be observed for children in a range of settings, from one to one, small nurture groups or larger classroom settings?

As discussed earlier, such research is scarce and as a result teachers and professionals alike need to be critical about both the significance of the findings and the application to a context that is hitherto little understood. More research is now needed to determine why children with FASD have such deficits in mathematics and what area of mathematics is most difficult for these children, which is important to tailor teaching and learning and increase teachers' professional and pedagogical knowledge in order to improve mathematics. But in parallel, and the topic of the next section of this chapter, there is also much scope for individual interventions and creative approaches of individual teachers: the history of literature on inclusion and inclusive teaching (Walker-Gleaves, 2015) shows us clearly that where responding to individual children's difficulties is concerned, it is frequently the knowledge and motivation of particular teachers that is able to make an educational 'breakthrough' with some children in difficulty.

Mathematics: a combinatory realistic and language approach to addressing some FASD-related issues

Mathematics is a powerful method of communication and is central to human understanding of pattern and order in the world. There are many, often competing, theories of mathematical learning and in turn diverse theorisations how these might be achieved through particular pedagogical practices and processes. A dominant theory in education is the constructivist theory of learning mathematics. Within this framework, children construct their understanding of mathematics through 'hands-on' experience, investigations, discussion, mathematical problem-solving and reflection. Their interaction with their teacher is central to this process of understanding, so the teacher needs a clear understanding of the mathematical concepts and mathematical connections between the concepts.

For many teachers, of English, art and other curriculum subjects, their teaching could be described as social constructivist (Vygotsky, 1984). And mathematics is no different: many – if not most – teachers believe that children do construct their understanding, based on their mathematical experiences. An enduring concern of mathematics educators is, however, the precise nature and extent of children's involvement in their mathematical education, specifically their emotional reaction to, and agency within, the pedagogies adopted. Much research has addressed the issues, for example, of whether enjoyment or fear are critical precursors of success in mathematics (Bibby, 2002), and a plethora of studies have assessed the significance of socially and culturally situated approaches (Nunes, 1998).

However, many also assert and agree with Papert's (1980) constructionism that children should be supported in their constructions by the way that their learning is organised. It is in the organisation of learning that children with FASD have much from which to benefit. Research into the cognitive ability of children with FASD demonstrates that while such children have little problem generalising learning from one context to another on the basis that this is a recognition process rather than an analytical process, it is in the generalisation in the first place that children with FASD find difficulty, since generalising is a complex comparative, decisional and high-level associative process that also necessitates significant contextual knowledge. Existing research, although sparse, suggests strongly that all individuals (not just those with FASD) respond to opportunities for contextual and linguistic learning, but in the case of children with FASD, it is especially potent – it both bootstraps information that would otherwise have to be acquired in formal learning situations (that is, the classroom) so providing a foundation for generalisations, and it also minimises the social and emotional baggage that many children with FASD carry as a result of difficulties navigating the formal classroom 'grammar' of mathematics in the first place – that is the basis of it in frequent whole-class teaching, problem-solving, investigations, content resting on memory and so on.

Research has demonstrated that, although it is scarce, children with FASD respond to situated and personalised approaches to learning mathematics. Realistic Mathematics Education (RME) falls into that category and sits at the heart of a growing movement of mathematics education that aims to align the subject with children's social and cultural milieu and their unique personal capabilities whilst utilising constructivist frameworks for the development of personal mathematical understanding. Central to the constructivist idea is that knowledge has to be 'constructed' by the individual learner and that it is situated and heavily located within personal experience and thus has personal salience; also key is the fact that knowledge cannot be simply transmitted from one person to another; and it is this philosophy that is developed in RME (Gravemeijer, 1994).

Why should children with FASD benefit from a realistic maths approach?

This is a key point in the design of mathematical activities for children with FASD, since although it is an important element of the National Curriculum in mathematics, it is critically important for teachers to consider the demands of what are very popular and indeed central approaches to mathematical learning – that is problem-solving approaches. Problem-solving requires a different style of thinking to rapid recall of addition and multiplication facts. Sometimes it is necessary to consider if 'speed' is a key marker of mathematical ability (Askew, 2012) that is appropriate for all children. Children sometimes need fluency and precision to find the exact answers to calculations; on the other hand, problem-solving involves different skills and, indeed, contrary to some teachers' practices in relation to problem-solving, may range in scope from small-scale activity to multilayered, iterative investigation. Furthermore, it is interesting that the National Curriculum (DfE, 2013) includes perseverance as one of those skills rather than rapidity: sometimes children who work quickly are often considered able mathematicians, and children with FASD often present confounding and contradictory behaviours in relation to speed – sometimes such children may progress through a task that they have mastered on their own or through practice and give the impression that they are working quickly so suggesting higher ability. On other occasions, such children find their difficulties to be a source of anxiety and will master quite complex behaviours either to convince teachers of their success in particular tasks, or become so adept at copying superficial skills that teachers assume progress in mathematics. Nevertheless, the National Curriculum (DfE, 2013) says that pupils who grasp concepts rapidly should be challenged through being offered rich and sophisticated problems before any acceleration through new content. Realistic Mathematics Education lends itself perfectly to such variation and changes in contexts within the primary curriculum, and is therefore suited well to developing opportunities for mathematical education for children with FASD. But it is not a silver bullet: RME can take time to implement and there is evidence that although UK primary teachers would prefer to use a gradual, careful and investigative approach, they are under pressure to cover the content requirements of the UK National Curriculum (Bolden and Newton, 2008). Teachers also identified the emphasis on teacher accountability and methods of assessment at KS1 and KS2 and school league tables as other potential barriers to more investigative approaches.

In the National Curriculum (DfE, 2013) using and applying mathematics is a central aim of the curriculum. The three aims for Mathematics are for pupils to:

- become fluent in the fundamentals of mathematics, including through varied and frequent practice with increasingly complex problems over time;

- reason mathematically by following a line of enquiry;

- solve problems by applying their mathematics to a variety of routine and non-routine problems.

However, the National Curriculum can be taught in exciting and varied contexts that provide more possibilities for children to learn in unique and multifarious ways. Educational visits to open air museums provide inspirational contexts for mathematical problem-solving. Visits to local industries, museums and many other venues can provide opportunities for 'initiatives', activities and meaningful learning. The concept of an outdoor classroom is an exciting opportunity for teachers and children. We have participated in the development of several outdoor classrooms and the exciting problem-solving opportunities that they provide. In one traditionally designed North East school we developed the internal school quadrangle as a learning area and it became the heart of problem-solving in the school. In fact a school's 'backyard' can provide a dynamic outdoor learning experience (Kenney et al., 2003; Dyment, 2005). Therefore we believe schools should use the outdoor school environment as a context for learning especially for children with FASD.

Case study

Entering the mathematical world of a child with FASD

It was on a first trip to an Army Camp at Aldershot that I developed my understanding of Rafferty's interests and energy and our awareness of specific learning difficulties and FASD. As the winner of a weekend stationed at Aldershot (the home of the British Army) donated by Rafferty and his family who were a forces family, his father frequently serving overseas, I ventured out around the camp and the adjoining museum, examining the munitions, tanks and the ranges, and being guided by Rafferty and his father as he navigated complex training equipment and reeled off highly technical knowledge about guns, ordnance and combat. It was one of my most profound learning experiences because I found myself completely dependent on Rafferty and his father, in the oppressive, daunting and often harrowing environment of war and strife. My ten-year-old pupil, with FASD, usually in turns, taciturn, hyperactive, troubled, sad, unengaged and completely removed from much of the classroom activities that I had hitherto witnessed, was completely at ease in his world, and kept asking if I was OK, if I understood all that I was learning, and whether I would now be able to take part in a gun fight or drive a tank in the face of impending disaster. Rafferty understood the unwritten rules of weapon safety, he understood the repeated actions that a soldier must go through when preparing munitions, he understood the impact of unsafe gun handling and he understood the physical impact of guns and bullets of all shapes and sizes, the speed of the shells, and the impact of the barrels on the trajectory of shells and bullets. I knew that no matter how many months or years that I spent on an army camp, I could not achieve this level of deep, lived knowledge, this level of situated understanding and complete familiarity with every single detail, and moreover, the expert application to contexts that I couldn't even imagine.

One month later, after returning to class, and discussing what I had witnessed and repeatedly reflected upon, and going to the literature on FASD and reflecting upon what I had witnessed some more, I decided that rather than ask Rafferty to struggle to read the mathematical word problems that I had prepared that I had deliberately based on the contexts of weaponry across the ages and cultures, I asked him to do a presentation about the kinds of munitions used in the British Army and the history of tanks and tank design. The class were fascinated by Rafferty's informal mathematic calculations concerning bullet speeds, rotation and trajectory, and his explanations of complex ballistics. This was probably the most outstanding and unexpected application of realistic mathematical problem-solving that I had ever witnessed, and changed entirely my understanding both of what the language of mathematics meant for some children, what realistic mathematics might be, was and how it worked, and not least the experience of the language of mathematics for children with FASD.

Cross-curricular problem-solving can be advantageous to all children. With the support of local sponsorship we have been able to lead several educational visits to London. In two schools, most of the children had never travelled outside of the North East England and most had only travelled outside of Middlesbrough while on educational visits. We asked the children to think of mathematical questions and to record them in their mathematical diaries. Some of the questions were answered 'in flight' on the London Eye and others we explored on the ground. It was possible to time our 'flight' and other flights and to note that the first and second half of the revolution of the

London Eye were usually the same times. Where possible we enjoyed involving the children in the organisation of the visit and used tables to record meal preferences, journey times and favourite London venues. This moment reflects our overall attitude to mathematics because we believe that there should be a degree of spontaneity and creativity about mathematics and it should be as free as possible from the constraints of tests and targets. Our overall attitude to mathematics is that it should be meaningful to the participants because it is set in a context that they want to investigate and because they understand its relevance to their lives. This is particularly important for all children with FASD who may feel that they have so few opportunities to enjoy forms of learning that naturally and routinely exclude them on the basis of language before they even approach the more ambitious curriculum content.

Furthermore, inclusion for all children is central to our personal philosophies of teaching and therefore, wherever possible, all children should be educated in a mathematical classroom that offers success and challenge to everyone. The solving of mathematical word problems that relate to a class theme or a context, in our experiences as teachers and educators, are usually motivating experiences for primary children, and especially involving for children who may experience, for example, the multiple and multilayered nature of FASD. Therefore our planning and preparation involved researching the context and organising educational visits to the location on the one hand, and on the other, researching and thinking carefully about all of the cognitive, emotional, decisional and physical elements of FASD, all before embedding the mathematics within the context. One particular pupil that one of us taught, presented in the case study with language problems arising out of FASD, found the reading of the word problems so challenging that he did not enjoy the mathematics that he retrieved from the problem. In our conversations afterwards, he taught us that a personalised approach is sometimes more appropriate and that teachers should never underestimate a child's potential ability.

 Concluding thoughts

As in constructivist approaches to learning, the RME student is an active participant in the teaching and learning process. Learning activities in constructivist classrooms are characterised by active engagement, enquiry, problem-solving and student collaboration. Collaboration is another similarity between constructivist and RME approaches as the students are given opportunities and encouraged to discuss their ideas and the strategies that they use to solve problems. On the micro-didactic level, RME is similar to constructivist approaches. However, RME states explicitly that the problems need to be embedded in a long-term learning trajectory. Such trajectories are profound concepts in the education of children with FASD. The maximisation of opportunities for children to be comfortable with, and capitalise on, their own loci of control, the continual focus on increasing richness of the environment as an arena of learning rather than a direct focus on control and conformity within the classroom, as well as enabling children with FASD the opportunity to excel at what they know and can do, rather than what is deficient or must be somehow urgently addressed, are all critical staging points in the mathematical education of children with FASD.

References

Askew, M. (2012) *Transforming Primary Mathematics*. London: Routledge.

Autti-Ramo, I. (2002) Foetal alcohol syndrome – a multifaceted condition. *Developmental Medicine and Child Neurology*, 44(2): 141–4.

Bolden, D.S. and Newton, L.D. (2008) Primary teachers' epistemological beliefs: some perceived barriers to investigative teaching in primary mathematics. *Educational Studies*, 34(5): 419–32.

British Medical Association (2007) *Fetal Alcohol Spectrum Disorders: A Guide for Healthcare Professionals*. London: BMA.

Carpenter, B. (2009) *The Challenge of Children with Complex Needs: Seeking Solutions and Finding Resolution. A Discussion Paper*. London: Specialist Schools and Academies Trust.

Coles, C.D., Kable, J.A. and Taddeo, E. (2009) Math performance and behavior problems in children affected by prenatal alcohol exposure: intervention and followup. *Journal of Developmental and Behavioral Pediatrics*, 30: 7–15.

Coles, C.D., Strickland, D.C., Padgett, L. and Bellmoff, L. (2007) Games that 'work': using computer games to teach alcohol-affected children about fire and street safety. *Research in Developmental Disabilities*, 28: 518–30.

Connor, P.D. and Huggins, J. (2005) Prenatal development: fetal alcohol spectrum disorders. In K. Thies (ed.), *Handbook of Human Development for Healthcare Professionals*. Sudbury, MA: Jones & Bartlett.

DfE (2013) *The National Curriculum Handbook for Primary Teachers in England*. London DfE.

Dyment, J.E. (2005) Green school grounds as sites for outdoor learning: barriers and opportunities. *International Research in Geographical and Environmental Education*, 14(1): 28–45.

Government of Australia (2002) *Fetal Alcohol Syndrome: A Literature Review*, National Alcohol Strategy 2001 to 2003–04 Occasional Paper, August. Government of Australia.

Gravemeijer, K. (1994) Educational development and developmental research in mathematics education. *Journal for Research in Mathematics Education*, 25(5): 443–71.

Hughes, K. (2006) *Fetal Alcohol Spectrum Disorders: Module 3 – Primary Disabilities* (presentation and video). Prince George, Canada: Provincial Outreach Program for Fetal Alcohol Spectrum.

Jacobson, S.W. (2002) *Neurobehavioural Deficits in Alcohol-Exposed South African Infants: Preliminary Findings*. Paper presented at the 25th Annual Scientific Meeting of the Research Society on Alcoholism, San Francisco.

Jirikowic, T. (2007) Sensory integration and sensory processing disorders. In K.D. O'Malley (ed.), *ADHD and Fetal Alcohol Spectrum Disorders*. New York: Nova Science.

Jones, K.L. and Smith, D.W. (1973) Recognition of the fetal alcohol syndrome in early infancy. *Lancet*, 2(7836): 999–1001.

Kenney, J.L., Militana, H. . and Donohue, M.H. (2003) Helping teachers to use their school's backyard as an outdoor classroom: a report on the watershed learning center program. *Journal of Environmental Education*, 35(1): 18–26.

Kesmodel, U. and Kesmodel, P.S. (2002) Drinking during pregnancy: attitudes and knowledge among pregnant Danish women in 1998. *Alcoholism Clinical and Experimental Research*, 26(10): 1553–60.

Lebel, C., Rasmussen, C., Wyper, K., Andrew, G. and Beauliei, C. (2010) Brain microstructure is related to math ability in children with fetal alcohol spectrum disorder. *Alcoholism: Clinical and Experimental Research*, 34(2): 354–63.

Lemoine, P. (1997) *Historique des embryo-foetopathies alcooliques*. Nantes, France: University of Nantes.

Lemoine, P., Harouusseau, H. and Borteyru, J.P. (1968) Les enfants de parents alcooliques: Anomalies observées, a propos de 127 cas. *Ouest Med.* 21:476–482.

Mattson, S.N., Calarco, K.E. and Lang, A.R. (2006) Focused and shifting attention in children with heavy prenatal alcohol exposure. *Neuropsychology*, 20: 361–9.

Mukherjee, R., Hollins, S. and Turk, J. (2006) Fetal alcohol spectrum disorder: an overview. *Journal of the Royal Society of Medicine*, 99(6): 298–302.

Nunes, T. (1998) *Developing Children's Minds Through Literacy and Numeracy. An Inaugural Lecture.* London: Institute of Education.

O'Connor, M.J., Kogan, N. and Findlay, R. (2002) Prenatal alcohol exposure and attachment behavior in children. *Alcoholism: Clinical and Experimental Research*, 26(10): 1592–602.

Papert, S. (1980) *Mindstorms: Children, Computers, and Powerful Ideas*. New York: Basic Books.

Peadon, E., Freemantle, E., Bower, C. and Elliott, E.J. (2008) International survey of diagnostic services for children with FASD. *BMC Paediatrics*, 8(12): 1–8.

Ryan, S. and Ferguson, D.L. (2006) On, yet under, the radar: students with fetal alcohol syndrome disorder. *Exceptional Children*, 72(3): 363–5.

Sigman, A. (2008) 'Dangerous measures', *Times Educational Supplement*, 26 December.

Streissguth, A.P., Barr, H.M., Bookstein, H., Sampson, F.L., Olson, P.D. and Carmichael, H. (1999) The long-term neurocognitive consequences of prenatal alcohol: a 14-year study. *Psychological Science*, 10(3): 186–90.

Taylor, M. and Houghton, S. (2008) Difficulties in initiating and sustaining peer friendships: perspectives on students diagnosed with AD/HD. *British Journal of Special Education*, 35(4): 209–19.

Timler, G.R., Olswang, L.B. and Coggins, T.E. (2005) 'Do I know what I need to do?' A social communication intervention for children with complex clinical profiles. *Language, Speech, and Hearing Services in Schools*, 36: 73–85

Ueckerer, A. and Nadel, L. (1996) Spatial locations gone awry: object and spatial memory deficits in children with fetal alcohol syndrome. *Neuropsychologia*, 34: 209–23.

Vygotsky, L.S. (1984) *Thought and Language*. Cambridge, MA: MIT Press.

Walker-Gleaves, C. (2015) Understanding the educational achievements and difficulties of looked after children. In S. Martin-Denham (ed.), *Making an Impact: Preparing to Teach in Specialist Provision*. London: Sage.

13

PMLD and language: the impact of teachers' beliefs upon the pedagogy of the unspoken word

Catherine Stewart

 This chapter

This chapter will explore how teachers' identity, ecology and belief systems shape, envisage and enable Profound and Multiple Learning Difficulties (PMLD) students' language, expression and communication (which is often non-verbal, unspoken and unwritten). There is a great need to consider the uniqueness of students with PMLD, the reality of curriculum objectives delivered and how communication and language needs can be supported, encouraged and understood within special needs schools. The emphasis within this chapter is that PMLD students often as not have substantially less neurological ability to articulate linguistically as well as physical and mobility deficits making the usage of the written and oral communication as both an act and a communication tool non-viable.

What are language and speech difficulties for children with PMLD?

Unlike mainstream students, such deficits have implications for speech (if one takes speech as the ability to articulate sounds that can coherently be understood as words), communication (here taken as the ability to make oneself understood, be it emotions, knowledge or sensations) and expression of thought (verbal and written) overall which in turn impacts upon learning taking place and the assessment of language, written skills and transferability of concepts to be verified.

Students with PMLD have such complex needs and difficulties that teachers need to be acquainted with the concept that language lends itself to non-verbal communication such as eye contact, body posture, tics and utterances and it is here that the teacher must ensure that students are understood, supported and encouraged as part of mutual communication and learning. Teachers must be revolutionary in engaging with students in a reciprocal partnership where both parties make sense of lives and emotions as seen through very different pairs of eyes. Here students interpret and communicate with the world through the senses, an area that is not at the forefront of mainstream literacy curriculums.

Within this chapter, language will take a different form from that in a mainstream educational setting. In fact language here is seen as the ability to be understood, to express emotions, sensations, thoughts and needs through non-verbal sensory mediums. Where mainstream teachers talk of curriculum objectives, reading and writing ability, working memory, grammatical understanding and language as oral organic concepts, here the curriculum becomes enacted through sensory factors such as eye movements, body postures, utterances, tics and vocalisations. Assessment of understanding and ability is enabled through the teacher's ecologies, experiences, beliefs and post-teacher training pedagogic practice. Unlike mainstream pedagogy, new avenues are opened up; the teacher becomes the curriculum. Teachers' emotional language and their ability to engage, understand and enable students to communicate impacts upon how well the students' world can be understood. In turn teachers have the privilege and responsibility of allowing students to be part of and contribute to a world that denies them existence due to their non-verbal style of language acquisition and expression which does not sit well within National Curriculum objective tests.

How do PMLD settings differ from mainstream?

Specialist settings are different from mainstream – the students require multiple types of teaching styles, they all learn in a very unique way, class sizes are smaller and, because all students have differing neurological, physical and cognitive ability, multiple curriculums are running all at once. Overall good practice can only come from viewing students as a different entity in a positive manner. Within mainstream, a static curriculum utilises aims and objectives with literacy learning goals to be followed, which is akin to Yero's (2002, p.31) 'road to race notions'. Teachers aspire to include all and ensure students 'get to the end' somehow in various chaotic formats with many falling at the hurdles; such barriers to language as a spoken concept are sometimes almost insurmountable for PMLD students.

Barton (1986) argues that, despite good intentions, educators and professionals do not know a great deal about 'handicap' and grossly underestimate people. Certainly concepts of capability postulated by Sen (2005, in Terzi, 2005) add weight to such arguments where teachers possess low academic expectations of 'mentally retarded' students in mainstream with regard to potential (Aloia et al., 1981). Special needs students' academic performances are affected by the ways in which teachers treat them and failure to achieve often correlates with expectation to fail (Good, 1981).

While the teaching workforce might not be prepared for the difficulty and complexity that meet them in many schools, that does not mean teachers cannot learn to work more effectively with students who have SLD or PMLD (Soodak and Podell, 1998; Clements, 2004; Mackenzie, 2012a, 2012b). Nor does it mean that teachers cannot understand their own cognitions in relation to the attributions they may make about and to children with SLD or PMLD. Many teacher education programmes, schools and local authorities have recognised and addressed the need to find ways to better prepare pre-service and in-service teachers to teach and serve pupils in special needs schools whose abilities and backgrounds are often outside the realm of their own experience and training (Buell et al., 1999; Humphrey and Lewis, 2008; Slobodzian, 2009; Frederickson et al., 2007). Because the education profiles and experiences of children with SLD/PMLD are varied and have multiple elements, it is impossible to pathologise or categorise them in relation to their abilities and capabilities and thus how teachers might interpret inclusive teaching for children in such settings. We can gain insights related to patterns of teachers' responses to various curriculums but must be cautious as to how we use these generalisations as plans for the design of future PMLD curriculums. We must always follow the admonition 'do no harm' as we seek to understand and support such children in their educational endeavours (Bronfenbrenner, 1979).

Certainly, teachers' pedagogic practice is entwined with their identity as practitioners (Jones, 2004). Teachers' characteristics, experiences and personal decisions regarding how to diversify and deliver education in multiple forms means working with students rather than a top-down hierarchical stance. Teachers working with PMLD cohorts must understand why they do not progress and have a deeper understanding of child development. One should want to care for students and respond to them, allowing their unvocal voices to be heard and unwritten style of learning to be facilitated.

Mainstream pedagogic practice is far removed from specialist provision, viewing difference as impairment. Research suggests that teachers become the curriculum (Stewart, 2016) and where SEN schools see diversity, teachers see each student's personality and the attractiveness of non-verbal sensory communication as the key to their unique pedagogy. To enable the child to be understood one needs to work with parents as, critically, parents of children with SLD or PMLD play a far larger and more significant strategic and curriculum role than other parents whose children attend mainstream schools (Fisher, 2007). For example, for some children in SLD/PMLD schools, the parents are the pedagogical and cognitive experts in their child's progress, often having had to exercise far more strategic and inter-professional power than similar parents in mainstream schools; they know the child's likes and dislikes and are well versed in the slight nuances of non-verbal communication that to the untrained eye appear obsolete.

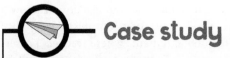 **Case study**

The context of language for a child with PMLD

Claire has no formal speech and her physical and neurological difficulties mean she is wheelchair bound and her head is held in a brace to ensure she is fully supported so mobility is limited. Her hand malformation makes holding articles impractical but she can make her feelings known by finger gestures, vocal sounds, head movements and eye contact. Prior to term time, the teachers and assistants have had a lot of contact with the parents to discuss how Claire prefers to communicate and what her nuances mean (happy, sad, disgust, frustration, etc.).

Today, the educational objective is the human body incorporating the notion that people differ in size and shape. Soft music is playing in the background as this creates a peaceful setting suited to all students' sensory needs. The teacher wheels Claire (along with other students, although some have less mobility and have to be strapped to a board and fully raised up vertically to be included) over to a table and strokes her hand to allow her to feel and look at the variance in the teacher's hand size while verbalising that all are touching hands. The objective is to make plaster of Paris moulds of hands and feet which can be cold and so a lotion using Claire's favourite scent is applied. She responds with a half smile and loud vocal approval and finger twitches are used as indicators to communicate when the lotion and stroking should stop. Pictures are taken of everyone's feet (including those of the teacher and assistants) and displayed on the large whiteboard, lots of 'guessing' the 'smelly foot' ensues along with conversations around whose fingers are long or short and students are very vocal in responses.

The teacher and assistants make the sounds 'brr it's freezing' and place their fingers in the plaster of Paris and shake and hug themselves. They place Claire's finger in the plaster and repeat the cold role play, they ask if they should put her hand in, she vocalises and finger twitches. Teachers and staff take this as a yes and slowly place her hand finger by finger in the plaster, stating how wet, cold, soothing it is, constantly gauging if she is becoming agitated, which she isn't. The teacher and assistants constantly reinforce the learning by saying 'wow, look how big your hand is compared to David's' (another student). The process is repeated with her feet. After this her favourite lotion is smoothed on and the teacher discusses how lovely it smells, how it feels soft on her hands.

The next day, when the moulds are set, the teacher puts up the pictures on the whiteboard again in order to discuss size, shape, etc. In turn all are asked whose foot is on the board and so on to engage students and enable learning and include everyone in the class. The teacher then announces that someone's 'foot' has gone missing and the hands have been mixed up. All the teachers and students in turn look at the different sizes of feet and hand moulds and whiteboard pictures to assess whose is whose! A lot of vocalisation is present here - students' foot moulds are held next to their feet and the teacher constantly talks about sizes, shapes (some hands and feet are smaller/larger and have varying types of formation). This in actual fact is part of the learning process, as is the painting, touching and feeling of materials used to decorate the hands and feet. Claire's feet (from the mould and her actual own) are given a nail polish make-over - the polish is held near to her nose and the teacher comments it is a beautiful colour and smells different from her favourite lotion. Later that day the finished products are held up and once again via the whiteboard and looking at the moulds and actual hands and feet, students are involved in responding to the concept. Claire is visibly enjoying herself, her fingers twitch, her mouth forms a half smile and her verbal responses are loud. This learning has been a joyous occasion for student and teacher alike via the media of touch, sight, sound and smell.

Teacher identity and beliefs and the impact upon PMLD students' non-verbal language skill sets

Teacher knowledge is an overarching concept that summarises a large variety of cognitions, from conscious and well-balanced opinions to unconscious and unreflected intuitions (Verloop et al., 2001, p.46). Such intuition and balanced opinions are immersed within the identities of SLD and PMLD students as well as teachers and professional practice, all of which are founded on personal ecologies. Issues about content, curriculum and pedagogy cannot be separated from emotional issues and all are inseparable from a teacher's practice (Zembylas, 2007).

Overall teachers' beliefs draw power from previous episodes and colour subsequent events (Nespor, 1987); pre-service vivid images influence interpretations of classroom practices playing powerful roles in how one undertakes pedagogy in teaching environments (Calderhead and Robson, 1991). Teachers feel that they have a moral purpose to work in partnership with the students to endeavour to aid spirituality and overall self esteem. Often they are not sure if they are doing things right, or even if there is a right way, a better way – there's no measuring stick (Stewart, 2016). In truth PMLD students are disadvantaged on so many levels – they need love expressed to them, and empathy. They need to know that they are understood, supported and cared for, that someone is listening to their often silent world – it's a very different practice from mainstream.

There is a need to expand current conceptions of teachers' pedagogic practice within specialised settings overall. To do so one has to explore the full range of what Clandinin and Connelly (1996) have called 'teachers' professional knowledge landscapes' – a territory of private and public knowledge, of curriculum requirements and passionate explorations, of emotional knowing and cognitive outcomes. Such notions become even more important when considering the complexities and differing concepts and attitudes found within SLD and PMLD schools which is harboured by the lack of academic conceptual knowledge about teachers working within specialised settings.

Overall there should be a sense of unity and similar pedagogy within the teaching team, so it is intrinsic to one's role and thus ensures that students receive appropriate care and are understood, that articulation on the smallest level is acknowledged and encouraged. Pedagogy stems from the heart and head (Shulman, 2005), and impacts deeply upon the student's ecological experiences in school. The emotional curriculum is entrenched in allowing communication, enabling the child to belong and non-verbally make themselves heard and understood.

However, there appears to be major confusion and deficits within academic literature regarding how to articulate such a 'special' curriculum, how to differentiate the curriculum (Heubert and Hauser, 1999; Kelly, 1989), how to decide in practice what topics should be covered (Senyshyn, 2012; Zigmond et al., 2009) and whether teachers have enough training and pedagogic knowledge to be able to differentiate at all (Maddern, 2010). Much disagreement appears to rest on the complex dichotomy of whether and how to balance the aspirations of an overarching curriculum theory with a design that is able to understand the capabilities of a complex group of students and their multiple needs, with the resources to help them flourish and prevail. It is the teachers who teach in these curriculum contexts that hold the possibility of change with regard to translating curriculum theories into practices that are able to build upon capabilities in a progressive and productive manner. Teachers need to be able to 'teach', 'enable' and 'educate', but implicit messages that are shaped by historical ecologies of what they are trying to achieve comes from themselves as being decent human beings and not educators.

In the past two decades, 'teacher pedagogic knowledge' or 'teacher practical knowledge' has emerged as a major area of exploration for educational researchers (Carter, 1990; Hashweh, 2005; Shulman, 1986, 1987). The work of Shulman (1987) focuses on a specific form of teacher knowledge: pedagogical content knowledge (PCK), defined as:

> That special amalgam of content and pedagogy that is uniquely the province of teachers and their own special form of professional understanding. (1987: 15)

In order to respect students' needs and individuality one should acquire humility and ignore the curriculum altogether (Senyshyn, 2012) or offer a more spiritual approach to curriculum activities, for both SLD and PMLD students.

The teacher's work is informed by practical interactions with the student and meaningful objectives developing as teachers and students work together often in an experimental fashion. Such notions strengthen the idea that a teacher's identity is a crucial factor in the construction of SLD and PMLD pedagogy. It is the most interesting area of education. Teachers can use their creativity, do things related to their topic, so it's up to teachers to make what they do interesting rather than force feeding them an ill-fitting curriculum. Overall uniqueness makes the job enriching (Mackenzie, 2012a, p.153); one needs to be unafraid to try the ridiculous or the unimaginable, to be a rebel and never give up (Stewart, 2016).

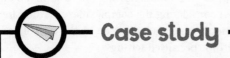 **Case study**

Designing language and literacy activities in a PMLD setting

Ingrid is a teacher working within a class with a PMLD cohort. She has children of her own and spends many hours trying to think of innovative ways to make her classes engaging and yet individually tailored to each student. On a particular windy afternoon her children are bored at home and need some physical outlet. She grabs their coats and hats and they head outside into the harsh winds and autumnal season.

The children relish throwing the leaves at each other that she has spent a long time collecting at the bottom of the garden. They jump up and down in the piles listening to the sounds and make paper kites and watch as the wind carries them away as they are too light to sustain the blustery weather. Later that night Ingrid thinks about the next day at school – the students are learning about the seasons and Ingrid knows that an explanation or video of such knowledge will not be enough to sustain their interest or lend itself well to those with limited sight and hearing difficulties. She is aware that making drawings of the seasons will not fit any student needs as most have little mobility in their hands and two are strapped to boards and harnesses due to their complex needs.

Ingrid is determined that all her students should experience the notion of seasons. She knows that merely verbalising the seasons will not grasp their attention and so decides to offer a more sensory educational version that will allow students to acquire the concept of words such as cold and air to enable them to enjoy and communicate to each other the enjoyment her own children orally verbalised to her the previous day.

She begins with stroking the leaves of an indoor plant across students' hands and faces. The leaves are green and soft and summery; in the background soft music is playing and scented plug-ins give off citrus smells. On the whiteboard images of summer, fresh leaves and bright sunshine are displayed. The students vocalise their relaxation through individual responses.

Ingrid introduces autumn, the music changes to louder sounds of wind and air. Ingrid has recorded the sounds of leaves and the wind gushing around her garden on her phone. She uses straws to puff air onto faces and if the student appears to find this acceptable she gently turns on a fan and throws a handful of brown leaves into the air. The leaves are scrunched into the students' hands and near to their ears and brushed gently across hands, feet and faces.

Those that non-verbally suggest they appear happy with this (via eye contact, or utterances that teachers know signal a particular feeling) are taken into the garden via French doors where they see the wind whipping up the leaves. Ingrid and the teaching assistants throw more leaves she has collected and piled up into the air. Pictures are taken of students engaging with nature; Ingrid buries herself in the leaf piles and jumps up and out shouting 'autumn!'. The students are given balloons and watch as the wind carries them away. Some students are lifted out of their chairs into the large piles of leaves and covered slightly if Ingrid and staff feel that they will find this engaging. Ingrid allows them to verbalise their feelings and constantly talks of autumn – 'it's windy, scrunchy and crunchy' – as she pairs each word with a sensation, holding up the colours red, brown and yellow.

Back in class the images taken are shown on the whiteboard. Ingrid talks through each student's picture, reinforcing what is happening in them. The students are asked to track the images with their eyes, while Ingrid and the teaching assistants place piles of leaves in their hands and turn on the fan softly, the music returning to a relaxing beat to help calm the students.

PMLD classrooms: the language of love and individuality

In asking whether pupils with special educational needs require distinct kinds of pedagogic strategies, we are not asking whether pupils with special educational needs require distinct curriculum objectives. We are enquiring whether they need distinct kinds of teaching to learn the same content as others without special educational needs (Norwich and Lewis, 2005, p.7). In reflecting upon how teachers define children, Jones (2005) reported that historical understandings of PMLD are directly related to the degree, intensity and multiplicity of disabilities present in an individual person, and the consequent levels of support needed for that person to function in society. Jones' (2004) research notes similar views about teachers' perceived notions of PMLD. They identified students as

a group of pupils with complex and multiple learning disabilities, pupils who can be very different from one another, who may present as very individual and unique, who may share common characteristics, yet whose individual pictures are very difficult to define in a group definition and therefore are all special. It's hard to describe a typical child because they're often very different, they can be ambulant and mobile and they can also be profoundly disabled. (2004, p.160)

Teachers are rarely exposed to deep and sustained inclusive pedagogical theory and practice during their initial preparation that would equip them adequately for such contexts (Stowitchek et al., 2000, p.142; Hodkinson, 2009; Ekins and Grimes, 2009; DCSF (The SALT Review), 2009). Overall there were significant practical and conceptual gulfs a within teacher ecologies, where lack of training or direction caused tension both personally and professionally.

> To be honest I got into school and wondered how on earth I could integrate any special needs in class. It was just not mentioned when I trained, I sort of trained to deliver knowledge rather than enable.
>
> (Stewart, 2016)

Due to ineffective training, the nature of teaching and the teacher's work is often so ill-defined that educational beliefs are particularly vulnerable to becoming what Nespor (1987) called an entangled domain. When a teacher encounters these domains, previous schemas or experiences do not work and the teacher is uncertain of what information is needed or what behaviour is appropriate. I argue that if teachers are unable to fathom out what to do in such situations, then they must rely on their belief structures, with all their problems and inconsistencies. While for some this may be frustrating if one continues to try to deliver a curriculum via a 2D approach (talking, discussing, writing about it) that does not fit the PMLD student, teachers need to view the curriculum via another lens, their personal beliefs and innovative approaches to ensuring knowledge is delivered and that students can communicate within it.

This can be enriching for teachers because special educational needs students are dynamic, aiding personal transformation, all leaving their personal footprints upon the teacher's shoreline. Merging with the beach rather than remaining separate entities that sit within an ecological construct, they become part of the teacher's narrative. With each new experience and child encountered teachers evolve and change practice. Their 'professional landscape' (Clandinin and Connelly, 1996, p.28) becomes an embodiment of the nuanced way of being as opposed to the mainstream teacher that Jones (2005) speaks to. Mackenzie (2012a: 22) suggests that where some teachers are resilient to the challenges special educational needs students pose and cannot imagine doing anything else, gathering joy from working with students, others see only difficulty and continual barriers to enacting externally imposed curriculums; in such circumstances, students and pupils move from being assets to being liabilities. There is also a greater need for adaption for those with more severe needs which goes beyond the normal adaptations often found in mainstream. While often unprepared for the difficulty and complexity that meets them in many schools, research findings offered support for previous academic research (Clements, 2004; Mackenzie, 2012a), verifying that teachers can learn to work more effectively with students with SLD and PMLD. Teachers learn on the job, seeing what works and what doesn't. It's like playing the piano – you have to learn the classics before you can do jazz. Years of research and working with great colleagues who had very different ways of working positively and reading up on everything has helped a great deal, but you have to live it every day, you have to have a desire to change students' lives (Stewart, 2016).

Overall teachers appear to be affected by the worlds they try to affect (Britzman, 2003, p.5). Teachers have to care about students' needs, be aware of what they find tolerable and intolerable and embrace how their histories can serve to shape practice. I argue that this reflection upon the unknown self or life-affirming incidents is not merely an experience that leads to correcting and perfecting teaching but constructs the ecology of becoming an empathising practitioner for special needs. Explicit messages are conveyed that teachers need to be able to 'teach', 'enable' and 'educate', while implicit messages are shaped by historical ecologies, where what they are trying to achieve comes from themselves as being decent human beings and not educators. Vivid images influence the interpretation of classroom practices playing powerful roles in how one undertakes pedagogy in teaching environments (Calderhead and Robson, 1991).

Noddings (1984: 113) maintains that needs and wants are not necessarily the same thing in curriculum and justice terms. The 'needs' of children with SLD or PMLD are contested and subsumed frequently under discussions of philosophical wants that relate more to frameworks of rights than concrete outcomes and an intentionally fitted and designed curriculum. Grigorenko and Sternberg (1998) focused upon a person's abilities rather than their impairment leading to an overall more social and 'best fit' curriculum. One needs to adapt the curriculum, to be unafraid and draw on life experiences no matter what: do not hold back, just give them a chance to use a different pair of binoculars. There should be a sense of similar humanitarian and altruistic ideals for the welfare of these students as a basic right to ensure students feel a sense of being included, belonging and accepted in a world which assessments and ability grades often deny them.

 **Case study**

Developing pedagogic skill in PMLD - a question of evolution and continual reflection

Shona is a new teacher to the PMLD setting but has five years' experience within SLD. She was thought of as gifted and talented with students in her previous class but wishes to extend her knowledge and pedagogy further and look at other ways of enabling and communicating with students.

The students all have limited mobility and communicate with verbalisations, head motions and noises, etc. She has considerable experience of play therapy and enjoys the more hands-on approach to teaching.

Today is a relaxed day for students and they are allowed a choice of options to do whatever they wish. Shona has undertaken in-depth conversations with teachers who have worked with the students before and has also read around their files regarding mobility and physical and linguistic abilities. Shona wants to get to know all the students on a personal level before engaging in curriculum objectives.

She approaches one girl, Anna, who is laid on her side among soft cushions in a play tent. Anna has limited movement and is taking a rest from her wheelchair and enjoys the comfort of the cushions and the tent sensation that envelops her. Shona climbs into the tent and says hello lying down beside her to gain good eye contact and ensure that no nuances of communication are missed. In the background a favourite artist of Anna's is playing and she makes soft mouthing notions and low verbalisations. Shona takes this to mean she is happy and content. Shona begins to sing along with the song and Anna's eye contact becomes more steady and fixed. Shona taps Anna's hand to the beat of the song and when she stops Anna gestures through low verbalisation she wishes Shona to continue the interaction.

When someone changes the music Anna registers her disapproval with louder vocalisation and mouth pursing. Shona supports Anna through this telling her it's Callum's turn now and tapping her hand to the new beat of someone else's favourite song.

Here the communication between student and teacher has become mutual and a sense of trust and the social skill of turn-taking and enjoying others' favourite songs have been utilised. Moreover, Shona has bonded with Anna and future interactions can build from here. Overall there has been an unspoken language of socialisation and respect between both parties. Students need to feel supported before they can begin to learn and engage.

 ## Concluding thoughts

Working within specialist settings offers an emotionally charged work life that involves a lot of personal internal strife and yet gives teachers a reason to stay (Mackenzie, 2012a, 2012b). One must develop a steely attitude towards empowerment for special educational needs students and shift professional landscapes in one's mind for the better. Overall, having a unique ecology that exudes empathy and having beliefs grounded in inclusive practice and a strong commitment to special needs students can anchor teacher identities. These tend to bode well for achieving positive outcomes when faced with powerful external and political macro systems. While SEN is often unchartered territory, the impact on teachers appears to be dependent on personal ecology, identity and morality. Attainment levels are low and so access to an appropriate curriculum means a sound and light room, not academic manuals – they need a physical, social and emotional syllabus, one that is in tune with their needs. Lacey and Ouvrey (1998) propose definitions of PMLD should encompass a collaborative approach, looking at the abilities of, as well as appreciating the extensive difficulties encountered by, those young people.

Within specialist settings inclusion is not merely a right but a way of appropriately teaching, and serves a more emotional and spiritual practice. Rather than inclusion being merely curriculum-based within special settings it becomes a sense of belonging overall, a way of enablement through diversity, and ultimately of turning every opportunity for learning into a life changing moment. Indeed, in this way, it is the essence of what literacy is and does: changing people's lives, often in incremental but profound ways forever.

References

Aloia, G.F., Maxwell, J.A. and Aloia, S.D. (1981) Influence of a child's race and the EMR label on the initial impressions of regular classroom teachers. *American Journal of Mental Deficiency*, 85(4): 619–23.

Barton, L. (1986) The politics of special needs. *Disability Handicap and Society*, 1(3): 273–90.

Britzman, D. (2003) *Practice Makes Practice: A Critical Study of Learning to Teach*. Albany, NY: State University of New York Press.

Bronfenbrenner, U. (1979) *The Ecology of Human Development: Experiments by Nature and Design*. Cambridge, MA: Harvard University Press.

Buell, M., Hallam, R., Gamel-McCormick, M. and Scheer, S. (1999) A survey of general and special education teachers' perceptions and in-service needs concerning inclusion. *International Journal of Disability Development and Education*, 46: 143–56.

Calderhead, J. and Robson, M. (1991) Images of teaching: student teachers' early conceptions of classroom practice. *Teaching and Teacher Education*, 7(1): 1–8.

Carter, K. (1990) The place of story in the study of teacher and teacher education. *Educational Researcher*, 22(1): 5–12.

Clandinin, D.J. and Connelly, F.M. (1996) Teachers' professional knowledge landscapes: teacher stories of schools. *Educational Researcher*, 25(3): 24–30.

Clements, L. (2004) Carers – the sympathy and services stereotype. *British Journal of Learning Disabilities*, 32: 6–8.

DCFS (2009) *SALT Review: Independent Review of Teacher Supply for Pupils with Severe, Profound and Multiple Learning Difficulties (SLD and PMLD)*. Nottingham.

Ekins, A. and Grimes, P. (2009). *Inclusion: Developing an Effective and Whole School Approach*. Milton Keynes: Open University Press.

Fisher, P. (2007) Experiential knowledge challenges 'normality' and individualized citizenship: towards 'another way of being'. *Disability and Society*, 22(3): 283–98.

Frederickson, N., Simmonds, E., Evans, L. and Soulsby, C. (2007) Assessing the social and affective outcomes inclusion. *British Journal of Special Education*, 34(2): 105–15.

Good, T. (1981) Teacher expectations and student perceptions: a decade of research. *Educational Leadership*, 38: 415–22.

Grigorenko, E.L. and Sternberg, R.J. (1998) Dynamic testing. *Psychological Bulletin*, 124(1): 75.

Hashweh, M.Z. (2005) Teacher pedagogical constructions: a reconfiguration of pedagogical content knowledge. *Teachers and Teaching: Theory and Practice*, 11(3): 273–92.

Heubert, J.P. and Hauser, R.M. (1999) *High Stakes: Testing for Tracking, Promotion and Graduation. A Report of the National Research Council*. Washington, DC: National Academy Press.

Hodkinson, A. (2009) Pre-service teacher training and special educational needs in England 1970–2008: is government learning the lessons of the past or is it experiencing a groundhog day? *European Journal of Special Needs Education*, 24(3): 277–89.

Humphrey, N. and Lewis, S. (2008) What does inclusion mean for pupils on the autistic spectrum in mainstream secondary education? *Journal of Research in Special Educational Needs*, 8(3): 132–40.

Jones, P. (2004) They are not like us and neither should they be: issues of teacher identity for teachers of pupils with profound and multiple learning difficulties. *Disability and Society*, 19(2): 159–69.

Jones, P. (2005) Teachers' views of their pupils with profound and multiple learning difficulties. *European Journal of Special Needs Education*, 20(4): 375–85.

Kelly, A.V. (1989) *The Curriculum: Theory and Practice*, 3rd edn. London: Paul Chapman.

Lacey, P. and Ouvrey, C. (1998) *People with Profound and Multiple Learning Disabilities*. London: David Fulton.

Mackenzie, S. (2012a) 'I can't imagine doing anything else': why do teachers of children with SEN remain in the profession? Resilience, rewards and realism over time. *Journal of Research in Special Educational Needs*, 12(3): 151–61.

Mackenzie, S. (2012b) 'It's been a bit of a rollercoaster'. Special educational needs, emotional labour and emotion work. *International Journal of Inclusive Education*, 16: 1067–82.

Maddern, K. (2010) SEN teacher skills under threat, government adviser warns. *Times Educational Supplement*, 12 March, p.3.

Nespor, J. (1987) The role of beliefs in the practice of teaching. *Journal of Curriculum Studies*, 19(4): 317–28.

Noddings, N. (1984) *Caring*. Berkeley, CA: University of California Press.

Norwich, B. and Lewis, A. (2005) How specialised is teaching pupils with disabilities and difficulties?. In A. Lewis and B. Norwich (eds), *Special Teaching for Special Children? Pedagogies for Inclusion*. Milton Keynes: Open University Press, pp.1–18.

Sen, A. (2005) Human rights and capabilities. *Journal of Human Development*, 6(2): 151–66.

Senyshyn, Y. (2012) Respecting students, acquiring humility and ignoring the curriculum. *Journal of Educational Thought*, 45(2): 145–63.

Shulman, L.S. (1986) Those who understand: knowledge growth in teaching. *Educational Researcher*, 15(2): 4–14.

Shulman, L.S. (1987) Knowledge and teaching: foundations of the new reform. *Harvard Educational Review*, 57(1): 1–23.

Shulman, L.S. (2005) Signature pedagogies in the professions. *Daedalus*, 134(3): 52–9.

Slobodzian, J.T. (2009) The devil is in the detail: issues of exclusion in an inclusive educational environment. *Ethnography and Education*, 4(2): 181–95.

Soodak, L.C., Podell, D.M. and Lehman, L.R. (1998) Teacher, student and school attributes as predictors of teachers' responses to inclusion. *Journal of Special Education*, 31: 480–97.

Stewart, C.M.B. (2016) Teachers' Pedagogies and the 'Special' Curriculum: A Study of the Beliefs and Practices of Teachers that Shape the Ecologies of SLD/PMLD Schools. EdD thesis. Durham University.

Stowitchek, J., Cheney, D. and Schwartz, I. (2000) Instigating fundamental change through experiential in-service development. *Teacher Education and Special Education*, 25(2): 142–56.

Terzi, L. (2005) Beyond the dilemma of difference: the capability approach to disability and special educational needs. *Journal of Philosophy of Education*, 39(3): 443–59.

Verloop, N., Van Driel, J. and Meijer, P. (2001) Teacher knowledge and the knowledge base of teaching. *International Journal of Educational Research*, 35(5): 441–61.

Yero, J. (2002) *Teaching in Mind: How Teacher Thinking Shapes Education*. New York: Basic.

Zembylas, M. (2007) Emotional ecology: the intersection of emotional knowledge and pedagogical content knowledge in teaching. *Teacher and Teacher Education*, 23(4): 355–67.

Zigmond, N., Kloo, A. and Volonino, V. (2009) What, where, and how? Special education in the climate of full inclusion. *Exceptionality*, 17(4): 189–204.

Concluding thoughts

Literacy is a human and civil right: all individuals have a right to read the word and the world so that they can make sense of their lives, express themselves and engage in informed decision-making about their own futures. Because difficulties with communication and expression and the resultant frustration and marginalisation frequently characterise the lives of many children struggling with language and literacy, it is also the one area that has the biggest single impact on their capacity to learn in all other areas. Every child's progress within literacy is critical to their development in ways far beyond the everyday process of learning: it impacts on every part of their life, emotional, physical, social, spiritual and relational.

This book has attempted to address some of these difficulties in children's language and literacy development and offer research-informed and practice-led approaches for carers, parents, teachers, teaching assistants and other professionals working with children of primary age who are experiencing language and literacy difficulties. Drawing on the latest research in education, psychology, neurology and sociology, this book has illustrated how such children's progress in literacy and language may often be mapped against difficulties in other areas of their lives, which lead to cognitive, emotional and social difficulties. These, in turn, impact upon educational progress, leading to lasting impacts on their lives as they grow. Focusing upon literacy gives an opportunity for critical interventions in children's lives, and this is what this book has aimed to do. As well as explaining the connections between language and literacy development, emotional regulation, social context and social progress, the book has described in detail particular activities for specific aspects of these children's major areas of literacy-related difficulty. It is hoped that this very novel and insightful approach makes it an accessible book for all carers, parents and professionals working with young children who are experiencing difficulty with reading and the written and spoken language.

Index